CREATING COLONIAL PASTS

History, Memory, and Commemoration in Southern Ontario, 1860–1980

Creating Colonial Pasts explores the creation of history and memory in southern Ontario through the experience of its inhabitants, especially those who took an active role in the preservation and writing of Ontario's colonial past: the founder of the Niagara Historical Society, Janet Carnochan; twentieth-century Six Nations historians Elliott Moses and Milton Martin; and Celia B. File, high-school teacher and historian of Mary Brant.

Examining the grand narratives of colonial Ontario – the Loyalists, the War of 1812, and the creation of settler society – Cecilia Morgan argues that place has played an important role in shaping memory and narrative in locations such as Niagara-on-the-Lake, the Six Nations territory at the Grand River, and the Mohawk community at Tyendinaga. Illuminating the pivotal role of women and Indigenous people in historical commemoration and uncovering the existence of a lively and interconnected circle of historians and heritage activists in late nineteenth and twentieth-century Ontario, *Creating Colonial Pasts* is a virtuoso study of history-making.

CECILIA MORGAN is a professor in the Department of Curriculum, Teaching, and Learning, at the Ontario Institute for Studies in Education, University of Toronto.

Creating Colonial Pasts

History, Memory, and Commemoration in Southern Ontario, 1860–1980

CECILIA MORGAN

UNIVERSITY OF TORONTO PRESS
Toronto Buffalo London

© University of Toronto Press 2015
Toronto Buffalo London
www.utppublishing.com

ISBN 978-1-4426-4837-1 (cloth)
ISBN 978-1-4426-2615-7 (paper)

Library and Archives Canada Cataloguing in Publication

Morgan, Cecilia, 1958–, author
    Creating colonial pasts : history, memory, and commemoration in southern Ontario, 1860-1980 / Cecilia Morgan.

Includes bibliographical references and index.
ISBN 978-1-4426-4837-1 (bound)   ISBN 978-1-4426-2615-7 (paperback)

1. Collective memory – Ontario, Southern.   2. Memorialization – Ontario, Southern.   3. Ontario, Southern – Historiography.   I. Title.

FC3059.M67 2015   971.3'02   C2015-903080-3

University of Toronto Press acknowledges the financial assistance to its publishing program of the Canada Council for the Arts and the Ontario Arts Council, an agency of the Government of Ontario.

 **Canada Council   Conseil des Arts
for the Arts   du Canada**

 ONTARIO ARTS COUNCIL
CONSEIL DES ARTS DE L'ONTARIO
an Ontario government agency
un organisme du gouvernement de l'Ontario

University of Toronto Press acknowledges the financial support of the Government of Canada through the Canada Book Fund for its publishing activities.

This book has been published with the help of a grant from the Canadian Federation for the Humanities and Social Sciences, through the Awards to Scholarly Publications Program, using funds provided by the Social Sciences and Humanities Research Council of Canada.

To Beth and to Paul

Table of Contents

List of Illustrations   ix

Acknowledgments   xi

Introduction: Pulling on Threads – Unravelling Histories and Historians   3

1. Books and Mortar: Janet Carnochan's Historical Town   11
2. "To Turn the Light on the Other Side": History and the Six Nations   59
3. "Among the Six Nations": Celia B. File and the Politics of Memory, History, and Home   91
4. "Where Nature had joined hands with man": History, Tourism, and Landscape in Niagara-on-the-Lake   112

Conclusion: Mending the Threads of the Past   172

Notes   179
Index   215

Illustrations

1.1 *Janet Carnochan* by E. Wyly Grier, 1921.   15
1.2 Memorial Hall, 1907.   17
1.3 Susan Chubbuck sampler, 1848.   18
1.4 Josiah Plumb's waistcoat.   19
1.5 Receipt issued by William Riley.   21
1.6 Sketch of William Riley's house, 1816.   22
1.7 Presbyterian weathervane, 1831.   23
1.8 Haudenosaunee wampum beads.   24
1.9 Haudenosaunee doll, mid-late eighteenth century.   25
1.10 Isaac Brock's Proclamation of War of 1812.   26
1.11 Isaac Brock's (never-worn) hat.   27
1.12 Lieutenant McDougal, Upper Canadian Militia, coatee, c. 1813–14.   28
1.13 Handbill announcing Brock's burial, 1824.   30
1.14 Memorial Hall interior, 1927.   32
1.15 Upper Gallery, Memorial Hall, 1927.   33
1.16 Eliza Morris's trunk.   45
1.17 Elizabeth Johnson Kerr's headstone.   47
1.18 Janet Carnochan's headstone.   53
1.19 Janet Carnochan Memorial.   54
1.20 Close up of the inscription, Carnochan Memorial.   55
1.21 Ontario Heritage Foundation Plaque, Memorial Hall.   56
1.22 Janet Carnochan Rose.   57
2.1 "Opening of the Brant Historical Museum," 1952.   68
2.2 "Ontario Indians Come to Exhibition to Demonstrate Their New Independence," 1939.   70
2.3 Milton and Lillian Martin with "Pat," 1944.   81

4.1 Putting Niagara-on-the-Lake on the tourist map. 114
4.2 Cover page, Niagara-on-the-Lake tourism brochure, 1897. 115
4.3 Deck of the *Chippewa*, c. 1890s. 121
4.4 "Sweet Memories" on board the *Cayuga*, c. 1913. 122
4.5 Postcard of Michigan Central Railroad train, 1923. 123
4.6 Lansing House, originally built in 1899. 124
4.7 Souvenir postcard of the Queen's Royal Hotel. 125
4.8 Queen's Royal Rotunda, c. 1890s. 126
4.9 Dining in style, Queen's Royal Hotel, c. 1890s. 126
4.10 Niagara Assembly/Canadian Chautauqua, c. 1880s. 127
4.11 Selling historic Niagara, 1919. 128
4.12 The army comes to Niagara-on-the-Lake, c. 1914. 129
4.13 The CEF Camp, First World War. 130–1
4.14 Chautauqua assembly of YMCA group. 132
4.15 Ladies' Lawn Bowling Club. 133
4.16 Caddies, Niagara Golf Club, 1902. 134
4.17 "Randwood," c. 1940. 135
4.18 Tourist map of the 1950s and detail of the map. 152–3
4.19 The tourist route of the 1950s. 154
4.20 Niagara's history in the 1950s. 155
4.21 "History" meets development in the 1970s. 158
4.22 "Dining in the colonial style of Upper Canada." 159
4.23 Theatre for patriotism, *Kathleen Mavourneen*, March 1915. 162
4.24 *Rural Matinee*, Capt. John D. Shawe, c. 1950. 163
4.25 Front page of the "Poison Pen Letter," 1971. 167
4.26 The "Poison Pen Letter" hits the front page. 1971. 168
4.27 Twenty-first-century tourism, Niagara-on-the-Lake, 2011. 169
4.28 Twenty-first-century tourism, Niagara-on-the-Lake, 2011 170

Acknowledgments

Numerous institutions and individuals helped get this book into print. It's a great pleasure to thank them publicly for their support and help.

The initial research was supported by funding from the Social Sciences and Humanities Research Council, for which I'm grateful. I also would like to thank my former department, Theory and Policy Studies (OISE/UT), for awarding me the small-scale SSHRC grant that allowed me to research Celia File's life. Thanks also are due to a number of archives, libraries, and museums, large and small, national, provincial, regional, and local: Archives of Ontario, Lennox and Addington County Museum and Archives, Library and Archives Canada, Niagara-on-the-Lake Historical Society and Museum (referred to in the photography credits as Niagara-on-the-Lake Historical Museum), Niagara-on-the-Lake Public Library, Queen's University Archives, and Woodland Cultural Centre.

At the University of Toronto Press, my thanks to Len Husband for his support, his good humour, and his willingness to champion a book that falls between the fowl of a monograph and a fish of a collection of essays. I am very grateful to Dilia Narduzzi for her thorough and careful copyediting of the manuscript and to Frances Mundy for overseeing the process.

I'd like to acknowledge the University of British Columbia Press for allowing me to use my article, "History and the Six Nations: the Dynamics of Commemoration, Colonial Space, and Colonial Knowledge," in James Opp and John C. Walsh, eds., *Placing Memory and Remembering Place in Canada* (Vancouver: University of British Columbia Press, 2010). It forms the basis of Chapter 2.

My thanks to audiences at the Canadian Historical Association, the Canadian History of Education Association, and the Niagara-on-the-Lake Historical Society for listening to earlier versions of this work and providing me with feedback. Thank you to Jim Opp and John Walsh for inviting me to the 'Remembering Place' workshop at Carleton University and to the workshops' participants, whose comments pushed me to think more seriously about the relationship between time and place. The anonymous readers of the manuscript gave me very good advice, not least about the need for an epilogue to "tie up the threads." A number of years ago – more than I care to reckon – Kathryn McPherson told me I should think about putting this research into a book of essays. I hope Kate doesn't mind my saying thank you for her inspiration and telling her she was right.

A number of individuals deserve special thanks. In particular, Sarah Maloney Kaufman and Amy Klassen of Niagara-on-the-Lake Museum were extremely generous, providing me with a number of photographs of articles from the Museum's vast and rich collection at no charge. I like to think Janet Carnochan would have approved of their generosity. In a similar vein, my sincere thanks to Rene and Eva Schmitz, Palatine Roses, Niagara-on-the-Lake, for their permission to use the photograph of the beautiful Janet Carnochan rose that appears in chapter 1. I also owe a debt of gratitude to Nancy and Ron Wood, whose hospitality in Kingston made my research into Celia File much more pleasant.

Finally, this book is dedicated to two people. My late aunt Elizabeth Whelan Parkinson, a teacher like Janet Carnochan and Celia File, taught me to read and to care about the past. Working on this book has made me realize how much she meant to me: I only wish I had told her that more clearly and more often when she was alive. Paul Jenkins is, fortunately, very much alive, so I'm glad to be able to tell him here and now how much he means to me.

CREATING COLONIAL PASTS

History, Memory, and Commemoration
in Southern Ontario, 1860–1980

Introduction

Pulling on Threads –
Unravelling Histories and Historians

The book you now hold has emerged from almost twenty years of researching, writing, and teaching about the role of commemoration and historical memory in particular historical contexts, especially those of nineteenth- and twentieth-century Canada. Being reflections on these areas and not a monograph, it is less tightly organized in its specific focus, as it ranges from the 1860s to the 1970s and deals with a number of sites in which historical memories were forged. Yet certain themes and connections link these chapters, both larger overarching ones as well as the individual people that move in and out, back and forth, through them. The chapters also examine the formation of historical memory and the use of historical knowledge in southern Ontario, particularly in the Niagara and Brantford areas.

The research in which this collection is grounded was initially undertaken for a study of Laura Secord's commemoration, one that became a book, co-authored with Colin M. Coates, *Heroines and History: Representations of Madeleine de Verchères and Laura Secord*. While exploring the ways in which Secord's story was told – by historical societies, school textbooks, the candy company, and promoters of tourism – in more or less disciplined ways, I kept finding other narratives and other narrators, stories that could not be told in that particular book but about which, I promised myself, I would write someday. Some of these promoters of "history" were ones I expected to find, such as Niagara-on-the-Lake's Janet Carnochan or those who encouraged the town's development of historical tourism. Other encounters – with Elliott Moses, a Delaware man from the Six Nations community, or Celia B. File, a high school history teacher from Napanee, Ontario – were unexpected.

In a number of ways the subjects of this book, then, showed up on my doorstep. However, their appearances were not quite the acts of serendipity that at first I assumed they might be. When describing this research I have often used the metaphor of "pulling on threads" to unravel the web of connections that linked these individuals – looking at one person or organization often turned up others that seemed too interesting or important to ignore or leave alone. Exploring turn of the century Brantford historian Augusta Gilkison, for example, led me to the Brant Historical Society. Pursuing their interest in the history of the Six Nations into the twentieth century, then, led me to Elliott Moses. In turn, Moses's papers at the National Archives led me to Celia B. File's memoir of her time with the Mohawks of Tyendinaga and the Six Nations. Searching for "more" on File's work subsequently took me to the Queen's University Archives and then to the Lennox and Addington Museum's collection, which turned up a wealth of correspondence between File and Mohawk historian Bernice Loft.[1] Exploring Janet Carnochan's conception of her town's history also meant including her notions of the place of First Nations in it, particularly the Six Nations, as they made significant and notable visits to her town both before and during her lifetime. Moreover, my initial interest in Secord's commemoration prompted me to look more closely at the ways in which she was remembered in a local context. That, in turn, drew me to explore the relationships between tourism and the use of the past in that landscape: a landscape that included a military camp that Milton Martin, who appears in the second chapter, attended. Southern Ontario, after all, was in some ways a very small society, even into the twentieth century – and its circle of historical commemorators was even smaller. To some extent, then, the fact that so many of these individuals moved in the same circles should not be overly surprising.

Yet during the years that this book covers, southern Ontario was also part of a settler society in which First Nations people have often been either physically, socially, and/or politically isolated from non-Aboriginals or, at the very least, perceived by the latter to live a separate existence from them.[2] Thus the fact that the webs and networks of connected individuals and groups that populate these chapters include Indigenous people is, I think, worth remarking upon. As my previous discussion should make clear, I cannot claim that my ability to explore such links stems from a focused inquiry on my part, as I too naively and uncritically accepted that divides between settler descendants and indigenous people would be both vast and unyielding by the late nineteenth century. What surprised and, I must confess, delighted me at times was finding "Indians in unexpected places"[3]: members of the Six Nations not just speaking at the Brant Historical Society's mid-twentieth-century meetings but also running the organization; the Mohawk soldier, teacher, and magistrate Milton Martin voicing his objections concerning Aboriginal people's representations in 1930s and 1940s textbooks; the Maracle and Hill families of Tyendinaga welcoming schoolteacher Celia File into their homes but also seeing her as an important ally in their struggles to live with security, dignity, and respect.

I am not trying to argue that somehow these were "typical" individuals, nor that their presence in "mainstream" organizations and media allows us to forget the weight of the Indian Act; Indigenous peoples' marginalization from the levers of political, economic, and social power; denials of treaty rights; or the sustained onslaughts on their culture and language, represented most clearly by residential schools.[4] Yet to dismiss or deny the significance of the lives and work of these First Nations men and women or to not pay close attention to their negotiation with settler society would be, I argue, to continue the latter's historical practice of dismissing Indigenous peoples and their history as inconsequential. It is possible, I think, to learn something more complicated about those negotiations if we include in our historical gaze local sites and lesser-known individuals – not to exclude national frameworks and the historically prominent but, rather, to juxtapose these approaches, to see both where they differed and where they might reinforce and complement each other. This is not to claim that such investigations into the contradictions and complexities of settler colonial relations will, in Audre Lord's well-known phrase, "dismantle the master's house" – namely because the individuals that appear here were not much interested in doing so. They did, though, wish to ensure that that house had room for them on the ground floor and in its main rooms, rather than being sent to the servants' quarters, basements, and garrets to which First Nations men, women, and children had been relegated by settler society and the nation-state.

Not all the book's chapters, though, deal directly with First Nations' people and the use of the past. The last, and longest, chapter explores the shifting relationships between history, culture, and tourism in Niagara-on-the-Lake, a small town that sits at the mouth of the Niagara River and in which tourism and "history" have been close, if at times reluctant, partners since the late nineteenth century. Despite the work of historians such as Carnochan, in this process Indigenous peoples' presence or absence generally did not feature as a question for discussion; the landscape that tourist promoters, local residents, voluntary organizations, and state bureaucracies wished to create would be marked with other preoccupations, other concerns. As American historian David Glassberg reminds us, "a sense of history and sense of place are inextricably intertwined; we attach histories to places, and the environmental value we attach to a place comes largely through the historical association we have with it."[5] Although in the case of Niagara-on-the-Lake I would substitute "tourist" for "environmental," Glassberg's point is more than well taken: the type of history linked to the town by both commemorators and tourist boosters bolstered arguments for a genteel, bourgeois tourism, one of educational and patriotic value, and distinguishing it from neighbouring Niagara Falls. In turn, the need to attract tourists to such a place could be used to argue for the preservation of the town's landscape and built heritage: who would be attracted to Niagara-on-the-Lake if nineteenth-century buildings were replaced with the brick bungalows of the mid-twentieth century?

The historiography on commemoration and the development of public historical memory in Canada is a rapidly growing and multifaceted area, exploring as it does the staging of pageants, the foundation of monuments, the development of the Historic Sites and Monuments Board, the creation of historically inflected tourist landscapes, the formation of museums and historic sites, the use of representations of Aboriginal peoples, and the creation of iconic historical figures (i.e. Jacques Cartier, John Cabot).[6] In recent years this scholarship has broadened its scope to include work that explores the creation of particular places through memory and narrative.[7] These chapters build on this work: they have been influenced by the questions and convictions that underpin this field, not the least of which sees the creation of historical narratives and history's public use as being a critical component of Canadian society's political, cultural, and social identity. Where, perhaps, they differ is in their scope and approach. Rather than looking at larger urban centres and at the activities of more prominent Canadians who staged pageants or fundraised for monuments, this book takes as its overall context small-town and rural Ontario, as well as the province's largest Indigenous reserve.[8]

To be sure, in some ways these geographical settings were less significant than we might think. These individuals had been influenced by the same kinds of historical narratives as their counterparts in urban Canada, not least because of their exposure to them in formal education (more about this later). On the other hand, though, the local contexts in which Janet Carnochan, Elliott Moses, or Celia File engaged with history were significant: first, because they attempted to create local landscapes through historical narratives and, second, because their work was produced in a nexus of concerns, constraints, and possibilities that were shaped by the immediate settings in which they worked. Memories and histories, then, were conditioned by the contingencies and contexts of place. By deciding to write the history of her town, Janet Carnochan, for example, might be seen as having limited her canvas. In doing so, though, she was also able to delve into a much wider range of archives and artefacts than if she had concentrated solely on the Loyalists or the War of 1812. Similarly, as chapter 2 argues, the Grand River setting in which Elliott Moses worked played a role in shaping his particular concept of Six Nations' history, albeit one that we might not expect.

Finally, my research also depends, in some cases quite heavily, on local archives – the Lennox and Addington Historical Society, the Brant County Museum, and the Niagara Historical Museum – to which I was led by the particular trajectories of my work. Much has been written, with great insight and perspicacity, about the "colonial archive" and historians' need to read either with or against its grain, interrogating its construction and structures and, especially, being attentive to its silences and erasures.[9] Yet much of what has been written about colonialism and the archive focuses on larger edifices created by imperial authorities, nation-states, and forms of provincial or regional governance. Less so, though, has the small-scale or local archive come under such sustained scrutiny (just as, in much of the historiography on museums, the archive's sibling, large-scale national or international institutions receive the most attention). Yet smaller archives also can be interrogated as sites in which colonial knowledge has been kept, organized, and produced, places where particular narratives can emerge that have helped sustain settler society's own fictions, such as that of a "pioneer past" almost entirely free of bothersome Aboriginals, for example, full of heartwarming examples of community spirit and self-reliance.[10] Although the question of local archives' relationship to colonialism generally remains to be explored by historians of Canada, such museums and archives – and the narratives that shape them – may have had a more immediate and central effect on communities' constructs of their past than we have acknowledged, both for adults and, especially, children, since their initial exposure to the past has often been in those institutions. These repositories also can hold, though, those fragments and traces of a past that suggest other possibilities, and show us that an untroubled history in which racial (and other) divisions and categories were respected and heeded was far from being "the whole story."

Not all the archives whose collections have shaped this book, though, were local: both the Archives of Ontario and Library and Archives Canada contributed their fair share to this book, both in the case of particular individuals (Elliott Moses' papers are held by LAC) and levels of the state. This is particularly so in chapter 4, which explores the role played by various levels of the government in shaping a landscape through certain narratives of the past, as well as its conceptions of what would attract tourists (the latter heavily derived from tourist entrepreneurs). Other chapters, though, focus more closely on individuals and the ways in which they grappled with living in their particular societies through the prism of the past. To be sure, my choice to focus on particular men and women is not a unique one: in the historiography on commemoration and memory in Canada, certain individuals – Helen Creighton, Ernest Cruikshank, Isabelle Skelton – have been singled out for the significant roles they have played.[11] However, while not without some degree of prominence and influence during their lifetimes, men and women such as Elliott Moses, Milton Martin, and Celia File cannot be said to have shaped the contours of public memory nor have they enjoyed the same kind of historical longevity as a Helen Creighton. Nevertheless, like any other cultural practice our understanding of the use of history and its significance remains partial and limited if we do not attempt to grapple with the ways in which individual men and women understood, deployed, desired, and were comforted or dismayed by it. As Susan Crane has argued, "all narratives, all sites, all texts remain objects until they are 'read' or referred to individuals thinking historically," an argument that has underpinned much of my work in this collection.[12] Sources such as Celia File's memoir, Janet Carnochan's *History of Niagara*, or Elliott Moses' talks, interviews, and written works provide hints and clues about how these men and women "thought historically," a process that involved complicated interplay between their conceptions of the past and their engagement with their present context.

I would be disingenuous, however, to claim that the state does not enter into this book. Chapters 1, 2, and 3 focus on men and women who were teachers, although their relationships with the teaching profession varied. Carnochan, for example, did most of her historical work after she retired from teaching. File's work as a teacher drew her into historical research on the Six Nations, while Martin's profile as an elementary school principal gave him a platform from which to challenge Canadians' historical knowledge, particularly that conveyed in textbooks. It could also be argued, of course, that Moses saw himself in the role of a public educator, as he strove to inform non-Aboriginal Canadians about his people's potential and, too, to educate both non-Aboriginal Canadians and his own community about the need for political and social change as he understood it. Moreover, while some of the actors in the last chapter were primarily motivated by the need to boost their hometown's economic fortunes, others also saw tourism as a way to educate both locals and visitors about Niagara's historical significance. "Public history," as expressed in the work of bodies such as the Historic Sites and Monuments Board or the Ontario Heritage Foundation, is, after all, public pedagogy. While the historiography on commemoration and historical memory has had less to say explicitly about the role of teachers in the creation of public history – and public history's link to the schools – there are hints in the scholarship that Carnochan, Martin, and File were not alone.[13] Guy Beiner's work on the creation of folk history in twentieth-century Ireland, for example, points to those secondary school teachers who collected narratives of the 1798 uprising, while Marla M. Miller and Anne Digan Lanning's research on historic Deerfield in Massachusetts demonstrates the involvement of female teachers in the town's late nineteenth- and early twentieth-century reconstruction.[14]

Portions of two of these chapters have appeared elsewhere. A version of chapter 2 has been published in *Placing Memory and Remembering Place in Canada*, while a section of chapter 4 is part of a chapter on landscape and historical tourism in *Heroines and History*. Although the arguments made in those earlier versions have not been overturned, I have added material that could not, for reasons of space and suitability, be used in the earlier versions, with the result that the chapters have been substantially enlarged in their scope. Moreover, working on this book and teaching the history of commemoration to students both within and outside the university has pushed me to re-evaluate some of the certainties that guided my earlier work on Secord and those who memorialized her. My chapter on Janet Carnochan, for example, represents a re-engagement with the question of white women's work in historical societies and the meaning of "the local." While I have argued – and still do – that the vast majority of those women involved in commemoration in late Victorian and Edwardian Ontario cannot be seen outside of imperialism's ambit, nevertheless treating Carnochan as the subject of an entire book chapter gives me more opportunity for depth and nuance in understanding her passion for the past. Celia B. File's desire for the colonial past was also rooted in her own experiences of teaching at Tyendinaga and her friendship with Bernice Loft. While undoubtedly shaped by her own racial privilege, her history, both personal and professional, cannot be as easily slotted into the framework of white women's historical writing that I identified for the earlier period. It is undeniable that Moses' and Martin's needs for historical knowledge were complicated ones, fraught with their own ambivalence towards both Indigenous and settler societies and shaped by competing conceptions of how Canadian history should be told. Yet what is remarkable about their narratives is not just their content. It is also their determination that they – not Indian agents, missionaries, or anthropologists – should be the ones to tell their stories.

This book, then, explores the ways in which individuals and groups struggled to define themselves and their contexts through the medium of historical narratives. There is also, though, the question of my own subjectivity.[15] Not only have I been, like Carnochan and File, a historian of Ontario's colonial past, concerned with the position of women and, increasingly, Indigenous peoples in it, like Carnochan I also live in her "historic town" of Niagara-on-the-Lake, a place that has come to occupy a portion of my research and writing and one where I have learned much about history's uses and significance outside the academy. Does that make me more subjective and less omniscient? Perhaps. Does that make my understanding of my subject matter more perceptive or overly myopic? I leave that to my readers to decide.

Chapter One

Books and Mortar: Janet Carnochan's Historical Town

"It is a beautiful spot with wonderful natural advantages," she wrote, "the broad lake, the blue river, forts, lighthouse, old elms, linden trees, weeping willows, broad, quiet streets, and almost every spot being of historic interest. It has been said that to know the history of Niagara is to know much of the history of Upper Canada." For Janet Carnochan, her hometown of Niagara combined great natural beauty – its shorefronts, Carolinian forest, and orchards – with a treasure trove of the past. Yet unlike the views, smells, and sounds of the lake and trees, sensory experiences that were accessible to all, uncovering and bringing the town's historical riches to the attention of audiences both local and beyond required great persistence and diligence. Such perseverance was needed since "history," for Carnochan, might be found in a number of places: in artefacts, documents, ephemera, landscape, and people. What's more, historical knowledge could be put to work in a number of genres and forums: displayed in a museum, reported at historical society gatherings, reflected upon in poetry, and transmitted in newspaper columns, articles, and books. To be sure, her research was time-consuming and taxing, at times involving solitary and tedious labour. Simultaneously, however, it was work that she delighted in, labour that engaged a range of her faculties: intellectual, moral, and, occasionally, sensory. Carnochan also hoped that her audiences would have similar experiences, that knowledge of the town's past would stimulate, educate, uplift, and entertain them.

Moreover, as the above quote suggests, while Carnochan's history was intensely local in its immediate scope, it also was interlaced with broader narratives of Canada's colonial origins. Such narratives might give the place significance and meaning for those sceptical about the need to highlight the town's past in such detail. Yet local history was not to be undertaken only as it manifested the effects of national and imperial events and processes, or read as a space where the aftershocks and reverberations of the nation-state and empire were registered. For one, the town of Niagara had been a place in which narratives of nation and empire took on concrete and embodied meaning and significance for men and women and for their descendants. Without the local context as a staging ground in which national and imperial affairs might be experienced, these processes remained abstract and disembodied, and their import could not be readily grasped by the public that Carnochan so dearly desired to reach. Moreover, although there was no escape, no safe haven from events such as the American Revolution or the War of 1812, for Carnochan the town's past also was more than military and political upheavals. It was a place made by the ideas and efforts of individuals and organizations, one that, in turn, she created for late Victorian and Edwardian audiences. Finally, a detailed examination of Carnochan's work allows us to see where and how she resembled her fellow historians in English Canada and, equally importantly, where Carnochan's historical vision and practice of history differed from those of her contemporaries.

Born in 1839 in Stamford (now part of Niagara Falls' north end), Carnochan was the second daughter of James Carnochan, a cabinet-maker and carpenter, and Mary Milroy, Scottish immigrants who had arrived in Stamford from Ayrshire around 1830. In 1841 the family moved to Niagara-on-the-Lake; with her four siblings, Carnochan spent her childhood and adolescence in the village, where she attended school and St. Andrew's Presbyterian church.[1] Like many young, single women in southern Ontario during the mid-nineteenth century, in 1856 Carnochan became a teacher by applying for a Certificate of Qualification. The next year, at seventeen, she began teaching at the Niagara Public School.[2] Carnochan pursued further teaching qualifications by attending the Toronto Normal School in 1859, where she received a First Class Provincial Normal School Certificate and went on to teach in Brantford and Kingston. Carnochan remained at this school for five years, until her mother's illness called her home to manage her parents' household. After her mother's recovery, Carnochan taught for a year in a rural school near Peterborough until the principal's position in the Niagara Public School became vacant.[3] She applied for the job and, upon being accepted, returned home in 1872.

Few sources have survived to describe Carnochan's years as public-school principal, although later tributes stressed her dedication to teaching and the esteem in which she was held.[4] Two years after the construction of a new high school building in Niagara was completed in 1876, Carnochan joined its staff and remained there until she retired in December 1900. While teaching, she also channelled her considerable energy into travel and voluntary work. She turned the story of her 1878 shipwreck on Sable Island, while en route to Britain, into a manuscript and also was chosen as one of twenty Canadian women to attend the Chicago World Congress.[5] Moreover, Carnochan began a long history of work for St. Andrews: she taught in its Sunday school, fundraised for the church, and from 1892 to 1895 sat on its Board of Managers. From 1897 until her death in 1926, Carnochan was the secretary of the church's newly founded Women's Missionary Society.[6] In addition to her service for the church, Carnochan sat on the board of the Niagara Public Library as its secretary and treasurer, and, from time to time, as a temporary librarian.[7]

While it occupied thirty-nine years of her life, less is known about Carnochan's work as a teacher. Instead, her "informal" educational work as a local and regional historian, historical preservationist, and museum director left its mark on the historical record. She began making forays into historical writing in the 1890s with her histories of Niagara's Anglican and Presbyterian churches.[8] In 1895 Carnochan became the president of the newly revived Niagara Historical Society (NHS) (an earlier endeavour by Niagara resident and historian William Kirby had been short-lived), where she was a leading figure until 1925, and served as president, corresponding secretary, and editor of its reports and publications.[9] After retiring from teaching, Carnochan became even more engrossed in historical work. As well as her activities with the NHS, Carnochan wrote a historical column in the local paper, the *Niagara Times*.[10] She became curator of the society's collections in 1901 and spearheaded the NHS drive for the 1907 construction of Memorial Hall, the first building erected as a museum in Ontario.[11] As well as representing the NHS at the annual meetings of the Ontario Historical Society (OHS), from 1901 to 1911 Carnochan also sat on its Monuments Committee and from 1914 to 1919 she was the Society's vice president.[12] In 1914 Carnochan published her *History of Niagara*, which was printed by William Briggs's Toronto publishing company, and had a foreword written by Dr. A. H. U. Colquhoun, Deputy Minister of Education.[13]

Not content with directing the museum and writing her histories, Carnochan expended much energy in attempts to preserve historical landmarks in Niagara, such as Butler's Burying Ground, Forts George and Mississauga, and the military reserve, or Commons.[14]

Of course, Carnochan was not unique or an isolated figure; rather, she conducted her local work within the larger provincial, national, and transnational contexts of a late nineteenth-century concern with the past.[15] Moreover, like her contemporaries Sarah Curzon, Mary Agnes Fitzgibbon, Emma Currie, Clementina Fessenden, and Elizabeth Thompson, Carnochan was an adherent of both Canadian nationalism and the British Empire. Yet while Carnochan shared their belief in history's power to inform the present with political, social, and, above all, moral examples, she differed from her fellow historians in a variety of ways. For one, unlike Fessenden's more conservative support of the imperial tie, Carnochan's was a liberal imperialism where support for Britain meant support for a history of abolitionism, religious toleration, and reform movements. While Curzon and Currie openly championed woman's suffrage – their writing of white women into history an overtly political act – Carnochan was far more circumspect about the need for enfranchisement. Although as we shall see she sought evidence of women's presence in various nooks and crannies of the historical record and defined "woman" as a historical category much more widely than the vast majority of her fellow historians, nevertheless there is no historical record of her own public support for suffrage. Her silence on the matter is intriguing, especially since Carnochan shared the associational life of many English-speaking, middle-class women of her time – temperance, missionary, and denominational work – which drew more than a few into calling for political change. Furthermore, she expressed publicly her admiration for Curzon and Currie; to wit, there is no hint in her tributes to them, during their lives and at their deaths, that her esteem was tempered by distaste for their political activism.[16] As well, in 1917 Carnochan gave a lecture to the Niagara Historical Society on the "extension of the franchise to women." Although the text was not published, a manuscript on the "First Years of the Canadian Woman's Rights Movement," which may have been her talk, sketched out its history, referring to Emily Stowe and Toronto Women's Literary Club, the growth in attendance of women students at the University of Toronto, the granting of the municipal franchise to women, and the growth of suffrage societies across Ontario and in Montreal, Saint John's, and Winnipeg. It appears that Carnochan approved of all of

Janet Carnochan's Historical Town 15

1.1 *Janet Carnochan* by E. Wyly Grier, 1921. This portrait was commissioned by the Niagara Historical Society for its twenty-fifth anniversary. Melbourne-born Grier, who was married to a Miss Dickson of Niagara-on-the-Lake, was well known in Canada and England and was knighted by King George V in 1935 for his contributions to Canadian arts and letters. Courtesy Niagara Historical Museum 988.246.

these happenings.[17] Whatever the case, though, Carnochan's passion for the past took up the bulk of her time. She may not have wanted to become involved in causes or pursuits that could have distracted her from her main goal: collecting, writing, and preserving the history of her beloved Niagara, a history that illustrated the grand narrative of the Dominion but that also testified to the importance of studying a particular location.

Carnochan and her colleagues in Niagara had been collecting a range of objects throughout the 1890s, artefacts that included portraits of early settlers, such as United Empire Loyalists, military heroes, or those who "either as men or women in any way helped to make our town and country."[18] By 1903, the Annual Report stated that two thousand articles had been amassed, making the need for a permanent museum even more pressing.[19] Carnochan played a key role in obtaining provincial and federal funds and raising money at the local level, work that was recognized by her peers and the local press.[20] The informal opening of Memorial Hall in March of 1907 was described by *The Daily Standard* of St. Catharines as a presentation of "many fine artefacts, many fine pictures in the revolving case; however, one important picture was missing: a portrait that should occupy the more conspicuous position, one that every loyal citizen of Niagara, and very member of the society hope some day to see adorning the walls of the building she has worked for so faithfully and zealously ... but for her we would never have had an Historical Society, a collection, or a building to store it in." The author also paid tribute to Elizabeth Thompson, a fellow member of the NHS who worked with Carnochan, for having arranged and labelled the collections.[21]

Once the museum opened, the society – and Carnochan in particular – accumulated an even greater variety of items. The 1911 Catalogue, which was broken down into Memorial Hall's thirty-one display cases and a number of other items that presumably were stored in its vaults, points to not only the plethora of material that the building housed (over 5000 items) but also the sweep and scope of the collection. In contrast with the collections amassed by local museums in New England in this period, which so often highlighted textiles and the implements used to fashion them (blankets, clothing, baskets, tablecloths, spinning wheels, and treadles) in order to represent the colonies' history as an "age of homespun,"[22] the objects held by the Niagara museum suggested that the town's history included a wide range of historical developments and historical actors. To be sure, the collection included textiles where

1.2 Memorial Hall, 1907. Courtesy Niagara Historical Museum.

possible. Case Eighteen was devoted to "women's work in early times, hand-made" and included an infant's cloak made in 1810; an embroidered cap from 1815; Honoria Jarvis's 1796 sampler; Laura Secord's beaded purse; and a wooden doll, complete with clothing, from 1835.[23] Case Fourteen highlighted collections of women's clothing: a shot-silk Empire dress made between 1806 and 1812; a silk shawl, cap, and white kid gloves brought from Paris in 1853 in a walnut shell; and a number of more everyday bonnets, shawls, slippers, and stockings.[24]

An even larger array of men's clothing and accessories sat next to the women's wear. Some of it spoke of daily use (hat stretchers, linen nightcaps), while other items testified to their owner's position in politics and associational life: Senator Plumb's white silk embroidered vest (figure 1.4), S. Sheppard's Masonic apron, and Rafe Clench's hat, worn

18 Creating Colonial Pasts

1.3 Susan Chubbuck sampler, 1848. Courtesy Niagara Historical Museum 901.112.

by him at the 1792 opening of Parliament in Newark.[25] Therefore, while china collections, cooking utensils, and a clutch of other household apparatus such as candle moulds, lamps, stoves, cradles, and andirons attested to sites of late eighteenth-century domesticity and intimacy in which women's domestic work and reproductive labour were significant, land grants, early maps, town plans, and sketches of Niagara's first buildings suggested the masculine worlds of colonial officials.

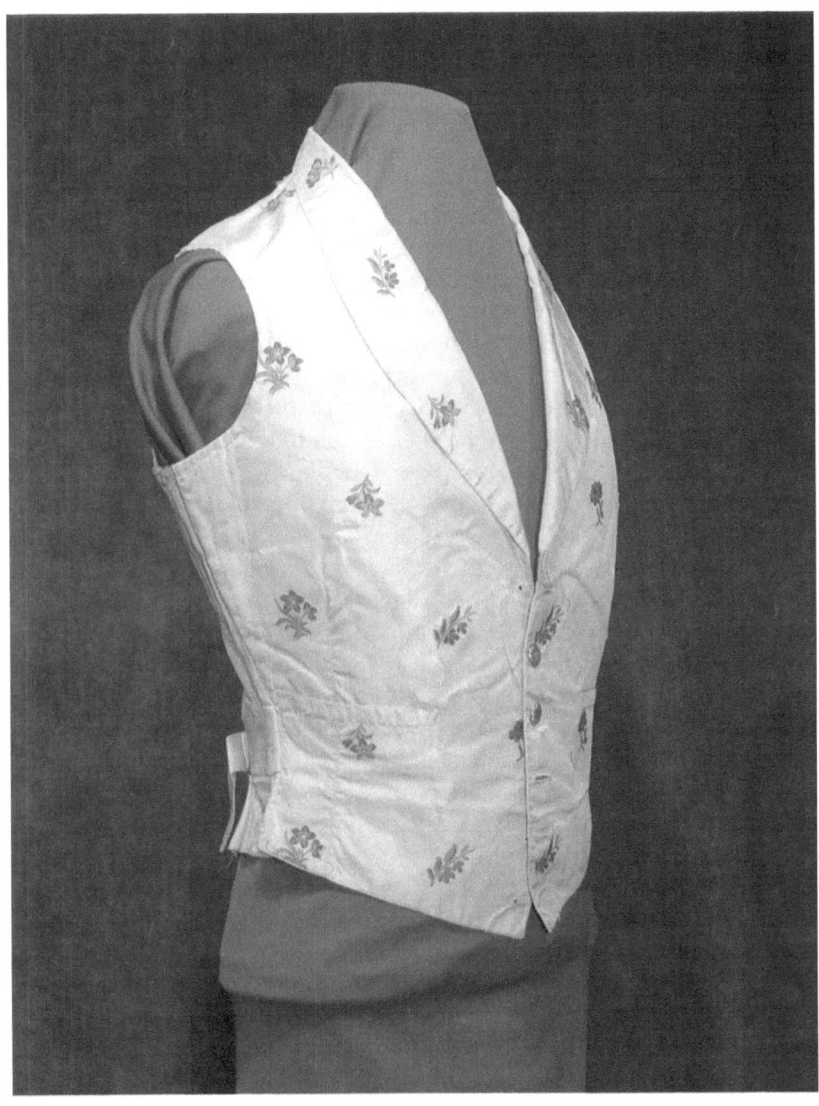

1.4 Josiah Plumb's waistcoat. Courtesy Niagara Historical Museum 972.221.

The museum's collection also sketched out another theme in the town's history, that of its political life. Carnochan and her fellow Society members eagerly amassed those documents and artefacts that testified to the town's position as the first capital of Upper Canada, presided over by Lieutenant Governor John Graves Simcoe: a speech and proclamation; land, liquor and tavern licenses signed by him; a copy of Elizabeth Simcoe's 1794 sketch of the Niagara River's mouth; and her husband's china saucer.[26] The reform movement in Upper Canada received its share of recognition in the collection, including: speeches, debates, and reports from the legislature leading up to the events of December 1837; as well as copies of William Lyon Mackenzie's proclamation from Navy Island, his newspapers from the early 1840s, published in Rochester, New York, during his exile in that city; and Lieutenant Governor George Arthur's proclamation asking for the capture of James Morreau, hanged in Niagara in 1838 for his share in the Rebellion.[27]

Although Carnochan would devote more time in her written work to the history of escaped slaves in Niagara, a few items suggested their presence in the town; a case of pewter and tin included a sugar bowl brought by anonymous escaped slaves and a small candlestick, the property of William Riley, "an escaped slave."[28] Riley's log house also appeared, in a pencil sketch done in 1816 (figure 1.6).[29] Moreover, in the display of women's work "Mrs. Riley's patchwork done in 1837 during the Slave Rescue" sat between mid-eighteenth-century work from England and a model of a doll's bonnet, sent from Paris in 1837.[30]

As well, Anglican, Presbyterian, and, to a lesser extent, Methodist churches all found their histories represented, in artefacts such as a pitch pipe, Communion tokens, a weather vane in the form of the Archangel Gabriel (knocked down from the steeple of the Presbyterian church in 1855's tornado) (figure 1.7), candle sconces, and a collection box, as well as documents that testify to the minutiae of running a congregation: lists of land and pew deeds, subscribers, and minutes.[31] The town's voluntary associations and its intellectual and social life were symbolized in multiple ways: in handbills advertising associations' gatherings and their rules and regulations, the Mechanic's Institute seal, artefacts and documents used in the town's schools, the library's catalogue, and books and newspapers published in Niagara (not to mention rare books that mentioned the area and rare books in general).[32]

Other items, though, told different stories. Some predated the Loyalist arrival and the formation of settler society. Case Twenty Five, placed in a gallery and described as "mostly Indian," held tomahawks, flints,

1.5 Receipt issued by William Riley. Riley had escorted a prisoner, John Harris, to the town jail and was paid a stipend of 2s and 6d for this work. Courtesy Niagara Historical Museum 2001.324.

arrowheads, bones, pottery fragments, a piece of Louis Riel's coat, Sioux weaponry, Chief Wandering Spirit's fire bag, and Inuit fishing gear and clothing. These items testified both to the presence of Indigenous people in the Niagara peninsula and from further afield – a collection that Carnochan was eager to augment.[33] Writing to Ontario Historical Society secretary and provincial archaeologist David Boyle in 1902, she conceded that her collection was becoming "very crowded," yet she also asked him to make "some judicious and thrifty purchases" of any Indian artefacts of which he had duplicates on behalf of the society. She had tried, with no success, to buy such objects on a number of occasions. Practical matters, of course, had to be considered, as she was collecting for a small-town museum and not a large institution funded by wealthy philanthropists. Carnochan reminded Boyle "we cannot of course pay fancy prices. We were to have had an Indian mask, turtle rattlers worn in dancing, a war club, of course this last would be a modern manufactured one as I suppose the genuine ones are not to be found."[34] (This was not the first time Carnochan had solicited such items. As Michelle Hamilton has pointed out, in 1899 Carnochan also corresponded with the Mohawk lecturer, performer, and international traveller John Ojijatekha Brant-Sero, who promised her a

1.6 Sketch of William Riley's house, 1816. Mary Ann Guillen, William Riley's daughter, donated the sketch to the Museum. Courtesy Niagara Historical Museum 991.090.

False Face mask, turtle rattle, and corn-processing tools).[35] While it's not clear if Boyle came through with the desired objects, her interest in Indigenous artefacts was not a passing fancy. During the 1906 OHS meeting at Collingwood, she was quite taken by the "valuable collection of the Huron Institute" that included Indian relics, botanical specimens, and mineralogy.[36] The collection also included material originally amassed by Kahkewaquonaby, the Methodist missionary and writer Peter Jones, as well as a copy of his *History of the Ojebway People*.[37]

However, if there was one event that can be said to have stood out in the Museum's collection, it was the War of 1812. Military flags, relics of General Brock (including his never-worn hat, which is still displayed in the museum's permanent exhibit), sashes, powder horns, spurs, coats, jackets, tunics, uniform buttons, weaponry, and commissions of Niagara residents, as well as engravings and sketches of individuals, events, and places associated with the War. All of these items composed not so

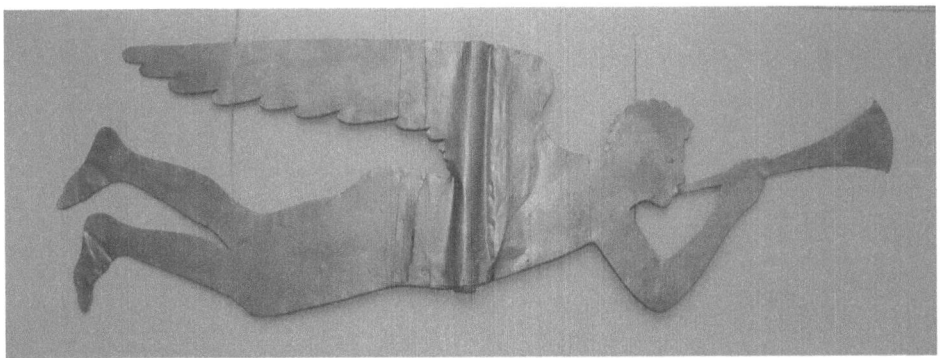

1.7 Presbyterian weathervane. It was set in place on St. Andrew's church in 1831, the year the reconstructed church was built (the original had been burnt in 1813 by American troops). Courtesy Niagara Historical Museum 969.409.

much a narrative, perhaps, but rather a montage of images and representations. The cabinets containing these items came first in the catalogue and, in all likelihood, they were the first things that visitors to the museum saw (unfortunately no floor plan of the Museum's layout survives). Like the town plans, surveys, and maps, these artefacts spoke of men's historical actions and agency, as it was men who took the commissions, wore the uniforms, fired the guns, and received the commendations. To be sure, the exhibit cases could not tell their viewers who made items such as clothing, sashes, and flags; in York, the Young Ladies' Patriotic Society made a banner for the town's militia in 1812, which they presented at a public ceremony and subsequently resurrected in the late nineteenth century.[38] Furthermore, Carnochan and her colleagues were committed to collecting items associated with Niagara's most famous heroine of the War, Laura Secord. Dispersed throughout the exhibits were multiple reminders of Secord, from encompassed engravings, sketches, and letters, to spoons, a sugar bowl cover, and a large hamper.[39] The Society also was proud to report that Miss Augusta Smith of Guelph, Laura Secord's granddaughter, had donated her grandmother's copper tea kettle "of which the story runs, that in the War of 1812, when in danger from the enemy, a quantity of gold doubloons were placed in the kettle hanging over the fire in the old-fashioned fireplace, both gold and kettle were undisturbed."[40]

24 Creating Colonial Pasts

1.8 Haudenosaunee wampum beads. Courtesy Niagara Historical Museum 970.143.

It was not only artefacts of the War of 1812 that were found in Memorial Hall's displays of military history. Other items represented imperial conflicts, past and present, both across Canada and around the world. In 1902 Carnochan told David Boyle she was in a "particularly good humour as I have just had a letter from South Africa from one of the 'boys' who writes a very good letter and encloses some little relics from S.A. [such] as a Kaffir girl's leg bracelet, a Boer pass, etc." The Museum also received a carpetbag left by a fugitive fleeing Culloden and an Indian silver brooch, engraved with two elephants, which supposedly had been discovered clutched in the hand of an unidentified victim of the 1857 Indian Mutiny.[41] Next to the War of 1812 displays visitors would find cases with Fenian muskets and bayonets, an 1832 United States Springfield gun, Boer guns captured by Canadian troops in 1901, a US Civil War carbine, a sword from Waterloo, and a Cuban machete.[42]

1.9 Haudenosaunee doll, Grand River, c. mid-late eighteenth century. This doll belonged to a Grand River chief's daughter and is made of wood and papier-maché. Courtesy Niagara Historical Museum 972.9.

PROCLAMATION.
Province of Upper Canada.

ISAAC BROCK, Esquire, President administering the Government of the Province of Upper Canada, and Major-General Commanding His Majesty's Forces within the same.

TO ALL TO WHOM IT MAY CONCERN :—... GREETING.

WHEREAS information has been received, that divers persons have recently come into this Province, with a seditious intent to disturb the tranquility thereof, and to endeavour to alienate the minds of His Majesty's Subjects from His Person and Government ; I hereby require and enjoin the several persons authorized, to carry into effect a certain Statute, passed in the Forty-fourth year of his Majesty's reign, intituled, "An Act for the better securing this Province against all seditious attempts or designs to disturb the tranquility thereof," to be vigilant in the execution of their duty, and strictly to enquire into the behaviour and conduct of all such persons as may be subject to the provisions of the said Act ; and I do also charge and require all his Majesty's Good and Loyal Subjects within this Province, to be aiding and assisting the said Persons, in the execution of the powers vested in them by the said Act.

GIVEN under my Hand and Seal at Arms, at York, this Twenty-fourth day of February, in the year of our Lord One thousand Eight hundred and Twelve, and in the Fifty-second of his Majesty's Reign.

ISAAC BROCK, President.

By Command of His Honor,
W<small>M</small>. J<small>ARVIS</small>, Sec'y.

1.10 Isaac Brock's Proclamation of War of 1812. Courtesy Niagara Historical Museum 978.5.463.

As well as the array of objects, documents, books, and artwork Carnochan and her colleagues gathered to illustrate the town's eighteenth- and nineteenth-century past (and the history of other places and times), the Museum's collection also testified to the nineteenth-century desire to commemorate. Medals struck for a number of occasions told of celebrations of British royalty, such as Queen Victoria's visit to London on the Lord Mayor's Day in 1837, her Diamond Jubilee, or her son's 1902 Coronation.[43] The Crimean battles of Alma, Balaclava, and Inkerman were remembered, as was the Paris Industrial Exposition.[44] However, commemorative practices were most completely represented by items that dealt either with the War of 1812 –posters for Brock's 1824 and 1853 funerals, a banner made for the 1853 unveiling of Brock's monument, photographs of it – or of other events deemed noteworthy to Canadian history, such as medals struck when Brant's monument was erected in 1886, ones made in honour of Simcoe in 1892, or those issued for Toronto's 1884 "Semi-Centennial."[45] Lest anyone think

Janet Carnochan's Historical Town 27

1.11 Isaac Brock's (never-worn) hat. Courtesy Niagara Historical Museum 972.275.2.

that the Niagara Historical Society was plying its craft in isolation, Case 30 contained "exchanges" (reports and transactions) from a host of historical societies across the province – Elgin, Hamilton, Lundy's Lane, York, Lennox and Addington, the Women's Historical Societies of Wentworth, Ottawa, and Toronto – and from the provincial, national, and university archives.[46] The Society's contacts also reached across borders; a list of exchanges with American historical societies included Michigan, Wisconsin, Buffalo, New York, Massachusetts, Rhode Island, New Hampshire, Long Island, Connecticut, Colorado, and California.[47]

The collection, then, was almost dizzying in the sheer magnitude of the items amassed by the Society, a magnitude that some felt detracted

28 Creating Colonial Pasts

1.12 Lieutenant Daniel McDougal, Upper Canadian Militia, coatee, c. 1813–14. McDougal fought at the Battle of Fort George and Lundy's Lane. Courtesy Niagara Historical Museum 972.902.

from the order into which the past should be put and, in turn, represent. In 1902 Boyle himself had attempted to help with its reorganization prior to the building of Memorial Hall. Despite the NHS's attempts to follow his precepts, though, he ended his efforts (albeit expended over the course of only two days) by describing it as still "semi-chaotic," since the building was simply too small for the number of artefacts it housed.[48] Forty-one years later, well after the building of the Museum, the situation had not changed much. A 1943 visit by museum collector and philanthropist Sigmund Samuel (accompanied by members of the Women's Literary Society of St. Catharines and the Women's Institute) left the Society pondering not just his interest in their holdings but his assessment of "the congested character of the building."[49] The Society probably did not need Samuel to tell them that, though, since photographs taken in 1927 show a building chock-a-block with the past. After Carnochan's death in 1926, her successor Elizabeth Thompson spent considerable time and effort reorganizing and relabelling the collection.[50] "The room looks so much better since it has been cleaned and is kept clean," she confided to Andrew Hunter, the Ontario Historical Society's secretary. "I never could see why historical material must be dirty just because it was old. So many are working up family history and the old maps help in this, but I find it very hard to find things Miss C had no [sense?] of order and left no records to help me."[51] It seems that Carnochan's methods, not to mention her imperviousness to dust, could not be easily duplicated. One imagines her successor tearing her hair in frustration as she wiped, swept, sneezed, and then moved things about (and probably sneezed again).[52] Already vexed by the state of the artefacts, Thompson felt even more exasperated by the large number of visitors – 1413 that year – who brought with them questions that, she admitted, challenged the extent of her historical knowledge.[53]

The reactions of visitors during Carnochan's tenure, to both the Hall's predecessor in the former town library and to Memorial Hall itself, are not readily available. However, approximately twelve hundred people came to view the collection in 1907, and over the next few years visitors came from other Canadian and American cities and, in one case, Wellington, New Zealand.[54] Both before and after the First World War, Memorial Hall and its collection became something of a local celebrity, advertised in the local paper as containing "over 6,000 articles of historical interest" and described by the Toronto press as one of the "points of interest" in the "most up-to-date and popular summer resort

30   Creating Colonial Pasts

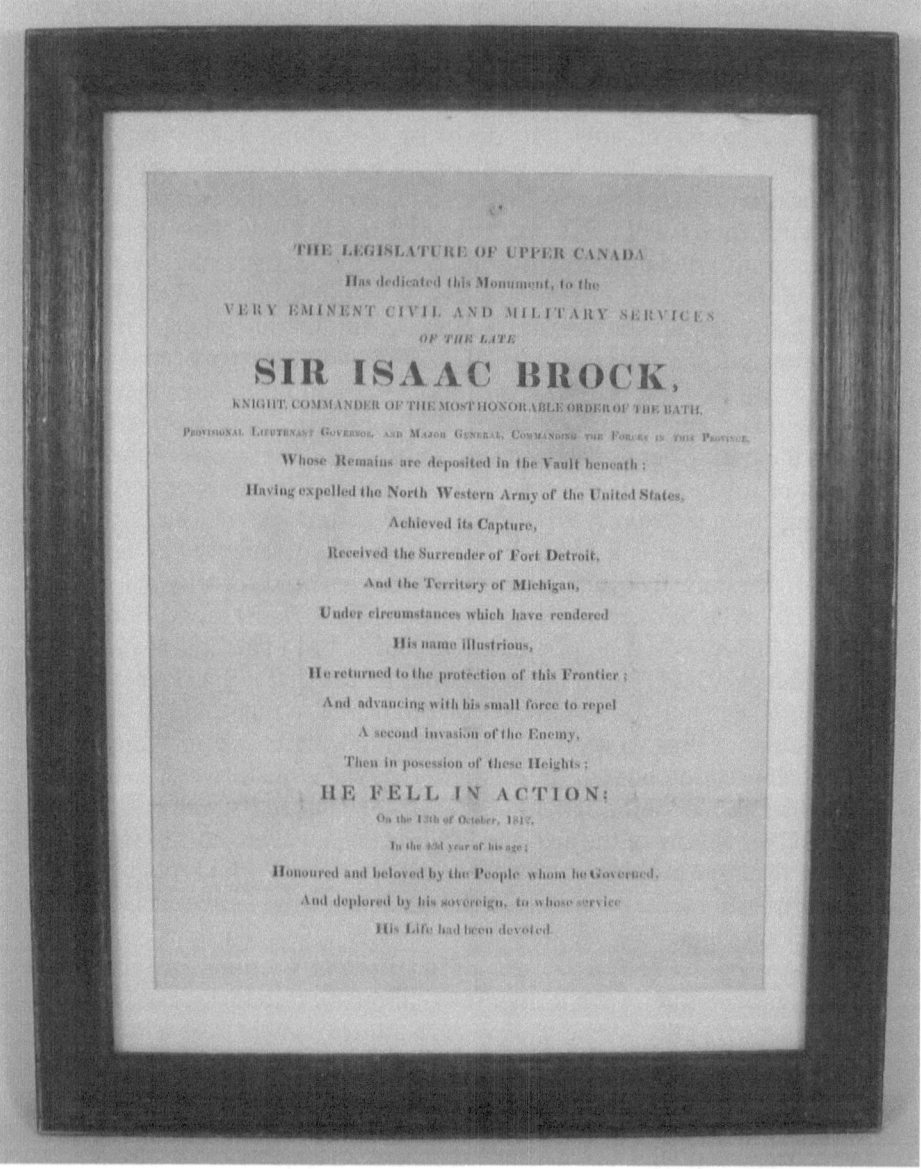

1.13   Handbill announcing Brock's burial, 1824. Courtesy Niagara Historical Museum 986.5.158.

in Canada."[55] Later in the twentieth century, school groups and local children were drawn to the museum, the latter so much so that in 1954 the executive committee tartly reported that the grounds and porch were being used as a playground and some parents viewed it as an appropriate place to send their offspring after school. The curators were not babysitters and did not consider childcare "a matter of historical import and discouraged its practice."[56] Carnochan herself also undertook to publicize the collection whenever she could. Her "Evolution of an Historic Room," published by the NHS in 1914, presented a short history of the collection's early years and selected a variety of items that, to her mind, were "the most remarkable." In her article the artefacts were arrayed in an order more kaleidoscopic than chronological: they spoke of the town's growth from the 1820s on but also its destruction in 1813, the consistent presence of the military, its religious life, reformers (Gourlay and Mackenzie), the library, individual white settlers, and the presence of Indigenous people.[57] Her 1908 piece "A Few of the Most Interesting Articles in Memorial Hall," meant to answer the commonly asked question of which article she found the most valuable, is almost breathless in its desire to draw attention to "so many valuable articles in the various divisions, Military, Literary, Artistic, Useful." Carnochan responded to the query with lengthy paragraphs that provided a compendium of historical objects. One imagines her walking the visitor through the Museum, almost at breakneck speed, in her desire to immerse them in the town's past.

To be sure, Carnochan's interest in collecting was a widespread one. It interested not only other Canadians, such as her colleague David Boyle or the Montreal lawyer and historian David Ross McCord, but was also transnational, as American, British, and Australian collectors amassed historical artefacts and natural history specimens that testified to national, regional, and local pasts.[58] As the reports and transactions of other historical societies held at Memorial Hall demonstrated, she was well aware of being part of a movement that spread far beyond southern Ontario. Yet Carnochan also was motivated by concerns shaped by both national and local contexts. For all of her support for Britain and Canada's tie to empire, Carnochan thought of her work as an important corrective to the notion that Canada lacked a history, a theme that she addressed directly in her writings. Moreover, and probably more germane to her role in the museum, Carnochan was driven to show that the depredations of the War had not depleted the area of its historical artefacts. "Much cold water," she wrote in her history of

1.14 Memorial Hall interior, 1927 Courtesy Niagara Historical Museum.

the museum, "had metaphorically been thrown upon the project of collecting articles relating to the history of the Town and Neighbourhood. It was said nothing had been left; everything had been given away or destroyed, or did any such article exist, no one would either give or lend anything for such a purpose. All such prognostications have proved false."[59] (Carnochan was not above depicting herself as waging a valiant struggle to do her work of history in the face of local scepticism, indifference, or hostility.) While documents, both in Niagara and elsewhere, and to some extent residents' memories, might illuminate the early years of European settlement, objects were invaluable. Citing Boyle, Carnochan spoke of the "superiority" of the local history museum as a pedagogical tool. "Wherever there is a good library, there should be a good Museum; one without the other is incomplete. It

1.15 Upper Gallery, Memorial Hall, 1927. Courtesy Niagara Historical Museum.

should supplement the library and be supported by the country as well as the library. Object teaching is the oldest kind of teaching, and every object should illustrate a point, embrace some statement, or elucidate something otherwise obscure."[60]

Object teaching, though, was far from being the only way to illustrate, embrace, and elucidate; discussions of objects, documents, and memories could be woven together in a written narrative. If not quite the culmination of Carnochan's historical work, since she continued to be active for twelve years after its publication, her *History of Niagara* certainly marked a very high point in her career (and to date it is still the most comprehensive and best-known history of the town).[61] Organized both chronologically and thematically, the book's forty-four chapters began with an overview of the peninsula, which included a discussion of its Neutral, Mississauga, and Seneca inhabitants. It then plunged the reader into highly detailed discussions of the multiple facets of the town's history, a multiplicity that began with the very name of the place. "Ouinagarah, Ongiara, Niagara – in the index of the 'Documentary History of New York,' there are over forty forms of the sonorous Indian word, sonorous yet soft and musical; the word is thought by some to be the only word left of the language of the Neutral Indians who formerly occupied this territory." But it wasn't just the Neutrals who were fond of plurality. The town had been known as "Loyal Village, Butlersburg, West Niagara, Newark, Niagara, and now Niagara-on-the-Lake – the unwary explorer of archives may easily be led astray, for in early records Niagara generally means Fort Niagara, and Little Niagara, the upper end of the portage road near Fort Schlosser on the American side." (Even in Carnochan's time residents might see their letters go missing, since Niagara featured in the names of a number of other places on both sides of the border.)[62] Carnochan did her best to impose order, though, with her division of chapters into discrete categories: politics (the first Parliament), the military presence (Brock, Butler's Barracks, the American Occupation), first settlers, local government (mayors and records, statutes and bills, the jail, the court house), economic and commercial growth (the Niagara Harbor and Dock Company), the professions, the churches, voluntary associations and lodges, education, the press and library, and the town's social life, found in "assemblies, balls and celebrations."

To no small extent, then, the book replicated those patterns and motifs found within the cases held at Memorial Hall. However, the events and developments of Carnochan's narrative could be intertwined more directly for her readers than, perhaps, for those who perused the artefacts, sketches, and photographs. For one, the military made a number of appearances, marking public space in the town with Forts George and Mississauga, as well as being the subject of discussions regarding Brock and 1812. It also, though, ran a hospital and garrison school; on Sunday mornings a regiment marched past "Mrs Radcliffe's ladies' school," its band playing as the young scholars marched in time to church. Military officers were also highly visible in the town's social life, hosting and attending balls, as well as helping to organize public rituals such as Brock's funeral.[63]

Perhaps not surprisingly for a small town, individual names recur in multiple locations and are woven through the narrative, particularly when their owners were involved in local politics, commerce, churches, and voluntary societies. It was not just that certain families had been more prominent or powerful and thus turned up more frequently in the records, although that was probably the case. Rather, Carnochan's all-encompassing approach to the history of the place resulted in the book's breadth of topics and repetition of names and, at times, events. For Carnochan, as in the museum collection, the written history of her town was to be found not just in one particular site, such as the courthouse, town council, or military barracks, or only in certain developments, such as the founding of schools and churches. Instead, *History of Niagara* found "history" almost wherever its author looked, embodied in an abundance of sites, people, and associations. To be sure, *History of Niagara* took some pains to insist that events in the town were central to and reflected the development of national political institutions, "Canadian" values and morality, and the maintenance of the imperial tie and national sovereignty (the first parliament, the abolition of slavery, the Loyalists' arrival, and the War of 1812). Carnochan was not impervious to or untouched by the more abstract narratives of nation building that were coming to dominate the teaching of history in English Canadian universities and schools. However, unlike the work of university-trained historians, the nation was not entirely the book's "centre of narrative excitement," a concept and methodology that displaced local lore and culture.[64] Instead, the local spaces of the town gave meaning to the enactment and embodiment of historical processes such as wars, diplomatic manoeuvring, and the formation of political institutions. While the book located its histories of churches, schools, associational and voluntary life within the context of transnational and imperial organizations and movements, the latter's significance could not be understood and fully appreciated until they could be seen to be operating at the local and individual level. In Niagara such larger histories took on direct meaning and immediacy through the actions of individuals living in a specific location, such as Robert Addison, the first Anglican minister; John Crooks, the town's first postmaster; or the group who struggled to maintain the Free Church. In Carnochan's book, local men (and, at times, women) were the linchpins through which national and international movements were effected and understood.

In treating the town's history in such a catholic manner Carnochan also called attention to the multiplicity of sources that she used to craft it. To be sure, like university-based historians Carnochan saw documents as holding an important key to the past but she did not eschew other materials, such as objects, the memories of individuals, and specific sites. Instead, unlike her academic counterparts who tended to relegate such sources to the realm of the trivial and feminine, Carnochan saw these sources as contributing to a complete history, to a past noteworthy for its fullness and amplitude.[65] Although one of her biographers pointed to the book's lack of footnotes and bibliography,[66] this does not mean that her sources became invisible. Rather, in the body of her chapters the primary materials are highlighted and foregrounded. Instead of being buried in notes or bibliographic citations, the newspapers, documents, objects, and reminiscences constantly and consistently stand out and are given pride of place – they almost become characters in the narrative itself. *History of Niagara*, then, is a work that calls attention to its own specific crafting and to the historian's craft more generally. In her chapter on the United Empire Loyalists, for example, the Report of the commissioners who examined Loyalist claims is not just referred to as a source to be mined (although it is that), for it also warrants its own history and provenance.[67] Later in the chapter Carnochan quotes letters and notebooks that testify to the Loyalists' distress and destitute condition, treating each source separately for its particular details and specific narratives. Her chapters on churches call attention to the minute books and other forms of records, seen as valuable not just for the information they hold but for their very existence. St. Andrew's Presbyterian church, for example, holds "the old record book of which we are so proud," while the monuments and tablets at St. Mark's testify both to the history of the parish and to the historically minded parishioners who erected them.[68] Sources, then, were repositories of history and memory that deserved their own commemoration.

As well as thinking of her primary material in a respectful and almost loving way, Carnochan probably also figured that readers of her history who wanted "more" would then make their way to the museum, where she would be able to guide them towards the requisite materials. Furthermore, it was not uncommon for local historians to ignore the growing convention of footnotes and bibliographies that were becoming so prominent a feature of academically trained historians' work.[69] Moreover, while Carnochan's work demonstrated the "archive fever" that also marked nineteenth-century historical research, it did not respect the growing divide that was emerging between "history" and other genres of writing.[70] Unlike her academic contemporaries, Carnochan had not banished literature from her "house of history." Poetry, for example, is woven throughout the narrative. It too could serve as a means of understanding the past and generating knowledge about it. At times her use of poetry was almost predictable, appearing in, for example, narratives about the Loyalists. Their journey to the Niagara frontier in the 1780s seemed to Carnochan to be "an exile without parallel in history, except, perhaps, the expatriation of the Huguenots in the time of Louis XIV, or that of the Acadians," a statement followed by poems by Rev. Leroy Hooker and William Kirby that lauded the UELs for their fearless devotion to England and their determination and hard labour that created an "England" in the wilderness.[71] Given the widespread influence of Longfellow's poem *Evangeline* in the nineteenth and early twentieth century, perhaps this was unsurprising.[72] However, poetry – Longfellow's, to be precise – also made its way into more prosaic subjects, such as a discussion of the Niagara Harbor and Dock Company that used a quotation to illustrate the excitement felt by the spectators when a vessel left the shore.[73]

Poetry was not confined to these chapters, though, as chapter 41 was entirely devoted to "poems relating to Niagara." These range from William Kirby's more elegiac lines on the burnt town of 1813 and his tribute to the town's pastoral delights, to celebrations of the Niagara winter, St. Mark's, and a number of Carnochan's own verses. Carnochan's subjects include "Fort George's Lonely Sycamore," Forts George and Mississauga, Laura Secord (both her 1901 monument and the woman herself), hymns for the local Chautauqua grounds' opening ceremonies and for St. Andrew's centennial, and a tribute to the goldenrod plant. She also reprinted her "Has Canada a History?" a seven-verse refutation of the charge, levelled by an anonymous accuser:

'Your Country has no history, you must own,'
they coldly say, with calm, superior tone.

Carnochan marshaled evidence that ranged from the Atlantic, Pacific, and Arctic Oceans, and her subject matter covered New France, the fur trade, Red River, Louisbourg, Acadia, Laura Secord, the Plains of Abraham, the Loyalists, the abolition of slavery, and the keeping of treaties. All of these events and deeds culminated in the final verse, which spoke of:

a long-enduring, glorious record, filled
With all brave acts, of pure unselfish love,
Of gentle, knightly deeds, inspired above,

That our fair country justly may be famed,
That never may its children be ashamed.

For those who might have any doubts that Canadian history was anything but a progressive tale, Carnochan ended with:

Let each his part build, strong, and true, and sure,
Then shall we have a history to endure,
And Canada-our Canada-shall be
A noble, Christian nation, great and free.

As this quote suggests, the stories Carnochan told in her chapters were narratives of progress, prosperity, moral beneficence (particularly the case with the churches but in other areas as well, such as philanthropy), and intellectual and social growth. Carnochan, it is fair to point out, was no Helen Creighton, Nova Scotia's twentieth-century folklore collector, nor was she a Thomas Raddall – both of whom, as Ian McKay and Robin Bates have argued, favoured approaches that either placed Nova Scotians outside of historical time or suggested that the province had experienced an inexplicable, almost mystical, yet more or less preordained decline since the apogee of the early nineteenth century.[74] For Carnochan, Niagara-on-the-Lake was very much part of the late eighteenth and nineteenth centuries; specifically, its struggle was to continue to embrace progress and change and to fight against decay and decline. If Carnochan had a "master narrative" of the town, it was that of economic, intellectual, and social growth and success from the 1820s to (approximately) the 1850s. After this time period the removal of the county seat to St. Catharines, the closing of the Harbour and Dock Company, the withdrawal of the British troops, and a plummet in shipbuilding and the subsequent failures of industries such as a tannery, steel works, and car and knitting factories saw the town's fortunes reverse.

However, hope was just in sight and all had not been lost. While no longer a traditional commercial and political centre, "the retrograde movement had been arrested" as the town was remade into a beautiful, lively, and, most critically important, modern tourist attraction. "The building of the Queen's Royal Hotel on its unrivalled site, the Chautauqua Hotel, the conference of Bible students, the tournaments, volunteer camps, waterworks, electric light, cement pavements, planting of shade trees on the streets, the town park, development of fruit farms, new residences, all show a new town."[75] Although, unlike some of her counterparts in the historical preservation movement, Carnochan was not entirely opposed to tourism, her approach was not that of Creighton's, which valued timeless folk tales and rural superstitions.[76] Instead, the visitor to her town would be delighted with the public library "with its over seven thousand volumes" and the six thousand historical articles in its museum.[77] Moreover, late nineteenth- and early twentieth-century tourists also had a history of their own; the last two chapters of the book focused on early travel writing about Niagara and the steady flow of visitors to the town. No quiet backwater, it had been – and continued to be – a pleasant, yet lively centre that attracted various kinds of celebrities and well-known figures, both from Canada and abroad, a veritable roll-call that included writers, explorers, political figures, reform activists, and royalty. "Almost every important event in the history of Ontario at least is brought up by the name of a visitor at Niagara," Carnochan proudly affirmed.[78]

Yet the *History*'s tone was not quite as triumphalist or confident as this quote might suggest. Not only had Niagara experienced serious economic blows mid-century, it had suffered an even more painful fate in 1813, when American troops first occupied and then set alight much of the town. Although Carnochan showed little interest in the minutiae of battles (unlike, for example, Welland historian and Historic Sites and Monuments Board member Ernest Cruikshank, her contemporary), she devoted Chapter Eight to the "American Occupation May-December 1813," first describing the battle at Crook's Farm won by the invading army, one that left a log house on the Crook property "swimming with blood." Those left were mostly women and children, "as the men were nearly all away, either as prisoners or fighting in the defence of their country." This was "the most difficult period to give" in the town's past, since the only available sources were "a few items gathered from conversations with descendants of those then living in the town, and a very few letters and documents." These surviving documents and "conversations" (we might call them recounted oral histories) depicted the capture and burning of the town as a brutal assault on the domestic realm. During the May bombardment "people retreated to their cellars, some hung blankets over their windows, some took refuge after the burning in caves dug in the side of a hill."[79] As the town burned in December, Mrs. William Dickson was carried from her sickbed to watch the destruction of her home, with its "fine library valued at £600," while Mrs. McKee's small daughter experienced frostbite (her mother had placed her on a tea tray to try to save her from standing in the snow while their home burnt).[80] An even worse fate awaited Mrs. Campbell, an officer's widow, and her three young children: they were not allowed to save warm clothing, saw their few valuables confiscated, and were "exposed to the elements for three days." Having carried her infant four miles to have it baptized, Mrs. Campbell then "had to dig its grave and cover its remains."[81] When the British returned to surround the town, the American occupation turned into a siege. "Numerous engagements took place, one in Ball's field, the ladies looking on from the windows," and another such "engagement" saw Mrs. Lawe entering the "field of battle" to remove her thirteen-year-old son who had volunteered for the fight.[82] It was not just the townsfolk who suffered. Heavy spring rains, summer heat waves, and cold fall downpours left the American troops miserable and suffering from serious illnesses: typhoid, dysentery, and diarrhea. Furthermore, while American troops inflicted the worst damage, nearby farmers saw their crops and livestock depleted by hungry British troops. Even after the Americans had withdrawn the town was still threatened, which led to the destruction of chimneys, walls, and orchards so that an invading force would be deprived of cover.[83]

Burning homes and turning women, children, and babies into the snow was bad enough; however, the consequences of the war went beyond the events of 1813. The burning of the town in many ways haunts *History of Niagara* – it is something that Carnochan returns to repeatedly. For one, the loss of the town's records resulted in a discontinuity in its history, one that Carnochan calls to her reader's attention in a number of places, a rupture and resulting scarcity of historical sources in what is elsewhere a narrative of plenitude. St. Andrew's church, for example, lost its records of 1812 to 1816, as the building was destroyed by the troops (as Carnochan's own church this was probably a loss she felt keenly).[84] It was difficult, she told her readers, to write a history of Niagara's early schools, since their records also were burned in 1813; instead, she relied on a pastiche of newspapers, letters, account books, materials from the national archives, and "tales of the oldest inhabitants."[85] However, despite the success of her reconstruction, Carnochan refused to let the loss be forgotten. On the next page she turned to the wartime closing of the schools, the town's endangerment and its occupation, and the scenario of 1814: "pupils scattered in all directions, and a heap of ruins representing the homes from which had gone forth the children the schools referred to, the records lost."[86] The town's built history also, of course, suffered losses. In the book's discussion of early buildings and early merchants, Carnochan pointed to the 1813 burning as the reason for the absence of late eighteenth-century architecture from much of the street scape.[87]

If *History of Niagara* set its sights on as wide a range of events and locations as possible, what of its cast of historical characters? How did Carnochan treat those often designated as "history's others": women, workers, immigrants, African-Canadians, and Indigenous people? Given the general tendency for university-based historians over her period to focus almost exclusively on men and, almost without fail, on white, middle-class men, Carnochan was in some ways distinct in her choices of historical actors. Women, for one, appear in a number of places in the book. Sometimes they are the victims of history's vicissitudes: they arrive, albeit hopeful and proud of their patriotism, as part of the UEL refugee population (if they have not already been killed by bands of decidedly unfriendly Indians on the other side of the border); they remember that in their girlhood they came close to starving in the "Hungry Year" of 1789;[88] and, as we have seen, they are ejected from their homes in 1813, surrounded by crying and, sometimes, dying children. Yet women are decidedly much more than victims. Even during the terrible events of 1813, they are canny and seize opportunities that come their way. When in 1813 Mrs. Cassady found her house occupied by American soldiers, who moved in and found her freshly baked bread on the table, she was able to strike a deal with them that allowed her to return home, bake bread for them from flour they supplied, and keep any additional loaves for herself. "This she did all summer," Carnochan noted approvingly, "a proof, no doubt, that Mrs. Cassady made good bread."[89] Sometimes they are heroines: Laura Secord, for example, and Maria Waite, whose courage and persistence in seeking a pardon for her husband Benjamin, transported to Van Dieman's Land after the Rebellion of 1837, met with Carnochan's wholehearted approval.[90]

Less exalted but still noteworthy women of the town also people the book's pages. They teach in the common schools or run their own, organize funds for missions, instruct in Sunday schools, found and conduct a successful choral society, contribute collections of books to the library, are the first to pass the departmental high school exam, work as postmistresses, join the local golf club and agricultural society, and write books.[91] In certain circumstances they might well take over masculine pursuits, as in the case of Dr. Miller's widow who, after her husband's death, "was frequently called in for medical advice, ran a drug store which she called "Medical Hall," and was called Dr. Miller. It was not that Dr. Miller had been missing from the historical record, as Carnochan had found a reference to her in 1832 left by Radcliffe in his letters to McGrath. Radcliffe described Dr. Miller as a "woman who compounds medicine and puddings with equal celerity, but not with equal skill," which Carnochan attributed to "a touch of masculine jealousy, as it is believed that Mrs. Miller was quite skillful, having learned much from her husband."[92] And when not pursuing employment or participating in voluntary organizations, women also attended a number of the "assemblies, balls, and celebrations" that helped create a realm of elite sociability in the town. "Twenty handsome ladies," along with sixty gentlemen, were present at Simcoe's June levy in 1793; fourteen years later those two hundred "ladies and gentlemen" who had been presented to Lieutenant Governor and Mrs. Gore danced until 1:00 a.m. and then sat down to supper.[93]

All of these were activities and occupations that many members of Carnochan's audience might approve, a group that was aware of – and perhaps involved in – middle-class women's engagement in voluntary societies, social reform, and woman's suffrage. Moreover, it is perhaps not surprising that Carnochan herself, an independent and active woman, might seek to restore such women's experiences to the historical record. There were, though, less-than-respectable women to be found in the archives. A survey of the town's newspapers from the 1790s to the 1840s produced an anonymous runaway female indentured apprentice (who could be spotted wearing a "blue callimanco petty-coat, and what is remarkable a great coat of Grey Bath coating made in the form of a long gown"), as well as a notice from Robert Cole that, having separated from his wife Mary "by mutual consent," she was not to be trusted with his accounts. The same fate had befallen Anna Dell, announced her husband Henry Dell, Sr. Perhaps the most notorious of the lot was Eve Conrad who in 1821, according to her husband Joshua, had left his bed and board, "not having the fear of God before her eyes, but being instigated by the Devil, has given herself to vice and immorality, etc."[94] We do not know what happened to the wayward Eve Conrad or what kinds of "vice and immorality" she had chosen that so affronted her husband: an affair, perhaps? However, Upper Canadian womanhood's reputation might have been rehabilitated for Carnochan's readers by the story of Miss Vanderlip, who in 1796 rescued William Jarvis' two children from a house fire, conduct that "'is spoken of with much applause.'"[95]

Carnochan was not oblivious to the difficulties involved in trying to find traces of women's pasts in the historical record, nor of the possibility that their experiences had been misrepresented. Her chapter on obituaries opens with that of Catharine Butler, who died 29 May 1793, the wife of Colonel John Butler. The obituary noted "few in her station have been more useful, none more humble. She lives 58 years in the world without provoking envy or resentment and left the world as a weary traveler leaves an inn to go to the land of his nativity." This description of Catherine Butler's life exasperated Carnochan: "Why do these old notices not give the maiden name of the wife? Mrs. Butler's life was not free from trouble, as she was kept a prisoner in Albany solely because she was the wife of Colonel Butler, and was finally released by exchange. Such vicissitudes frequently occurred in the Revolutionary War, according to the cruel customs of the period. It has recently been learned that Mrs. Butler's maiden name was Pollock."[96] After having been treated so inhumanely during her lifetime and with such disregard after it, Catherine Pollock Butler deserved a better accounting of her past. Moreover, as a lifelong single woman whose name did not change, Carnochan may have been more sensitive to a married woman's loss of her birth name.

While women were more likely to be spoken of than to speak themselves, there were exceptions. In particular, women offered their words as historical witnesses, whether passed down to descendants in documents, or in narratives told directly to Carnochan. The late Mrs. Quade, born in Niagara in 1804 at the lighthouse-keeper's house and a town resident until 1831, told her children the first parliament met at Navy Hall – her statement one of many that located the assembly in different sites.[97] Hannah Jarvis's written impressions of Niagara in the 1790s sketched its beauty, noting the meandering of Four Mile Creek (if in England, this body of water "'would be a place worthy of the King's notice'"), and the kindness of her Dutch neighbours, the Servos, who on discovering her American background sent her familiar food – lard, sausages, pumpkins, Indian meal, squash, and carrots. She reciprocated with a dinner invitation.[98] Mrs. Roe remembered her childhood home, Locust Grove, with its black walnut woodwork, metal roof from Montreal, and the eleven children who grew up there, well fed on peach dumplings, Johnny cake, sausages, and corned beef, thanks to the work of black servants, many of whom had been slaves.[99] While most of the female voices that readers would hear are British or European, a "colored woman" provided a reminiscence of her school days:

The first school I went to was to a yellow man called Herbert Holmes – "Hubbard Holmes" our people called him. Oh, he was severe. They were then, you know. But he was a fine man and had been educated by a gentleman in Nova Scotia. He used to drill the boys and when holiday time came he would march us all to a grocery kept by a black woman and treat us all to bull's-eyes and gingerbread. I went to a black man upstairs in the schoolhouse of St. Andrew's Church. The room was full, full of children. The benches were slabs with the flat side up and the bark of the tree down, with round sticks put in slanting for legs. The children all studied aloud and the one that made the most noise was the best scholar in those days. Then I went to a Miss Brooks, from Oberlin College, in 1838-9. She was sickly and died of consumption. Oh, what a hard time she had with some of the boys, bad, rough ones. But Herbert Holmes was a hero. He died in trying to save a black man from slavery.[100]

More of the African-Canadian community's history was provided by Mrs. Guileau (also spelled Guillen), William Riley's daughter – a "fine-looking mulatto woman" – who remembered the dispute between black and white Baptists over the church, one "'the black Baptists won'" (she also recalled baptisms that took place in a town creek and in the lake, near Fort Mississauga).[101] Carnochan did not dismiss these memories as insubstantial or unsubstantiated, nor did she dismiss those who passed them on to her as being prone to faulty recall or embellishment, attitudes that also would differentiate her work from that of her male colleagues in university history departments.[102]

Not all women, though, appear in Carnochan's history. We hear little about those who worked as domestic servants, for example, and there is only a cursory mention of Irish women (Carnochan had little to say about the Irish in the town). While Maria Rye's "Western Home" enters her narrative, Carnochan was mostly concerned about showing her readers that Rye's child-saving mission was a success. Rye bought the former jail for her "waifs and strays from the Motherland, and here over five thousand have been sent out as servants or adopted; many of these have taken good positions, and hundreds of letters and photographs are received at the Home, telling of their progress, sometimes in a home of their own and sending for a servant from the present inmates."[103] To be fair, Carnochan's methodology and sources may not have allowed her to "say" much about these female "waifs and strays," even if she thought the details of their individual lives compelling.

1.16 Eliza Morris's trunk. Eliza Morris was one of the recipients of Maria Rye's "child-saving." Courtesy Niagara Historical Museum 986.1.54.

Other women were of more interest to Carnochan. The figure of the Mohawk matron Molly Brant wends its way through book's pages, being introduced in the first chapter as one of a list of names – La Salle, John Butler, Joseph Brant, Brock, Robert Hamilton, Duke de Rochefoucauld de Liancourt, General de Puisaye – that lend significance and historical lustre to the town.[104] However, it is not clear how much time Brant spent in Niagara-on-the-Lake; she lived in Fort Niagara across the river during the Revolutionary War and spent the bulk of her life in Upper Canada in Kingston, where she died.[105] It is her daughters, then, who serve as their mother's representatives, reminding readers of her history of interracial diplomacy and intimacy. In 1793 they graced the dance floor at a ball held to celebrate 4 June, the King's birthday. According to General Lincoln's journal, the celebration was noteworthy for the

> ease and affection with which the ladies met each other, although there were a number of present whose mothers sprang from the aborigines of the country. They appeared as well dressed as the company in general and

intermixed with them in a manner which evinced at once the dignity of their own minds and the good sense of others. These ladies possessed great ingenuity and industry and deserve great merit for the education they have received, owing principally to their own industry, as their father, Sir Wm. Johnson, was dead. Their mother was the noted Mohawk princess, Mary (Molly) Brant, sister of Captain Joseph Brant.[106]

While this is the most detailed passage about the Johnson sisters – as with other women, Carnochan usually had to rely on the words of others – nevertheless she missed few opportunities to remind readers that Brant's descendants had lived in the town. St. Mark's graveyard was home to the last resting places of Elizabeth Johnson Kerr, Brant's daughter, and her obituary was one of the earliest Carnochan reprinted in her chapter on death notices.[107] Their male relatives also might benefit from the connection. An early Grand Master of the town's Freemasons, Robert Kerr was both a military surgeon and the husband of Molly Brant's daughter; indeed, his wife also was mentioned as part of his 1824 obituary, reprinted from the *York Gazette*.[108]

Why the insistence on remembering Molly Brant through the presence of her descendants? One might dismiss these references as Carnochan's attempt to introduce a tinge of romanticism to her narrative of a small town by pointing to the existence of "the exotic" in its early years. However, given the racial dynamics of history writing during this period, such an argument does not explain much, since there were other ways of introducing romantic grace notes. At the very least, it seems an unsatisfactory explanation. After all, not many historians of Upper Canada during Carnochan's lifetime cared to think too long or in too much depth about Molly Brant and her relationship with William Johnson. Few wanted to acknowledge that their union was significant, that she played a pivotal role in diplomatic relations between the Iroquois and the British, or that the Brant-Johnson alliance produced female offspring who would go on to intermarry with élite men in Upper Canada.[109] As we shall see in chapter 3, taking Molly Brant seriously as a historical actor was a rare act of scholarship. She may have been omitted in other historians' accounts of the Loyalists or in other historical narratives because of her gender and her race – only a very small number of white women and Indigenous men featured in these records. As well, it may be telling that she did not use these opportunities to link the Johnson sisters with their uncle Joseph: Molly, not her brother Joseph, is the name that Carnochan preferred to invoke.

1.17 Elizabeth Johnson Kerr's headstone, St. Mark's Anglican Church graveyard, Niagara-on-the-Lake. The inscription reads: "Sacred to the memory of Elizabeth Kerr, wife of Robert Kerr, who departed this life at Niagara, 24th January, 1794, aged 32 years." Photo Credit Paul Jenkins.

Carnochan also was certainly not afraid to acknowledge that at least one other descendant of a white father and Indigenous mother was part of the town's history. In her tour of St. Mark's graves, she introduced her readers to that of Dr. William McMurray, the Archdeacon of Niagara and, for thirty-seven years, St. Mark's parish rector. Buried alongside McMurray was his first wife, Charlotte Johnson, "sister of Mrs. Schoolcraft and daughter of Chief Johnson, an Irish gentleman of Sault Ste. Marie, and an Indian maiden."[110]

It was not just the figure of Molly Brant that allowed "Indians" to be part of the town's history. Brant's fellow Iroquois, as well as other Indigenous people, also made their mark, particularly in a separate chapter that focused on "Indians, Their Treaties, and Council Meetings." Although Carnochan was unable to say much about the earliest residents of the area, the Neutrals, Seneca, and Mississauga, she told her readers that her silence on this question had more to do with Europeans' historical amnesia about and their dispossession of "the red man," not to mention the British destruction of Indian remains. She also suggested that the "fierce Iroquois" extermination of the Eries, Hurons, and Neutrals may have resulted in Neutral territory in Niagara going unoccupied.[111] However, searching through archival collections from Michigan and Ottawa, Carnochan found evidence of many late eighteenth-century meetings between delegations of Indigenous people and the British: the Six Nations, the Shawnee, and the Seneca from Buffalo Creek (the latter included Red Jacket). (She was probably pleased to find a reference to Indigenous women in a speech delivered by Seneca leader Farmer's Brother in 1791: "when our chief women requested of us in Council to give Colonel Procter assistance ... this had great weight with us.")[112] The aftermath of Brock's death brought a large contingent of Six Nations, Huron, Pottowatomis, Chippewas, mixed-race members of the military, and Indian Department interpreters – John Norton and Jean-Baptiste Rousseaux – as well as Colonel William Claus and other military officials to Niagara for a council meeting. Carnochan also included Little Cayuga's address of consolation and offering of wampum for Brock's grave. 1815 saw another large council meeting – "Hurons, Mohawks, Oneidas, Onondagas, Cayugas, Senecas, Tuscaroras, Tutulies, Delawares" – with leaders from both the Grand River and Buffalo, as well as "about four hundred of their young people."[113]

While such large political and military meetings of Indigenous groups at Niagara ended with this one, nevertheless that did not mean an end to Indigenous gatherings. Mohawks from Six Nations and Tuscaroras from Niagara Falls, New York, held a number of lacrosse matches on the town's common, sometimes with war dances and always with a ritual visit to the Clench homestead, as the family were Johnson-Brant descendants. Furthermore, some of Carnochan's readers may well have remembered the 1897 meeting of the Ontario Historical Society in Niagara, when a deputation from Six Nations held a council meeting in the town's Court House to debate whether a historical society should be formed on the reserve. "This was argued pro and con with great eloquence and volubility, as well as with dignity and deliberation," Carnochan remembered. "The speakers spoke, some in their own language, some in very good English. The ritual was carefully observed, and the rules of debate ... All was conducted with dignity and utmost decorum."[114]

Dignity also marked the Shawnee leader Tecumseh who, after Joseph Brant, was probably the best known Indigenous figure in Upper Canadian history; indeed, Carnochan felt no need to provide any words of introduction in her discussion of him.[115] Although Carnochan did not know if Tecumseh had ever been to Niagara – probably a source of disappointment for her – she was happy to describe him and partially recount a speech he made near West Flamboro (present day Flamborough). Her source, Mrs. Van Every, heard him as a young girl and remembered an unforgettable man of over six feet, with a "Roman nose" and "piercing eyes," who was "quiet, lonesome, proud," not to mention being "a perfect Demosthenes in eloquence (who) swayed his readers like reeds, his words were like an electric charge."[116] Tecumseh's speeches focusing on the new republic's unjust treatment of his people left such an impression on Mrs. Van Every's family that, at the age of sixteen, her brother would "dress up like an Indian and repeat" them by heart.[117] In addition to Tecumseh's declarations of injustice, Carnochan also included Red Jacket's reproaching of missionaries for whites' execution of Christ and of his people's astonishment that whites who had the Bible could be "so bad and do so many wicked things."[118]

Not all "Indians," though, were dignified orators, political leaders, or members of historical societies. Like most of her contemporaries, Carnochan had her share of ambivalence towards Indigenous people's participation in the past. Her retelling of Loyalist narratives or accounts of the War, for example, includes the "vicious Indians" who kidnap whites, steal their goods, or threaten them with axes and tomahawks.[119] To be sure, such incidents not only occurred in the Revolutionary War but also had a history that stretched further back into the seventeenth century. However, Carnochan was unable to understand the reasons for their recurrence or to understand the specific kinds of violence that Indigenous people had endured in colonial wars. Yet at other points in her narrative she admitted – even if inadvertently – that not all white captivity by "Indians" resulted in gruesome death. At Fort Niagara in the 1770s, British officers and their wives "bought" white children from Indians who had been taken captive and adopted, for example.[120] The tale of the Gilbert family, originally from Pennsylvania and taken captive in 1780 by Indigenous people fleeing from the American army, also demonstrated that captivity could lead first to adoption and then, because of the captors' willingness to bargain with British officers and their wives, ransoms that resulted in family reunification at Niagara. While Carnochan lauded the kindness of the British military in ransoming these captives, her account is free of the lurid details of torture and cruelty that marked many captivity narratives of this period (one senses she also was thrilled to have found the source of this tale, a 1790 edition of the London publication that told the Gilbert's story).[121]

Indigenous peoples' presence at Niagara, then, was significant for Carnochan, as it demonstrated that the town had been an important staging ground in pivotal encounters between the British and Indigenous allies and between groups of Indigenous nations that had been torn apart by the wars of the late eighteenth century. To be sure, Carnochan's treatment of "treaties and council houses" also might have reminded her readers, some of whom could have heard of these gatherings from parents or grandparents, that the violence and terror of the eighteenth century was not quite as distant as some might have wished. These gatherings had marked the transition to and helped usher in – at least for European settlers in southern Ontario – the security and safety of the nineteenth century. However, Indigenous people did not quietly vanish from Carnochan's history after 1815, as they tended to do in most other histories of this period; rather, they returned to Niagara on a number of occasions and for their own specific reasons.

Carnochan also was interested in the history of African-Canadians, a group that played a number of roles in her narrative. As I have argued elsewhere, lauding their arrival in Niagara as fugitive slaves might affirm the benevolence of Upper Canadian and, by extension, British rule.[122] A portrait, for example, of a group who kissed the soil of their new home, one derived from a resident's oral history, or a newspaper account of an escaped slave from Tennessee who had floated across the Niagara River on a raft cobbled together from a gate, said little about the racism that they met in their new homeland.[123] Yet Carnochan also began her chapter on "Africans" by debunking the misconception that Simcoe's 1793 bill had abolished slavery outright, and she also told her readers that slaves had been held in the town from the 1790s until the early 1800s.[124] What is more, she applauded the agency and heroism of African-Canadians who resisted slavery and injustice, most notably that of Herbert Holmes ("an educated mulatto teacher") and Jacob Green. Holmes and Green were part of the crowd that gathered to prevent Francis Bond Head from returning Solomon Moseby, an escaped slave from Kentucky, to his master (Moseby had been held in the town jail while Bond Head decided what to do with him). Both Holmes and Green were killed by the troops sent to transfer Moseby from the jail to his owner: "the two heroes, for so we must call them, are buried in the Baptist graveyard, but no stone marks their grave," Carnochan noted with a tinge of sadness.[125] Carnochan also recognized dramatic activities of the town's African-Canadian population, pointing to celebrations of Emancipation Day, a meeting to celebrate Henry Boulton's election to the legislature, and the participation of the "coloured corps" as part of the colonial government's troops in 1837. She also reprinted a list, compiled by a former editor of the local paper, of the "principal colored people seventy years ago," remarking as well that since then the town had seen its "colored families" decline in number.[126]

Despite its plenitude of detail, one that at times threatened to veer into sheer extravagance, *History of Niagara* also was marked by absences, omissions, and exclusions. One of the most notable of those was Carnochan's lack of attention to the town's Irish community. To be fair, there may have been few sources for its history: even today local historians find it difficult to say much about it. Nevertheless, *History of Niagara* has little information about a group whose homes clustered in the eastern part of the town – "Irishtown" – and whose residents' graves filled the nineteenth-century sections of St. Vincent de Paul's cemetery.[127] And, even if Niagara did not have much of a "working class" for most of the period covered by Carnochan's history, the book does not give servants or labourers the same sustained attention, or treat them as a category, as it does Indigenous people or African-Canadians. Finally, while the Museum included a range of domestic and intimate items, *History of Niagara* tended to incorporate the household and family only as they were impinged upon by political and military events: their violent and chaotic rendering by the American Revolution and the War of 1812, the participation of particular family members in the town's political and social life, or their material culture. Unlike feminist historians' work of the late twentieth century, Niagara's households do not feature as distinct sites of reproductive, productive, or emotional and moral labour. In this respect, at any rate, Carnochan resembled academically trained historians' unease with domesticity, one that may have stemmed from her own apprehensions about heterosexual family life and the demands it placed on women. Although she did not speak publicly about this, her earlier years in teaching had been reshaped and diverted by the demands of tending to her mother. While she may have been joking, the opening lines of Carnochan's 1868 letter to her brother John, sent while she was teaching in Peterborough, suggest a degree of resentment, even uncharacteristic self-pity, at her family's lack of interest in her. "Judging by the time you took to writing," she told him, "I may suppose none of you care very much whether I write again or not, but I will let that pass and write myself."[128] Furthermore, Barbara McDonald told her friend Janet Carnochan in 1882, "you have very sensible views of a married life and a single one it is a sure case we can be happily single as well it is a sure case a single woman has not half the worry and charge that a woman that raises a large family."[129]

Carnochan's work did not go unacknowledged during her lifetime. Her contributions to and leading role within the NHS, her numerous articles and pamphlets on the area's history, *History of Niagara*, and her campaigns to preserve local landmarks under the aegis of the Dominion government: all of these resulted in her becoming a public figure in the years leading up to the First World War, with a listing in the National Council of Women of Canada's 1900 *Women of Canada*, compiled for the Paris International Exhibition, and interviews in newspapers and periodicals such as the *Canadian Magazine, Toronto Daily News, Toronto Star Weekly*, and *Toronto Sunday World*.[130] In a typical quote, *Canadian Magazine* writer Francis Drake Smith noted in his 1912 interview with Carnochan, "it is with a peculiar sense of pleasure and satisfaction that the writer places on record something concerning a woman who in her own retiring way has done much for the community and Province in which she lives."[131] In 1914 a chapter of the Imperial Order Daughters of the Empire was named after her; based in Toronto, the chapter was

1.18 Janet Carnochan's headstone, St. Andrew's Presbyterian Church, Niagara-on-the-Lake. Photograph by Paul Jenkins.

made up of teachers.[132] This tribute was followed by yet another one when, in 1921, the NHS unveiled an oil portrait of Carnochan that, along with a sonnet and letters from across Canada and the United States, was presented to her in a public ceremony (see figure 1.1).[133] When Carnochan died in 1926 she was memorialized in both the Niagara-area and Toronto press as a Canadian "historical figure," a "rare patriot," and "Niagara's foremost woman" and its "first citizen."[134] After her death Carnochan became a subject of commemoration herself in the Niagara area. The town's high school founded a scholarship in her name, local newspapers periodically ran tributes to her, the Niagara-on-the-Lake library named its local history room after her, books were written that celebrated her life and work, a local nursery bred a rose in her memory, and 4 June has been designated Janet Carnochan day in Niagara-on-the-Lake (an event that includes free admission to the museum).[135]

1.19 Janet Carnochan Memorial, St. Andrew's Presbyterian Church, Niagara-on-the-Lake. Photograph by Paul Jenkins.

1.20 Close up of the inscription, Carnochan Memorial. Photograph by Paul Jenkins.

As such tributes suggest and as I have pointed out earlier, in many respects Janet Carnochan was part of the cohort of patriotic and imperial minded women's historians of her time – Mary Agnes Fitzgibbon, Sarah Curzon, Emma Currie, and Clementina Fessenden – many of whom were her friends and colleagues in historical societies. Yet subsuming her and her work within that group would overlook some of the important, if subtle, distinctions that help set her apart from the rest: the wider range of her interests, her sustained and close attention to archival detail and her love of research, and her insistence on the centrality of a particular place, not just events, to the past. While the others focused their energies on figures such as Secord or Brock, Carnochan's devotion to writing Niagara's history resulted in descriptions of civil and associational life, as well as the sufferings and bravery of Loyalists or the turmoil of the War of 1812. Moreover, unlike her counterparts' depictions of Indigenous people, which tended towards the one-dimensional, or their lack of interest in African-Canadians, at the very least Carnochan was curious about the presence of these communities and attempted to provide historical detail about them and their activities. Furthermore, unlike Curzon Carnochan did not rely on her historical writing for a living. Her curiosity, not commercial imperatives, drove her research and allowed her to pursue her archival

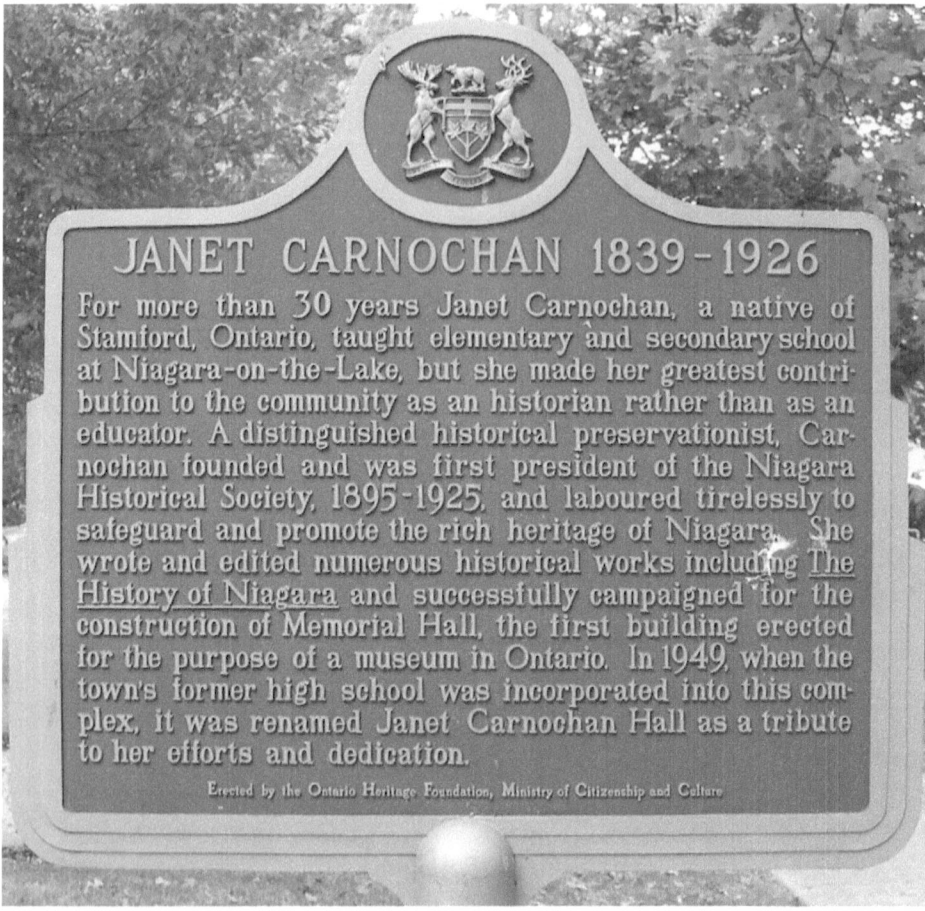

1.21 Ontario Heritage Foundation Plaque, Memorial Hall. Note that the OHF inscription describes her as both a "historian" and a "historical preservationist." The latter term suggests that even while dignifying her work with the term "historian," the OHF accepted the historical profession's relegation of Carnochan to the status of an amateur. My thanks to the anonymous reader who caught the OHF's slippage. Photograph by Paul Jenkins.

1.22 Janet Carnochan Rose, Palatine Fruit and Roses, Niagara-on-the-Lake. Photograph courtesy of Palatine Fruit and Roses.

desires as she wished. The multiple strands of her approaches to historical work – the newspaper article, the historical report, the display case, and the lobbying of governments – suggest not just the enthusiast but also the teacher, attempting to capture audiences, willing and unwilling, by whatever means might be useful.

Carnochan also straddled the different locations in which historical scholarship might be practiced and, to a degree, the kinds of divisions that were taking place between "scholars" and "amateurs." While the museum was often associated strictly or solely with her and her efforts, even a quick glance at the lists of individuals who donated to it testifies to a more collective endeavour, one that Carnochan herself acknowledged.[136] Both Memorial Hall and *History of Niagara* were not the products of a lone scholar toiling in the archives, the model of the historian that, however unrealistic, had become the ideal promulgated by university-based researchers.[137] Nor did Carnochan live the kind of narrow, cramped existence brought on by "archive fever," which Bonnie Smith argues characterized the lives of many prominent nineteenth-century European and American male historians based in universities. Instead, her work was shaped by a life of associations and community, whether within the historical societies or simply by her life in Niagara. To be sure, as her comments about the demands of family suggest, it is likely that the more solitary aspects of the historian's work appealed to her as well, not to mention the travel she undertook to other archives. Yet in a context in which the scholarly writing of history was becoming an endeavour increasingly confined and restricted – in its subject matter, its methodologies, and its practitioners – Carnochan's history and museum suggested more possibilities, that history might be practiced on a wider canvas. Far from being strictly the realm of European men and politics, diplomacy, and warfare, historical knowledge might be heterosocial and, at times, heterogeneous, particularly when practiced and performed in a specific and beloved place.[138]

Chapter Two

"To Turn the Light on the Other Side": History and the Six Nations

The 1898 meeting of the Ontario Historical Society was not a routine gathering for its members. Instead of assembling in Toronto, Kingston, or London to hear papers delivered on topics such as the War of 1812 and catch up on fellow members' activities of the previous year, in June the Society travelled to the Grand River reserve of the Six Nations for part of its proceedings. There they were greeted by Chief Dehhehnagaraneh, Speaker of the Confederacy's Council. Bidding them welcome to the Council fires in the name of the "chiefs and warriors of the Six Nations," Dehhehnagaraneh hailed the delegates "not as strangers, but as brothers whose forefathers fought side by side with ours in the past, in defence of our country – as brothers whose fathers were devoted and loyal through many dangers and difficulties, privations and sorrows to the this land and country, and to the throne of Great Britain, our great ally over the water." Hoping that his people would "benefit much by the deliberations of your council-meeting today," Dehhehnagaraneh also wished that the OHS delegates would, in turn, "carry with [them] to [their] own homes and people a better knowledge of [their] red brother, that [they would] know now that he has benefited by the years of settlement, civilization and educational advantages, and is not behind in the progress of all things good in this country."[1]

The 1898 meeting was, as Janet Carnochan would have known, preceded by the Six Nations' delegation to the previous year's gathering at Niagara. From the end of the 1890s until 1911 the Six Nations and the OHS maintained an ongoing relationship, one marked by the Confederacy's desire to see its history with Britain and Canada honoured and recognized and the Society's fascination with the community's artefacts and archaeological sites.[2] OHS members consistently expressed their admiration for the Six Nations' courtesy, oratory, and dignity; they also praised the "evidence of prosperity and progress" attested to by the Six Nations' homes, farms, churches, and schools, spaces that "manifested a determination to keep pace with modern times." The Six Nations could be justly proud of their history, for which they had "the sincere and heartfelt appreciation of their brother Canadians from end to end of this fair country."[3] For their part, Six Nations' delegates not only agreed with such assessments but also took them one step further by calling for more dramatic political change. Chief Nelles Montour (Delaware), an OHS executive committee member, told the Society in 1898 that his people's history, record of loyalty to the Crown, and well-ordered affairs warranted the appointment of an Iroquois Superintendent of the reserve: "among ourselves and of our own blood, there are men capable of filling the position with credit and dignity."[4] In 1911 the Six Nations adopted the OHS president, David Williams, in a ceremony held at Oshweken.

Euro-Canadians' fascination with Indigenous peoples has its own complicated and complex history, an interest manifested over the nineteenth century in myriad locations and genres. Historical pageants, history texts, novels, theatre, Wild West shows, exhibitions, museums, and advertising deployed representations of Indigenous people, much of it stereotyped, repetitive, one-dimensional, and racist. However, other possibilities existed. As Michelle Hamilton has recently shown, Ontario had its own history of settler interest in Iroquoian and Algonquian peoples' artefacts and material culture that, while certainly not free from stereotypes or appropriations, might demonstrate a greater respect for Indigenous culture and history.[5] Furthermore, as Janet Carnochan believed, highlighting Indigenous peoples' presence in particular events and locations was a way of claiming the latter's significance to Canadian history. Moreover, as we shall see in chapter 3, individuals found meaning, even solace, in the history of Indigenous-newcomer relationships.[6] While historians have pointed out how little control Indigenous people exercised in national spectacles of the nation, their research has demonstrated that, no less than their non-Indigenous counterparts, Aboriginal peoples often had their own political and strategic reasons and motivations for being involved in particular projects.[7] Far from being passive recipients of imperial gazes, members of the Six Nations also desired, in Mohawk historian and lecturer Ethel Brant Monture's words, to "turn the light on the other side."[8]

Through their work in historical societies and their writings and speeches over the course of the twentieth century, various members of the Six Nations presented narratives of Canadian history that claimed it as their own. In doing so, they sought to establish their presence as national subjects in these narratives and to contest the forms of colonial knowledge that placed them outside of the historical time of the nation. No less than their white counterparts, the Six Nations' commemorative activities were complex, being shaped by a range of social and political attachments, relationships – not least of which was gender – desires, and locations. The creation of historical narratives by individuals at the local level suggests "history," in addition to being intertwined with colonial projects and used to buttress relationships of power, simultaneously also was used to negotiate with and, at times, counteract colonialism. The Six Nations produced historical ways of knowing that, although forced to engage with the nation state and its borders, challenged them. In turn, they demonstrated just how complicated such knowledge and its practices might be.

Just as Niagara played a critical role in shaping Carnochan's historical work, the context of the Grand River was instrumental in shaping its residents' sense of time and place; it also helped make their narratives available to white historians.[9] Founded in 1784 on the banks of the Grand River on land purchased by the Crown from the Ojibwa Mississauga, the community was created out of the dispersal of Iroquois people by the American Revolution. It became home to members of the Six Nations Confederacy (Mohawk, Cayuga, Onondaga, Seneca, Oneida, and Tuscarora) and a number of Delawares, Nanticokes, Tutelos, Creeks, and Cherokees. In 1847 the Mississaugas, with tenure to their lands on the Credit River threatened by the colonial government, were invited by the Six Nations to move to the Grand River, where they formed the New Credit reserve.[10] While the reserve was not without tensions and problems created by the Dominion government's colonial policies, its members exercised a considerable amount of control over their affairs and enjoyed a much higher level of economic prosperity than did many other Indigenous communities in late nineteenth- and twentieth-century Canada.[11] By the 1890s, the Six Nations was a community with prolonged contact with Europeans; many people from both sides of the reserve boundaries were well aware of this history. Nineteenth- and twentieth-century transportation networks – first trains, then cars – linked the Grand River reserve to nearby

Brantford but also to Toronto, Buffalo, and other parts of New York State. Ethnographers and archaeologists, both from Canada and the US, were drawn to the reserve for their research; for instance, when OHS secretary and provincial archaeologist David Boyle became interested in conducting fieldwork on First Nations' societies, he turned to the Six Nations.[12] Such conditions facilitated Six Nations' contact with Euro-Canadians from the Ontario Historical Society (OHS) and Brant Historical Society (BHS).

Matters went further in 1911, when Chief W. M. Elliott asked the OHS to support the Confederacy's fight for legal equality, citing their long-standing history of "systematic government" that had produced an "Indian empire" before Columbus's arrival, followed by a history of support for Britain during the latter's time of need. That support in 1776 had led to the loss of their territories, a loyal service that Britain had recognized with treaties that the Dominion government was now infringing upon, robbing them of their rights, infantilizing Six Nations men, and lumping the Six Nations in with all other Canadian Indians, an insult that took no notice of their distinct and unique history with the Crown and British Empire. "If the Six Nations chiefs and warriors were men enough to fight for Canada and the supremacy of the British crown upon this North American continent ... why should the legislation of this country now place them in the category of minors?" asked Elliott. He concluded by requesting the OHS "use its influence in advocating our cause," appealing to them as fellow descendants of the United Empire Loyalists, men who were "comrades in arms in the fighting time, let us today fraternize as common brothers in peace and endeavour to accord to all the freedom which the British constitution grants us all under the British flag."[13]

Elliott's request for the OHS's support cannot have come as a complete surprise to its members. Over the course of the past two decades the previous President, James Coyne, and his colleagues had opened up the possibility of such discussions, with statements such as "to the Red, as well as the white, loyalists is due the credit which belongs to those who preserved Canada as an integral portion of the great empire."[14] Other members of Six Nations, such as the Mohawk lecturer, historian, and performer John Ojijatekha Brant-Sero, stated that his people's historical record legitimated a distinct national status within the British Empire, a position of alliance with, not subjection to, imperial power.[15] However, the delegates voted to steer clear of this potentially contentious issue, arguing that their constitution prevented them from discussing political matters. After 1911, the Six Nations allowed their membership in the OHS to lapse.[16]

Yet while they might have renounced formal affiliation with the Society, the OHS's caution did not prevent certain individuals from continuing some contact. In 1922 Asa Hill, the Secretary of the Six Nations Council, presented a paper to the OHS entitled, "The Historical Position of the Six Nations," in which he repeated the points made by his predecessors: the history of Five Nations Confederacy, the specific position of the Iroquois in colonial conflicts, the Six Nations' ability to preserve their traditions, and the Crown's recognition of the Cconfederacy's "rights and sovereignty." Hill cited treaties of the late seventeenth and eighteenth centuries to prove his point and establish that the relationship between the Confederacy and the Crown existed well into the nineteenth and twentieth centuries, one underscored by the War of 1812 alliance and Six Nation's presence "in the awful scenes on Flanders fields."[17]

Thus Hill's paper must be seen as part of an ongoing argument in which "history" was critical in legitimating certain forms of government and Six Nations' contemporary control over their affairs. However, like his predecessors involved with the OHS, Hill saw the history of Six Nations-British relations not simply as a narrative where the former brought Euro-Canadian civilization and nationhood to the latter, with the accoutrements and signs of progress such as schools, churches, and those "neat farms" so beloved of the OHS. Such was the "history" produced by Euro-Canadians about Indigenous peoples whom they saw as being on the path to enfranchisement, the final act of incorporation into the Canadian nation.[18] At times members of the Confederacy also claimed their community's ability to adopt such practices and institutions, although their arguments often seemed aimed at demonstrating the ease with which the community adapted and incorporated aspects of "Canadian" society, less so than simply demonstrating assimilation to white norms.[19] Equally important, though, Hill's narrative reversed the customary tropes of progress and enlightenment often favoured by non-Aboriginals in English Canada.[20] "History" was not something that had merely occurred to the Six Nations, nor was the latter's past a burden of superstition and ignorance. Instead, it was a liberating and protective force, one where they had been historical actors in the various theatres in which the modern Canadian nation had been staged: the War of 1812 and, in particular, the First World War. Moreover, these performances had been critically important sites in which Iroquois masculinity had been proven and reaffirmed, in forms both "traditional" and "modern," to be one of dedication to both the Six Nations' community and to the Canadian nation.

However, the events of the War that Hill celebrated and the context in which he wrote his narrative suggest the extent to which "remembering the past is shaped by the conditions of place."[21] The Six Nations' service in the First World War became a matter of contestation on the reserve, to no small extent as a result of conflicting interpretations of past practices and local political positions. During the War a number of men, including Milton Martin, had served under the Dominion government's command. Their volunteering sparked much acrimony between different groups on the Reserve, as the hereditary council did not believe the men should have answered any recruitment call not issued by the Six Nations. At the time Hill delivered his paper, the tensions that had been brewing before the war over the hereditary system of government versus an elected council were about to erupt openly. In 1923 the Cayuga chief Deskeheh (Levi General) travelled to Europe to argue the Six Nations' sovereignty case before the League of Nations; the following year, the RCMP arrived at the Oshweken council house door to seize the Six Nations' wampum and council records and announce the first band election.[22]

Nevertheless – and somewhat ironically – continuous and long-standing attempts by the Six Nations to include their history as part of the "national" narrative were more successful at the local rather than the provincial or national levels. Founded in 1908, the BHS specialized in both the history of Euro-Canadian "settlement" of the area and in the history of Indigenous-white contact at the Grand River. Indeed, from its inception the Society did more than just demonstrate an interest in the Six Nations' history, for it built much of its identity on the premise of its "authority" on such issues.[23] At times the Society's pronouncements and actions were tinged with imperial paternalism: in 1913, for example, it expressed concern for the safety of the artefacts housed in the Mohawk Chapel, and in 1918 formed a committee to investigate the education of Six Nations children in their own history, a suggestion that did not consider that they might have been learning their history from their parents and elders through oral histories and ceremonies.[24] However, on a number of occasions the Society supported the Six Nations in its opposition to federal initiatives and lobbied the federal government to take better care of important commemorative sites of Six Nations' history.[25] Moreover, members of the Six Nations themselves claimed the BHS as a place in which their versions of history could be presented and discussed. Over the course of the 1930s a number of individuals from the reserve had begun to attend BHS meetings – reading papers, performing musical solos, and participating in historical pageants.[26] By 1937, Six Nations' members also sat on the executive and by 1941 Elliott Moses, a Delaware, was the Society's vice president (two years later he became its president, a post he held over the course of the next decade).[27]

While the Society's records show evidence of this increased participation by members of Six Nations, they say little – at least explicitly – about the racial dynamics and consequences of these encounters between Indigenous people and Euro-Canadians. I wonder, though, if the latter might have been prodded to rethink what might have been understandings of colonial relations, Indigenous inferiority, and the "natural" decline of their cultures and society. For one, non-Aboriginal audiences were frequently reminded of the Six Nations' history and the fact that they could lay claim to an organized system of government, one in which women had participated, and which had only recently ended on the reserve.[28] Moreover, members of the Six Nations appeared as both constituents of the society and as representatives of their own nation/s. The number of times in which they claimed both territories simultaneously may have helped dislodge whites' notions that indigenous peoples, literally and metaphorically, occupied only their reserves. Instead, they came to sit in their Brantford neighbours' parlours and the library meeting rooms, wearing suits and dresses, discussing historical issues and participating in administrative matters. At other times they assumed "traditional" clothing for recitations of Pauline Johnson's poetry or performances of historical pageants staged on the reserve.[29] Despite the efforts of the federal government to delineate spaces neatly as "Indian" or "white," then, under particular conditions such boundaries were permeable, even though both parties might well have approached and negotiated them with degrees of hesitation and apprehension. Might it have been more difficult to see these members of the Six Nations as members of a "dying race" or as inhabiting, in Anne McClintock's phrase, "anachronistic space," removed from the temporality of modernity?[30] Were they able to comprehend the anger and frustration that underlaid Ethel Brant Monture's public statement, one delivered in another southern Ontario town in 1964: "We are tired of being presented as anthropological studies. We are human beings. We have been the object of years of research and investigation. We have long felt it was more than time to turn the light on the other side."[31]

Of course, it would also have been easy to have recognized the Six Nations as "exceptional Indians" or as simply having been assimilated, bearing a few vestiges of their history but in general having been so changed by their exposure to western cultural norms and, in particular, Christianity, that they no longer bore much resemblance to "authentic" or "traditional" Indians. Certainly some of the Society's reports hinted at this attitude. A 1931 talk given by Reverend Snell on the Mohawk Institute, for example, told members how two thousand Indians "had profited by (its) training," noting that the Institute's foresight in investing over one million in education and missionary work had raised the "local Indians" well above "the average of Indian mentality."[32] However, Six Nations' BHS members and speakers countered this discourse and, like their predecessors in the OHS, asked the Society for support for their separate status. At their January meeting in 1951, Arnold Moses (a member of the Delaware and Elliott Moses' brother) spoke about the "effect of modern culture on Indian life and outlined the attitude of the Indian people to the proposed new Indian act." The Canadian government, Moses argued, was trying to abolish reserves, so "Indians" were faced with either "living as a separate social structure or going out into the world and competing with the white man and being absorbed and losing their identities. This they had no wish to do." Moses acknowledged the government's provision of social welfare, as well as their medical and legal services, but his message concerning assimilation was clear. The Society thanked him for his "thought-provoking address" and passed a resolution to write to the Minister of Citizenship and Immigration, demanding "Indians must be consulted" before any changes were made to their treaties.[33]

The Society, then, represented a space in which both Indigenous and white people claimed an overlapping and at times shared history, one tied to the reserve, the nation, and imperial and transnational settings. For white historians, the nearby Six Nations reserve could be claimed as an intrinsically interesting space, an exotic attraction that brought educated outsiders to the area. It also served to remind themselves and others of Brantford's lengthy history, both national and imperial: it could not be dismissed as merely another small Ontario city with a history and landscape fundamentally interchangeable with that of other, similar communities. Local historian Jean Waldie, for example, who worked for the *Brantford Expositor* as a district editor in the 1940s and 1950s and was the first woman president of the BHS and the OHS, published a number of articles about the Neutrals and Six Nations that ranged from Brant County's "beginnings" as an Indigenous space to the erection of the Brant monument in the city's downtown park.[34] For the Six Nations, though, local history was a narrative that was intimately and inextricably tied to that of multiple nations and empires, one that intermingled with the narratives of their white neighbours but that also spoke to other territories and other conceptions of nationhood. These were not the abstract constructs of nation and empire that have marked much of the scholarship on commemoration, nor were they invoked in ways that simply reinscribed power and reinforced political boundaries.[35] Instead, as we shall see, Six Nations' historians argued that national and imperial histories had been marked by the nation-state's failure to uphold treaties and its imposition of the Indian Act, both of which affected the contemporary lived experiences of the Grand River residents on an ongoing, daily basis.

As well as the more collective and collaborative work in commemoration of the BHS, throughout the twentieth century individual members of the community also argued for the importance of historical knowledge, albeit from a range of perspectives. This group included historians and performers Brant Monture and Bernice Loft who, as I have argued elsewhere, strove to establish Indigenous peoples' central place within narratives of the modern Canadian nation, while simultaneously insisting on the significance of Indigenous cultural practices and traditions.[36] As well as Monture and Loft, Six Nations men, such as Elliott Moses and Milton Martin, also pondered the need for historical knowledge and produced work that engaged with such narratives.

While Monture believed that her community's history was one of progress, in which the Iroquois (and especially the Mohawk) had taken up various aspects of Euro-Canadian society to be incorporated within Mohawk identity, Moses' perspectives on these matters were more fractured and shifting.[37] Born at Six Nations in 1888, the second-oldest son in a family of eight boys and two daughters, Moses' father, Nelson, was a Delaware, his mother an Irish-Canadian housemaid at the reserve's Anglican rectory. Moses followed his father in becoming a farmer, although before taking up farming in 1917 he attended Guelph's Ontario College of Agriculture. Director of the Ontario Plowman's Association for thirty-nine years, Moses travelled to Britain in 1949 with the Ontario Champion Plowmen and held a number of positions in Six Nations' agricultural associations. As well as his work in agriculture, Moses was the Soldier Settler Inspector and Estate Clerk in Brantford's Indian Office and Chairman of the Ontario Provincial Indian Advisory

68   Creating Colonial Pasts

Crests Adorn Cake—Admiring the cake which adorned the tea table at the official opening of the Brant Historical Museum at 57 Charlotte Street, are, left to right, Warden Edward A. Wright of the County of Brant, Chief Councillor James H. Powless of the Six Nations, and Mayor Howard Winter of the City of Brantford. The cake was artistically iced with designs to represent the original seal of the County of Brant, including an Indian with a bow and arrow, and an oak tree and a deer, and the crest of the City of Brantford with an Indian, a pioneer and a beaver.

2.1 "Opening of the Brant Historical Museum," *Brantford Expositor*, 9 June 1952. The centre figure is Chief Councillor James H. Powless, Six Nations.

Committee. Throughout his life, then, Moses occupied and claimed a number of places: on the reserve, within the nearby institutions of the Canadian nation-state, and on an international stage (see figure 2.2).

In doing so, though, Moses also crafted positions on Indigenous history and Indigenous identity – particularly the relationship of the Six Nations to the Canadian nation-state – that were, to say the least, complex and in many ways contradictory. Like Monture, Moses argued that the Six Nations were a "progressive" people and had a history of which they should be proud. Their past both affirmed their contributions to the Canadian nation-state and demonstrated that they had advanced by learning from Europeans: they could not be denigrated as "primitive savages."[38] To be sure, Moses also attacked the Indian Act and its provisions as "perfectly racist," as it placed Indians in an inferior category and freed them from the obligations and responsibilities of "first-class citizens": they were not held responsible for debts owed to non-Aboriginals, reserve land was exempt from taxes and could not be used as collateral, nor could they have liquor stores or warehouses on the reserve. Moreover, the Act was frequently administered improperly to the Six Nations' detriment, as when illegal timber cutting on Six Nations had led to the "decimation" of the reserves' stands. "The whole Indian Act with more than one hundred clauses causes Indians to feel they are nothing more than tenants of the department of Indian affairs," Moses declared, rather than national subjects with a clear stake in their homes and country.[39]

In this and in many other speeches and articles, Moses insisted that the Act mapped out Indigenous peoples' lives from "cradle to grave," a form of racial discrimination that "separated them from all other citizens giving them an inferior rating compared to all other ethnic groups of Canada." Moses was not alone in his disdain for the Act; for many Indigenous peoples it symbolized the Canadian state's domination over them, right down to its definition of "Indian" status. But for Moses, the problem with the Act was the fact that it denied his people the advantages and benefits of "white" society, rather than focusing on Indigenous history and communities. The Act created distinct and distinctly inferior spaces for Indigenous people, ones in which they were denied access to other spaces that might improve their lives, such as educational institutions, businesses, or new types of families. Little or no consideration, he charged, was given "to the future advancement that might be made in copying and successfully mastering the white man's way of life."[40]

70 Creating Colonial Pasts

2.2 "Ontario Indians Come to Exhibition to Demonstrate Their New Independence." *Toronto Daily Star*, 23 August 1939. Elliott Moses's photograph is in the top right corner; he is described as one of the organizers of this demonstration. The other figures are Abby Schuyler (with loom), Arnold Moses (with violin), and Chief Little Bear George Green, from Six Nations.

As this passage suggests, Moses' public critiques of Indigenous-white relations in Canada were based on a liberalism that believed in equal treatment to produce equal results. He had little sympathy, particularly by the 1950s and 1960s, for other Indigenous writers and activists who called for a different and special status for their people, calling their work a "waste of time and energy" for they were based on notions of a way of life impossible to restore. Moses had particularly harsh words for those "non-Indian organizations" – the media, church and service groups, and women's clubs – that were "gullible and seemingly willing to believe ridiculous reports of the filth and poverty across Canada" on reserves (in many of his speeches Moses went to great lengths to deny that all Indigenous people were living in such conditions). Rather, the key to "Indian" success was education and integration, including intermarriage. "We find Indians working side by side, with non-Indians, many having come from the old land and possessing a very different national background by working together (and) sharing each others" tasks day by day. Such a state of affairs, Moses claimed, "causes them to accept each other on a human basis as fellow men and citizens, thereby helping to destroy of the world's greatest curses, that of racial discrimination and replaces it with a quality of true pride and loyalty, to their country which grants them equal rights and privileges and a standard of living second to none in the whole world."[41]

Moses may well have been influenced by the growing civil rights' discourse of the post-WWII decades. But his thoughts on equality for Indigenous peoples also might have been affected by an earlier eugenic discourse and knowledge of recent history, when eugenics in both Europe and Canada had been used to define who was and who was not a "first-class citizen." Repeatedly Moses stated that any problems "Indians" might face were cultural and not the result of biological inferiority. Here his use of Indigenous history (sometimes understood as that of the Six Nations, sometimes meant to include a variety of First Nations) was deployed in a number of ways to counter any suspicion of biological determination. "History" demonstrated that the Six Nations had had their own system of government before contact with Europeans, their own beliefs, languages, and values. However, Indigenous societies (at least the more "advanced" ones) had not stood still but, rather, had evolved, a state of affairs that all must emulate since "for Indian people, to stand still means stagnation whereas progress and enlightenment means cultural development." While government and non-Indigenous people must shoulder their fair share of the blame for problems that did exist, it was up to the latter to exercise their agency and "move forward."[42]

Time and again Moses stressed that there was no reason why this happy state of affairs could not come to pass, particularly with education. He suggested that those "Indians" who believed "Indians think differently to non-Indians and should not be disturbed in their natural thinking and ... advocate that due to this fact Indian children should be taught differently in school" were mistaken.[43] But Moses also denounced white society and the government for their opposition to Indigenous teachers who, at Six Nations, had a long history of employment in the reserve's day schools.[44] In a 1968 address delivered to the Waterloo Historical Society, Moses told his audience that it was crucial that his people took charge of their children's education: "In spite of the fact that missionaries on the reserve and other interested non-Indians claimed the system of Indians teaching Indians would be a failure, the very opposite is true and the system has proven to be a complete success." Out of thirty-five teachers, only three or four were non-Indian. "This underrating and lack of confidence by non-Indian people in the capabilities of Indians has always been and still is thinking of seemingly intelligent non-Indian people who view Indians racially," he argued.[45] A poem, "Time," memorized when Moses was seventy-two and had undergone cataract surgery that left him temporarily unable to read or write, contained the telling lines: "It doesn't matter if you are red, white, or black. Whether you're gentile or Jew, or the list of that. Time has no favourites. It doesn't turn back. So keep looking forward, keep your eyes on the clock. For there's time to be thankful for the whole of Life's walk."[46]

Moses did not go unchallenged by other First Nations. Angered by Moses' being introduced to the Ontario legislature as a Confederacy chief, the hereditary chiefs wrote to Ontario premier Leslie Frost to inform him that, as a Delaware, Moses could not hold the title and that they would sue if further misrepresentation occurred.[47] In December 1960, a fellow Delaware, "Big White Owl" criticized him for his depiction of reserves as backwaters that should be eradicated. Moses, Big White Owl charged, was born and raised on a reserve "and owes everything that he is and ever will be, to his Indian ancestry." Furthermore, Moses probably did not know "he and his family had been living under a borrowed name for the last century," as his proper ancestral name was Stonefish. Rather than sniping at reserves and their residents, Big White Owl contended, he should have proposed the creation of an all-Indian province, with its own government, premier, and federal representatives in Ottawa: "he would have been introducing a real ultramodern idea that makes sense and his people probably would have agreed with him."[48] "Not Quite White," a piece published in the *Brantford Expositor*, also disagreed with Moses' attitude towards Indigenous tradition and culture. "His arguments have always indicated an attitude of compromise, on any subjects pertaining to people of our race," wrote this author who, while having been brought up to respect elders, reluctantly broke with tradition on this point to contradict Moses, even if doing so meant risking showing a lack of respect towards him. "Indian tradition and culture are beautiful and wholesome, with the power to teach whites much about humility, gratitude, and reverence. I am amazed that a person of Mr. Moses' ripe years should be so naive as to think we can solve the Indian problem by integration when integration means, 'no Indians, no problem.'"[49] There are suggestions in these rebuttals of Moses that he was simply behind the times, that his position represented an older, more accommodating stance that did not speak to 1960s' First Nations' nationalism.[50] Talk of integration may have seemed incongruous during a decade when Indigenous people were increasingly publicly celebrating First Nations' identities and histories.

Notwithstanding these critiques, Moses' defence of Indigenous peoples on the grounds of their capacities and intelligence challenged the Canadian state's paternalism towards them, a detail that his critics did not point out. Moreover, by crafting these narratives of Six Nations' history and placing men such as himself at their centre, Moses was participating in a discourse with its own particular history. His deployment of history, both to counter and to participate in colonial knowledge of Indigenous people, had its antecedents in the work of Indigenous historians and activists such as Peter Jones or George Copway, men who, like Moses, moved across a number of boundaries and inhabited multiple places in nineteenth-century colonial society.[51] Even his activities within the Brant Historical Society suggest the degree to which Moses self-fashioned himself as a link between Indigenous and non-Indigenous histories and spaces, as he spoke on and introduced topics that covered both Six Nations' history and their contemporary experiences at the Grand River and across Canada.[52] Moses' perception of his role was, perhaps, best symbolized by the part he played in the Grand River pageant held to mark the bicentennial of William Johnson's arrival in America; during the event, Moses translated the various languages used by Indigenous actors in their re-enactment of an eighteenth-century council meeting for the large and, according to the international press, white audience.[53] Two years later Moses was credited with organizing a display of "Indian handicrafts" at Toronto's Canadian National Exhibition, one meant to demonstrate the range of skills Indigenous Canadians had displayed to "work their way" off relief and out of dependency during the Depression (figure 2.2). Like Jones, Moses' mixed-race background, albeit in his case a Delaware father and white mother, may also have shaped his choices of political tools and strategies.

As well, while he often identified himself as a representative of the Six Nations, Moses also pointed to his Delaware ancestry as a source of pride and means of differentiating himself. His papers suggest that Moses worked on a number of research projects that focused on Delaware history. "A Short History of the Chapel of the Delawares"; the "Delaware Story," a work that filled four stenographers' notebooks that Moses was writing just before his death; a Lenape-English dictionary from 1899; and a promotional leaflet from CBC's Northern Service, that featured fellow Delaware and journalist Russell C. Moses, who hosted the corporation's *Indian Magazine*: all testify to Moses' concern for his ancestor's distant past and twentieth-century achievements.[54] Delaware history also was the history of particular families: Moses collected Nathan Montour's "The Life Story of My Grandparents," a thirty-nine page narrative that focused on the life of William and Frances Ann Montour and included childhood memories, Delaware stories and customs, as well as the politics of the group's arrival at Six Nations.[55] Moses also was a collector, as he appears to have been instrumental in the 1955 recovery and return of a Delaware mask held by the Anglican Women's Auxiliary in London, which he initially discovered in the 1930s at a Brantford exhibition of missionary "relics." According to Moses, the mask's history was intertwined with that of his family in a number of ways. It came into the church's keeping when the Delaware at the Grand River, including his grandfather Cornelius, converted to Christianity; it had been passed down to the Auxiliary by the wife of the Anglican missionary Adam Elliott, for whom Moses was named; and Moses' quest to retrieve it (from under a "box of old clothes" in a London storeroom) was undertaken partly at the urging of his late uncle Jesse Moses, a Delaware historian. Although the reporter who covered the story emphasized the mask's alterity for a white audience, calling it "terrifying" and describing its "evil" whiskers that resembled those on a "malevolent old mandarin," Moses was much more matter-of-fact about its use, stating simply that it was a medicine mask that probably had other uses as well and that its authenticity could not be doubted.[56] While, as we shall see, Moses was ambivalent about certain aspects of the Iroquois Confederacy's past, Delaware history appears to have posed fewer problems or caused him less anxiety.

There was more, though, to understanding Moses than the issue of Indigenous acquiescence to dominant definitions of "Canadian" national identity versus distinct and separate "Indian nation(s)." Moses' repudiation of the "traditional" form of Six Nations' governance and his recognition of the Canadian nation-state's sovereignty also were shaped by the politics of gender and an acceptance of Euro-Canadian gendered norms, particularly vis-à-vis Six Nations' women's role in shaping both time and place, lineage and land, and in choosing hereditary chiefs. Moses was careful, though, not to denigrate the role of Iroquois women as clan matrons and believed that they had selected morally upright, honest, and temperate men. As well, the matrons could unseat a chief if he did not live up to the position's requirements. However, Moses did not believe that the clan matrons had any "special qualifications ... other than that I assume they would be selected from well known families." Moreover, while the hereditary system had worked well "so long as the Six Nations were a nomadic people" (particularly important because "no educational standards were required"), a more "progressive" system of government was needed once they settled at the Grand and became farmers and wage earners.[57]

Moses did not state explicitly that a government run by women and answerable to them, which was how he understood the hereditary system, was a "retarding" factor in the Iroquois' progress. However, it does not take much of a logical leap to note that his understandings of progressivism and modernity were gendered. Elected governments would be composed of educated Six Nations men who, in the context of the 1924 election, had attained their offices with the direct intervention of the Dominion government, itself implicated in stripping Indigenous women of their political status and history and thus insisting on their dependency on men, both Indigenous and non-Indigenous. Furthermore, Moses' account of the "push" for elected government made much of the role of those Six Nations' men who had volunteered during WWI (albeit with the support of their mothers and sisters "at home"). As loyal soldiers, they had had a "right" to proper, progressive political representation, for it was these men who saw that the more enlightened and contemporary solution was a "democratic" government, in which there was no hidden, feminine influence.[58]

And Moses seems to have made no secret of his father's public condemnation of the hereditary council on precisely that point. In 1908 Nelson Moses was summoned before the council concerning the publication of "verses of a libelous manner entitled 'To the Chiefs,'" which had appeared in the Haldimand Banner. In this poem, Moses made frequent references to the "rusty chiefs, all born that way, your grannies say, you must obey," who, "like the ancient Sanhedrin," had no judgment, "for granny's choice, and granny's pride, rules a nation." The poem ended with the advice and hopes that

> We long to see their places filled
> With men of judgment and self-willed
> Men who love a civilization
> Progressive things for the nation.
> The time is come, the change is near
> Warriors brave - you must not fear
> Strike for your rights and rest you not;
> Strike sir! While the iron is hot
> Go back ye chiefs to your grandmas
> For your advice and for your cause;
> Can you not see the tocsin knell
> Pealing forth the chief's farewell.[59]

For Six Nations men, then, abnegating the past meant embracing a newly independent and "civilized" form of masculinity, a militant and progressive gender role in which elderly women did not make decisions of both local and national importance. As well as Elliott Moses' understanding of modern political governance on Six Nations, his conceptions of Six Nations' society before the Iroquois' arrival at the Grand River was also shaped by conceptions of gender relations and roles. As a farmer who was active in various agricultural associations, and who often spoke proudly of the Six Nations' agricultural achievements, Moses frequently described the latter as a fairly recent phenomenon. Raising bountiful crops and tending healthy livestock was, he often argued, a feature of Six Nations society learned from Euro-Canadians. Here again, though, was a new meaning of Iroquois masculinity, as Moses insisted "his people" were "naturally" inclined to the hunt. However, Six Nations' men often superseded their instructors, becoming hard-working, successful men who disciplined themselves to the land and, despite the racist limits imposed on them by the Indian Act, also became successful owners of property, implements, seeds, and livestock. [60] In Moses' discourse on Indigenous "advancement" then, these men were indistinguishable from their white male counterparts whose farms lay just beyond the reserve's borders.

Such a vision of progress through changing gender relations was, of course, not confined to Moses; it had been precisely the policy of the Dominion government and the vast majority of missionaries who worked among Indigenous people, particularly in residential schools.[61] But what is also surprising in reading Moses' version of narratives of socio-economic (and, of course, political) change among the Iroquois peoples is his complete omission of women's roles in agriculture and their influence in shaping the local landscape. In his particular "national narrative," the Confederacy members survived on hunting and trapping, not because of Iroquois women's work in planting, cultivating, harvesting, and distributing squash, beans, and corn (as well as other fruits and vegetables). Women's work is completely absent in his narratives of his people's history. Thus the motor of progressive change, in Moses' view, was masculine: Iroquois men gave up their hunting, fishing, and trapping and instead adapted to an entirely new means of subsistence, that of the farmer (with the happy result that subsistence became surplus, a surplus that, although he rarely made the point explicitly, was also controlled by men). The "grannies" that drew Nelson Moses' scorn could not be historical actors in this narrative of the "modern" Iroquois nation.

At times Moses expressed an admiration for existing patterns of "traditional" Iroquois culture. He frequently lectured on the longhouse peoples, believing that non-Indigenous Canadians should receive the correct view of their religious beliefs and practices. Six to seven hundred people on the Six Nations' reserve belonged to this group; the Great Spirit was their supreme being, who taught them to live upright and honest lives, perform religious dances, and mark the year's agricultural changes with festivals. Moses described these events with great respect, adding "through their religion, the Long House people have kept our traditional Indian dances alive and authentic. Now many of us Christian Indians are concerned about the Long House religion dying out, for, should this be the case, our Indian dances would soon be gone forever." He argued that most of the longhouse members had been integrated into the rest of the reserve's industry, recreation, and social life. Over time they would embrace Christianity, a process that would not pose many problems, given their existing worship of a power believed to control the universe. But Moses ended this speech on a note more wistful, more ambiguous, and possibly more defiant than in many of his other talks to non-Indigenous audiences:

> In many respects it seems unfortunate that the Indian has to sacrifice most of his culture in accepting the non-Indian way of life. In closing I recall a story which has a bearing on such conditions. An old Indian said, "When white man come to our country we had great forests, lots of wild game and fish. White man, he kill all game, take all fish out of the river and lake; then he go away. Soon he come back. He cut down big trees – big trees all gone. He start to cut small trees. Trees, game, furs, fish now all gone; he go away for a long time. Now, 'by gosh,' he come back for rock." How true this is from an Indian point of view. [62]

Despite Moses' eagerness to point to the ways in which historical changes had produced new types of spaces within the Grand River Territory – churches, productive farms worked by male heads of households, and European-style homes presided over by wives and mothers – nevertheless he could not entirely detach himself from the space of the longhouse, one in which gender relations were configured differently from his mapping of political space.

Moreover, Moses would discover that rejecting traditional concepts of Iroquois gender relations, particularly that of matrilineal descent, would directly affect his own family's residency on Six Nations. The elected council refused Moses' daughter, Ethel Rose, and her two children permission to remain in her parents' home on the reserve, as she had married a white man and had been struck off the band's list. While public speculation attributed the council's decision to Moses' lack of popularity within certain sectors of the community, nevertheless the Indian Act's excision of Indigenous women married to non-Indigenous husbands from official treaty status also underpinned and, in the eyes of the state, legitimated the council's decision.[63] Moses' position underscores the need, as Arif Dirlik has pointed out, for us to consider that places are not only "locations of inherited inequalities and oppressions" but "the struggle over history" may also take place between colonized peoples themselves, not just colonizer and colonized.[64]

Elliott Moses' perspective on the Six Nations' past, present, and future was not the only means of imagining and configuring time and place. His contemporary Oliver Milton Martin suggested that other approaches to these fraught and fractious questions might be possible. Born on Six Nations in 1893 to Mohawk parents Robert Martin, a carpenter, contractor, and part-time farmer, and Lucy Miller, Martin also was a descendant of the well-known Dr. Oronhyatekha (Peter Martin). Although he would be known for his educational achievements, Martin interrupted his schooling in Ohsweken when at sixteen he "became restless" and moved to Rochester, where he worked as a delivery boy in a drugstore. While in Rochester Martin caught the attention of an Anglican minister who encouraged him to return to school and to Canada, where in 1914 he graduated from Caledonia High School. During high school Martin developed an interest in the military, joined the Cadet Corps, served as a bugler at the Niagara-on-the-Lake military camp, and then became a member of the 37th Haldimand Rifles. The outbreak of the First World War saw Martin enlist in the Canadian Expeditionary Force, 114th Battalion, and travel overseas to join other Indigenous volunteers to France. Along with his friend James Moses, Martin was able to arrange his secondment to the Royal Flying Corps and spent the rest of the war training to become a pilot.

On his return to Canada Martin, like many other Indigenous veterans, found his military service did not open many doors. He sold war bonds (unsuccessfully, by his own admission), applied for a Dominion government education grant (again, unsuccessfully), took up a teaching post on the reserve, and managed to save enough to complete teaching training at Toronto's Normal School. Martin then took up a post at Secord Elementary School in Toronto's east end, where he met his future wife, special education teacher Lillian Bunt; he also became the secretary of the Ontario Public School Men Teachers' Federation. In 1935, a year after marrying Bunt, Martin became the principal of Danforth Park School, a career that was cut short in 1939 with the outbreak of the Second World War and his recall to the army as a brigade commander. Martin had retained his links to the army during his teaching career, as he and his wife were invited to attend George VI's Coronation in 1937 in his capacity as a member of the Canadian military contingent. During the war Martin travelled across Canada and to Scotland with the military; in 1944, though, he retired from the army and became a magistrate in York County, a position he held until his death in 1957.

Ostensibly, then, Martin epitomized the model of assimilated Indigenous manhood so beloved of many Department of Indian Affairs officials and, to no small extent, Elliott Moses: the former in particular may have been pleased by Martin's successful 1921 application for enfranchisement.[65] Yet that did not mean that Martin's Mohawk background was forgotten or obscured, as his public career was frequently categorized as that of an "Indian" man. Newspaper announcements of his appointments and promotions, for example, often bore the headlines such as "Indian School Principal Heads 4th Inf. Brigade," "Indian Officer Appointed York County Magistrate," "Indian Colonel Regrets Brigade Has Lost Kilts," and "Full-Blooded Indian Named to Command 13th Brigade."[66] Those articles that did not trumpet Martin's ancestry and birthplace in their headlines usually worked in references to it. A short piece run by Toronto's *Evening Telegram* on Martin's appointment as a magistrate, for example, which featured a photograph of Martin, Lillian, and the neighbour's fox terrier "Pat" at the Martins' O'Connor Drive home, noted Martin's Iroquois ancestry, birthplace, and status as the "first Indian" appointed to the province's judiciary. The reporter referred to Lillian only as "his wife" while telling readers that Pat belonged to next-door neighbour, R. H. McGregor, MP.[67]

To be sure, Martin himself was proud of his ancestry and in all likelihood wanted reporters to include it as proof that Indigenous people – and in particular the Iroquois – had the abilities to be leaders, to hold positions of authority and responsibility. In response to a reporter's suggestion that his trajectory from the "little red schoolhouse" of Ohsweken to command of the 4th Infantry Brigade of Canada's militia was a "pretty broad jump," Martin replied that it was "just a logical development in an ordinary militia career." Moreover, he was simply following in Joseph Brant's footsteps, arguing that Brant held the rank of a colonel when he fought alongside the British. Martin also was eager to portray himself as simply one of a group of contemporaries, telling the press that not only had "thirty-five percent of the eligible male Indian population" served in the First World War but that his home community had produced medical doctors, a Doctor of Pedagogy, nurses, school teachers, and a lawyer.[68] Press coverage of his career was laudatory, even flattering, as it focused on his service to "King and Empire," his notable achievements as a teacher and principal, and his fair, kind, and merciful conduct as a magistrate.[69] Martin, one of his obituaries noted, was "one of the finest persons in Toronto, and one of the most remarkable in Canada."[70]

Fine and remarkable Martin may been in these reporters' eyes: he did not, though, believe that all was "fine and remarkable" for his people in

2.3 Milton and Lillian Martin with "Pat." *The Evening Telegram* 23 November 1944.

Canada. While Martin insisted on his pride in being Canadian and part of the British Empire, it may have been a pride maintained despite, not because of, their treatment of his fellow Aboriginals. Although praising his conduct on the bench, one obituary also noted that he did not lose opportunities to remind those who appeared before him of their status as settlers on Indigenous territory. When a man to whom Martin gave a suspended sentence for assault called one of his co-accused a foreigner, Martin rebuked him, stating, "this is a country of many nationalities and people should not go around calling one another foreigners. As far as that goes," he added with a smile, "you are all foreigners – except me." He also corrected a witness who had described a woman complainant's behaviour as that of a "wild Indian," suggesting "sternly" that the woman "might have been acting like a wild Irishman, Scotsman, or something like that. Isn't that what you wanted to convey?"[71] Most of the newspaper coverage of Martin's career, though, refrained from explicitly naming Canadian racism towards Indigenous people as an obstacle that he had overcome. Gordon Sinclair, however, showed no such reticence, as he told a story of "'local boy makes good' against tough odds ... because anybody will tell you an Indian has a harder time making the grade in his native Canada than a foreign-tongued immigrant." While Sinclair's own anti-immigrant bias may have shaped his perception of Martin, he returned to the theme of the latter's unequal status within Canada throughout the article. Despite being born "a native," Martin had "become" a Canadian and thus was now unable to buy land and build a house on the reserve where he was born. "The new colonial home he is building, incidentally, is the finest wigwam in Canada," Sinclair stated.[72]

Sinclair described Martin's demeanour in discussing his passage from "Indian" to "Canadian" as good-humoured, almost nonchalant. "Going through a form of enfranchisement which is pretty much the same as a foreigner taking out citizenship papers ... might irritate, or even infuriate, some home-grown Canadians, but the colonel has a merry-eyed capacity for being amused at such things. He gets many a gay but silent grin to himself when people see in his dusky face the look of foreigner. It's they ... you and I ... who are the foreigners; the colonel is the native."[73] Martin, though, may simply have been very self-controlled when he dealt with the press; perhaps he believed that to show any degree of anger would be to invoke stereotypes of Indigenous men's "savagery" (he was noted for having adjourned his courtroom on one occasion because he was upset and did not want to pass judgment in the heat of emotion).[74] On other occasions and in other venues, he was far from reticent about Indigenous peoples' poor treatment by Canadian society and, especially, the Canadian government.

Furthermore, in his public lectures and writing, Martin foregrounded two kinds of history, targeting Canadian narratives and representations that were based on untruths and stereotypes about his people. Instead, he insisted on relating the "real" or authentic histories of his people. In a speech to the Ontario Educational Association Conference, for example, Martin vehemently denied that the "Red Indian" was a "primitive savage as expounded by the standard history book used in Ontario public schools," adding "naturally I am somewhat hurt and humiliated when I am obliged to teach my class that my ancestors were great thieves, dishonest, barbaric and essentially primitive." "I have no savage instincts," Martin continued with a smile,

> at least, I do not think so. I hardly know of any Canadian Indians who have. Hence it is certainly strange and against all logic that my race could have lost their savage primitive character in the eight generations that have elapsed since the white man first had dealings with the red. There is nothing to prove that they were cruel, dishonest and primitive. As a rule, you will find that the records of the Indians were written by enemies, persons who had fought against them in the early wars. The Indian is called savage because it is alleged he scalped his captives.

However, Martin pointed out that scalping was not carried out until the victim had died. "And if that is barbarous, I beg to inquire to what extent our standards of barbarism exist. Scalping is to my mind not half so cruel, heartless, as the bombing of defenseless towns by planes in the night, or the stifling of noble souls with poison gas. The sinking of the Lusitania was an exceedingly more barbarous act than all the scalpings the Indians were ever guilty of." Martin ended his talk with a demand that public school history texts be "amended" and all disparaging references to Indians deleted. He did not accuse their authors of malice, though, just "mere thoughtlessness."[75]

Martin made similar points at an annual agricultural fair on Six Nations. After a ceremony in which Ontario Premier Mitchell Hepburn's wife Eva Burton was adopted by the Mohawk (in the Premier's absence) and that featured a historic pageant, speeches, songs, and dances by men and women "in full tribal regalia," Martin gave a lunchtime speech, appearing alongside Ethel Brant Monture. He called for the extension of the franchise "in a voice ringing with sincerity, and using English pure and well-phrased" and "for changes in history textbooks so that Indian children would stop being ashamed of their ancestors." He went further, enumerating many of the heroes of his race and declaring that he had no hesitation in saying that it was the Indians who saved Canada for the British. "Teach the children the good things, the real things about the Indians," Martin concluded.[76]

Those "good things," those "real things" could be found in, for example, his 1951 two-part series "The Indians of Canada," published in *The Canadian Friend*'s January and February issues. Based on a lecture he had given at the Friends' House the previous December, Martin first explained his need to tackle his people's problem: they were "forgotten" and the little knowledge that existed about them in Canadian society came from the schools, "or the false impressions gathered about them from movie thrillers," "which [was] of no help to them." Martin sketched out a narrative of pre-Columbian Indigenous society which, while not untouched by war – "they fought well against heavy odds to preserve and defend what was theirs," including homes, lands, ideals – nevertheless had no "organization for war, no war chief, no war plans, no manufacture of weapons of war, and no preparation for future war ... Quite unlike the civilized nations of today, most of whom are continuously preparing for an attack against them by other civilized nations."[77] Furthermore, Iroquois history was full of examples of collective work for peace, the Five Nations Constitution "contains many ideas which we of today consider modern, e.g. female suffrage, the referendum, league of nations, disarmament, religious freedom."[78] When Europeans arrived – Spaniards, French, and English – despite Indigenous peoples' assistance and lessons in agriculture, hunting, and medicine that kept them from freezing, starving, and dying of disease, they destroyed civilizations and took land. "Isn't it amazing," Martin told the Friends, "that in those days civilized Christian Europeans seemed to think they had the perfect right to claim our land just because they ran into it. They didn't seem to think there was anything wrong in claiming something that didn't belong to them." Although Indigenous people were content to live alongside their new neighbours, the latter's greed erupted into wars between themselves in which the former became embroiled and entangled.[79]

Matters did not improve even when European title to North America was "settled," as treaties and promises to Indigenous allies were broken, particularly concerning hunting and fishing rights, health services were bad, "and it's as difficult for an Indian boy or girl to get a high school education as it is for the average Canadian to get a university education." Despite Indigenous men's service in both world wars and Indigenous women's participation in the Second World War, they were denied basic rights of citizenship unless, like Martin, they gave up being "Indians." Because of the inequities of the Indian Act, Indigenous people were forced to choose between Canada and their own communities and "the price they [were] asked to pay for citizenship in their native land [was] too high." Should they choose "Canada," they were forced to renounce homes and farms they might have spent a lifetime establishing and might even be banned from paying visits to their birthplace, the reserve. Since they could not vote, Indigenous people were denied redress of these wrongs. Recently proposed legislation, Martin stated, did not "contain any semblance of a new deal, and was met by strenuous objections from friends of Indians and Indian organizations" and thus was withdrawn. Such avenues proving dead ends, Martin exhorted his audience to help his people. "They are starving," he ended, "not for food or clothing. They are starving in spirit for that understanding from their fellow Canadians, for that justice and fair play which they have been taught to look for in the British flag, for the square deal which they were led to believe they would get when they gave up the land where you live now. I know you will do what you can to help them."[80]

It is possible that Martin's reference to "recently proposed legislation" was a dig at the federal government's combining of Indian Affairs with immigration, with the result that Indigenous people were treated like "newcomers" in the country of their birth.[81] Whatever the case, though, Martin was even more forceful in an unpublished paper that he considered calling "Dictatorship in Canada," "A Square Deal for Indians," or "The Indians of Canada." In its forty-eight pages there is little hint of amusement or tolerance for white Canadian foibles: instead, its narrative is one of the latter's loss of memory, the need to educate whites (a theme addressed by Brant Montour as well), and of colonial oppression over the centuries. While Martin did not believe that returning to an age prior to contact with Europeans was possible and supported "gradual assimilation to Canadian citizenship," nevertheless he strenuously objected to the way in which Indigenous children were educated. They were not taught about their ancestors' central role in Canadian history, for example, and the schools seemed aimed at turning out "poor imitations of the white man." If not for their parents and grandparents' teaching within the home, Martin contended, this project would have succeeded.[82] It had some effect, though, as Martin pointed to young Indigenous women's fondness for lipstick and face powder and the attempts of those who left their reserves to deny their background and instead claim Spanish or Italian ancestry "because their education [had] led them to feel that their race was inferior."[83] Indigenous teenagers faced almost insurmountable problems in getting to high school, while in residential schools children were used as cheap labour. Those promises in which Indigenous parents had put their faith – that their children would be provided with the means to make their way in Canadian society – were hollow ones.[84]

As well as relying on larger historical narratives, such as historic alliances and equally historic betrayals, Martin also narrated his own history and enfolded it within those imperial and national accounts. His tale began with the decision of the Six Nations Council, a body that, while it might have been slow to come to its decisions, was run by able men who had the promotion of their people's welfare at heart. The Council's decision to send two young men to Osgoode Hall was overturned by the federal government and ended up with both of them (one being Martin) joining the CEF. On returning to Canada in 1918 Martin was told by an official of the Indian Department that he must chose between becoming a farmer and or a teacher. In a detailed account, he set out the difficulties he faced and his lack of options, all of which led him to decide that he had had enough of "living under a dictatorship." With the help of his regiment's Commanding Officer, Martin decided to opt for enfranchisement and become a Canadian citizen.[85] In spite of, in his words, the "exemplary *and* voluntary" wartime record of First Nations' people, his people across the country lacked the right to vote, hold their own mortgages, and, in the case of those who worked as itinerant agricultural laborers, could not form unions to protect themselves.[86] Although wards of the Crown, they did not even have their own Ministry and were instead "placed below" natural resources. However, organizations such as the Native Brotherhood of British Columbia, the Indian Association of Alberta, the Union of Saskatchewan Indians, and the North American Brotherhood demonstrate "Indians" had realized "in unity there [was] strength."[87] Martin's short history of these groups ended both in an acknowledgment of the difficulties in founding large-scale federal and provincial groups – language differences, lack of funds, "old tribal animosities," "occupational and economic differences" – and a tribute to "those leaders who by their persistence are succeeding in its [sic] accomplishment."[88]

But real problems persisted, not least because of the racial prejudice engendered by the teaching of history in the nation's schools. However, that could be fixed, since "Indians are generally liked by the people who know them and this unfortunate racial prejudice can be overcome in one generation by teaching in our schools the full and true story of the part played by the Indians in the growth of Canada."[89] Movies, again, were partly to blame, as they showed only "supposed attacks on peaceful settlers in the covered wagon." Schools, though, with their ability to influence both white *and* Indigenous children, were most harmful:

> I remember when studying in public school the short chapter on the Indians of Canada; I learned "that they were a copper coloured race of savages who lived in America before the white man came. The men lived by hunting and fishing and the women did all the hard work. They were a cruel bloodthirsty race fond of fighting and torturing their captives." That is about the gist of what we learned of the Indians while we were in our impressionable age and the sad part of the story is that that is about all that the average Canadian knows about them now which is nothing at all and the consequence is prejudice against him for what he was supposed to be.[90]

Martin called for changes to the government's enfranchisement policy, stating again "the price was too high." Indigenous people should not have to choose between living in their communities and becoming Canadian citizens; the latter choice resulted in them becoming "outcasts from their own people" and facing "an uncertain future among strangers who are not always willing to receive them on an equal footing." The answer was both the vote and the privileges of tribal membership.[91] Martin also suggested that Canada should implement the New Zealand parliamentary system in which indigenous people had their own representatives.[92]

Not all the problems could be blamed entirely on the federal government. Martin wanted a change in his people's attitudes as well, as he felt that their leaders must do more to inculcate faith and goodwill in their communities and counter the "false rumours and insinuations of agitators among them, who are so ready to attack any new measures" out of fear and suspicion. In turn, though, government officials needed to be more tolerant, sympathetic, and honest if things were to improve.[93] Martin ended his paper with a call for a "better deal" for Indigenous people so that they might assimilate "into the life of the

Canadian community." "Every one of my readers," he reminded them, "is living on land which in the not very distant past belonged to the Indians of Canada who gave it to your grandfathers. The advance of civilization was too fast for the Indians and they were left behind. They are catching up but are finding obstacles in their way which must be overcome if they are to be good Canadians. All they ask of you know is a square deal and the right to live as free people. Will you give it to them?"[94]

Martin's texts and public pronouncements struggled with the legacies of the past for his people's present and future, not least of these legacies being the confined spaces that Canadian society and, in particular, Canadian governments had fashioned for them: the reserves on which they could not create their own domestic spaces and live as both Indians and Canadians, the schools in which their education was substandard, and the other spaces, such as universities, from which they were excluded. At times his stance resembled that of Moses in his desire for assimilation and his belief that Indigenous people needed to "catch up" with civilization. However, he also argued even more vociferously for a clear and unambiguous acknowledgment of their centrality to Canada's past, a narrative in which their presence and significance could no longer be denied or obscured. Moreover, Martin's own personal history, particularly a life lived away from his birthplace and his multiple careers in which he often was greeted as an "Indian in an unexpected place," also may have shaped his warning about living as an unwanted guest among strangers. Perhaps what Martin wanted, above all, was the freedom to choose both worlds: not a freedom to live untethered from the past but, rather, one that meant openly proclaiming his Indigenous history and ancestry, participating in community decision-making at the Grand River while simultaneously attending Osgoode Hall, serving in the Canadian military, and presiding over a Toronto courtroom, all the while being a proud Mohawk who, to paraphrase Martin's comments about racial passing, did not have to put on "white-face" powder and pretend to be Italian. Martin, it seems, saw through a nation-state's attempts to "assimilate" Indigenous people that, as Philip J. Deloria has argued for the American context, "had nothing to do with the sameness that might have characterized social or political equality. Rather, [it] had everything to do with the practice of perfecting conquered people into similarity – ghost forms of the white conqueror, coexistent but not equal."[95] Neither Martin nor, it must be admitted, Moses, had any intentions of becoming ghosts in their own country.

Just as Moses' use of history had its precedents in nineteenth-century Anishinabe texts, Martin's trajectory was a path already travelled by fellow Mohawks John Brant-Sero and Frederick Loft, men who sought to link lives lived outside of the space of Six Nations – including their marriages to white women – to their birthplace and its history.[96] It is only relatively recently, I suggest, that they have been treated as more than interesting exceptions or anomalies who were not really "true" Indians: late nineteenth-century notions of authenticity have had exceptionally long reaches. Yet as Deloria points out about their American urban dwelling counterparts, a group that included men such as Charles Eastman, Ely Parker, and Carlos Montezuma, "to read this cohort simply in terms of assimilation is to mistake the rhetoric used in planning white domination for the actual encounter, which proved far more complicated – even among those who accepted the idea of assimilation itself. In that encounter, new generations of Indian people – some with prereservation memories, others raised in reservation contexts, still others brought to culture in cities or on the road – figured ways to move within the institutions that did, in fact, constrain, dominate, and transform them. Likewise, they often learned to move within the rhetoric – of assimilation, for instance – that structured expectations."[97] Men such as Moses and Martin targeted the rhetoric of the nation-state, albeit in slightly different fashions and for somewhat different purposes, in ways that exposed the hollowness of its vaunted program of assimilation – even when they agreed with some of its goals.

The Six Nations' remembrances of place and time thus suggest the need for a more nuanced perspective, one that bridges those commemorative processes preoccupied with narratives of nation-states and, in turn, Indigenous forms of memory focused primarily on local spaces and their temporalities.[98] While both approaches have been extremely significant in demonstrating the power of nation-states and the ability of colonized peoples to resist them, they do not entirely capture how complicated identifications with both colonial powers and Indigenous agency – ones in which were mingled strength and loss, pride and mourning – might structure these narratives. As we have seen, members of the Confederacy insisted in their inclusion in official commemorations of Canadian nationalism while simultaneously arguing that their participation demanded that the "nation" be understood in more intricate ways, ones that emanated from and incorporated places beyond the boundaries of the nation. I do not want to suggest, though, that all of them wished to completely dissolve the political boundaries of mid-twentieth-century Canada. Certainly that was not the case for Moses and Martin, for whom returns to the Mohawk Valley were no longer possible. Nevertheless, both men were clearly tied to the space of the Grand River Territory in multiple ways and felt keenly a burden of responsibility to their birthplace and community. For example, while it is not clear if Moses sought enfranchisement, he may not have done so because it would have meant leaving his home at the Grand River, however conflicted and complicated his position there might have been. For Milton Martin, the Canadian state's binaries of "white" versus "Indian" made even his return to the Grand River territory impossible. However, the past could be mobilized for the future, becoming a source of both solace and strength: it suggested things *had* been different and, thus, that they could and should *be* different. Turning the light on the other side might result in a vision of Canada that would create new places, new histories, and thus new futures for the Six Nations.

Chapter Three

"Among the Six Nations": Celia B. File and the Politics of Memory, History, and Home

"In the fall of 1921, I reluctantly made application to teach the Central Mohawk School on the Tyendinaga Reserve near Desoronto." With this confession Celia File opened her narrative, "Among the Six Nations," an eleven-page document lodged within Elliott Moses' papers at Library and Archives Canada and written, according to a handwritten note on its first page, in the early 1960s. The depth of her reluctance could be gauged by the exigencies of her situation: only an "overwhelming desire to teach," a temporary but long-expired and no longer renewable teaching certificate that closed "white" schools in the area to her, plus a need to recuperate from a bout of ill health brought on by the hardships of farm life could induce her to take up such a position. Her fears of living among savages were abruptly dismissed by the Indian agent, who instructed: "go and see for yourself." It was "either that or nothing," since File had absolutely no personal contacts with the "dark-skinned, silent, stern-looking" strangers that she had seen in the streets of Desoronto, so off she went, embarking on a journey that she would come to remember as personally and professionally transformative. In both the work that she would undertake as a historian and in her writing of her own history, File's acts of remembering demonstrate yet another angle through which to view the intertwined and tangled nature of settler and indigenous narratives in southern Ontario.

Born Celia Vandervoort in 1887 in Napanee, File's mother, Frances Roblin Vandervoort, died in 1894 when Celia was seven; her father Charles Wilbur Vandervoort remarried twice. Although the Vandervoort family does not seem to have been particularly wealthy, they were not without political influence in the area, as Charles Vandervoort was the Sheriff of Lennox and Addington County. File attended Napanee

Collegiate and then Model School in the area, from which she graduated in 1905.[1] Three years later she married a fellow teacher, Herbert File; according to the 1958 newspaper coverage of their golden wedding anniversary, they celebrated their marriage with a week-long honeymoon in Belleville.[2] Celia and Herbert had no children of their own but they looked after and educated some of her nieces.[3] The first and second decades of the twentieth century are a fairly murky period in File's life; most of her correspondence starts in the 1930s and, as we have seen, her life "Among the Six Nations," began in 1921. Herbert taught for some time and farmed outside of Napanee; however, evidence in File's papers suggest it is doubtful that he was able to make much of a living from either enterprise.

After three years at Tyendinaga, File enrolled at Queen's as an extramural student and then decided to become a full-time student. At Queen's, File completed a BA in History and English; she won the Alexander Laird Scholarship in English and in 1930 – after the initial prizewinner decided not to return to Queen's – was awarded the Sir James Aiken Fellowship in Canadian history. The $500 scholarship probably helped clinch her decision to enrol for an MA, as did the urging of Duncan McArthur, Queen's History professor and soon to be Deputy Minister of Education in the Hepburn government. With the graduate degree, McArthur told her, she would be able to obtain a better teaching position.[4] File decided to study the "history of the Mohawks," specifically the life of Mary (Molly) Brant and her diplomatic influence on both the British and Six Nations during the American Revolution. File's topic took her to the National Archives, where she worked with sources such as the Johnson papers, the Claus papers, and published documents. However, she also conducted research on the Grand River reserve, where she talked to various people and gathered information on both Brant and other aspects of the Confederacy's history, rituals, and material culture.[5] File continued to do so even after the thesis was accepted by Queen's, as she spent the summer of 1933 conducting research on the members of the Longhouse religion. It was during her research trip in 1930 to the Grand River reserve that she met Bernice Loft; as I have discussed elsewhere, they became particularly close friends in the 1930s.[6] In 1934, in a ceremony covered by Queen's alumni magazine, File was made an honorary member of the Six Nations who bestowed on her the same name, Kanoerohnkwa, given her at Tyendinaga.[7]

After completing her MA, File taught at Napanee Collegiate, specializing in History and English.[8] For most of the 1940s File taught at a number of schools in southwestern Ontario. While working in the village of Oil Springs southeast of Sarnia in 1945, she lost the only complete copy of her thesis, destroyed in a fire that levelled her apartment building.[9] After leaving teaching in 1952, File became a journalist, writing a gardening column in the 1950s and 1960s for the *Napanee Beaver*.[10] File was also involved with a number of voluntary organizations, such as the local historical society and the county hospital.[11] However, as her correspondence demonstrates, she also maintained an interest in Aboriginal issues, particularly those concerning the Six Nations, long after her active contacts with the Grand River and Tyendinaga communities had ended.[12] File died in Napanee in 1973.

Celia File wrote history in at least two registers: first, in her thesis on Mary Brant, and, second, in her narrative of her time at Tyendinaga. While the first is a formal piece of historical scholarship that conformed to the Queen's History Department's standards and the latter is a memoir, nonetheless the relationship between the two texts is more symbiotic than the genres might suggest. It is highly likely that her experiences concerning her time on the reserve led her to study Brant since, by her own admission, before working at Tyendinaga she felt nothing but suspicion and hostility towards "Indians." Moreover, although it is difficult to prove, I suspect that her work on Brant inflected her relationship with Bernice Loft, in that her respect and admiration for a late eighteenth-century Iroquois woman faced with negotiating colonial society may have been transferred to Loft, a mid-twentieth-century Iroquois woman poised between both the Grand River community and settler society. While it is not possible to draw upon the apparently irretrievable final version, the draft of the thesis deposited in the Queen's archives suggests how File approached Brant, the concepts and methodology that underpinned her research, and the reasons why she chose Brant as a significant and worthy historical figure.

The 133-page draft deals with Brant's background and family, her life in the Mohawk Valley with Johnson, the history of the Five Nations' Confederacy and their expulsion from the Valley, and her time at Niagara, Montreal, and Carleton Island. File concluded her work with a reflection on recent commemorations of the Six Nations. In File's estimation, Brant was a central figure in keeping the Iroquois loyal to the Crown and was thus a diplomat and political actor during a period of intense military and political upheaval. She played a "stellar part," File argued, both in protecting her people and brokering their loyalty to the British cause.[13] Respected by all whites whom she met, Brant also gained "increasing influence" over her own race. Moreover, in File's analysis, Brant's powers of leadership were greater than those of her brother, Joseph. Her speech to the Five Nations council persuaded them to cast in their lot with the British, a speech that either white men or Joseph, mistrusted or envied by some members, would not have been able to make.[14] Brant also exerted a diplomatic influence over her people at Carleton Island, ensuring that their resentment over British failure to prevent the destruction of the Five Nations' territory did not erupt in violence.[15] Her leverage with the Iroquois was recognized by Captain Fraser who, "despite his dislike of the Indians in general, is shrewd enough to recognize ability when he sees it, and man enough to give credit where credit is due" (File frequently used the present tense).[16] While File admitted that from the fall of 1781 on the official correspondence had little to say about Brant, she believed that regardless Brant continued to work as a mediator between the British and her people. "These were indeed dark days, and we are safe in assuming that Molly Brant was doing her part at Carleton Island, even though we have no record to prove it."[17]

The thesis did not stint in its treatment of the details of politics, war, and diplomacy: there is much in File's discussion of Carleton Island about the Five Nations' strategic position, for example, and the motivations and actions of Daniel Claus, Gilbert Tice, Joseph Brant, and John Johnson are given full scope. It is the Johnson household, though, over which Brant presided, and the households that she created in the Canadas, that lie at the heart of her history. In Brant's Mohawk Valley "home" she was the

> "brown Lady Johnson" who played a stellar part, holding the affection of this man of affairs, making a home to which he could come, sure of rest and sympathy, mothering his children, advising him in his treatment of her race, admonishing the men of that race when they proved intractable, welcoming the distinguished men and women who sought out this home in the wilderness which was at the same time the centre of so many activities. Not only did she gain an ever increasing influence over the people of her own race, but, what is more amazing, she gained at the same time the respect esteem of white men and women who came in contact with her.[18]

This esteem was all the more striking, File believed, since Brant "held but questionable right to be called the wife of the man to whom she bore at least nine children."[19] File cited manuscript sources that she believed proved Brant was not legally married to Johnson, yet also argued that according to Mohawk customs Brant was Johnson's "true wife" and had been seen as such by her people.[20] Brant was a devoted mother to her children (about whom File conducted genealogical research aimed at discovering their fates); when the British found her difficult and demanding, it was usually because of her ambitions for her family and her concerns for their well-being.[21]

Brant's narrative, then, linked the domains of family, sexuality, and reproduction to those of transatlantic diplomacy and imperial warfare. File remembered and commemorated Mary Brant as both wife and diplomat, both mother and politician, roles for which Brant was rarely honoured. Those that thought about her as a historical actor generally posed her as a question or problem: Johnson's "wife" or concubine?[22] For File, Brant was able to unite these realms partly because of her people's customs and practices, those that involved both gender and imperial ties. She spoke to them in council as a clan matron, for example, and inherited a Mohawk history of friendship and loyalty to Britain.[23] Yet Brant's own personality was, for File, key to her centrality to these events. She was "a beautiful woman, one with 'fine, natural courtesy,'" who also possessed "personality, quick wit, ... powers of adaptability, [and] ... keen intelligence."[24] By the time Johnson died Brant was no longer "Brown Lady Johnson" but had become "Mrs Mary Brant" to her white contemporaries and, to the Mohawk, "Degonwadonti" or "she against whom rival forces contend."[25]

Above all, File saw Mary Brant as a heroine, a woman who led her people through perilous times with courage, pluck, and dignity. File's narrative oscillates between the stance of a historian interested in political, military, and diplomatic events and a biographer who sought to capture the romance of Brant's individual story. Being true to the former mode meant engaging in her own "romance of the archives," digging deep to find genealogical details, poring over male colonial officials' correspondence to catch glimpses of her subject, and fuming at Augustus Buell, whose history of the Johnson family she consulted, for his lack of reliability and, above all, footnotes. "Throughout his book Buell seems to have access to information of which no one else has ever heard, and the mysteries of his bibliography have never been unravelled. Then, too, we have instances where he has misquoted manuscripts which are accessible to all," File lamented.[26] File also believed there was no need to rely on unsubstantiated sources since, between materials generated by the colonial archive and the Six Nations' own written histories – Tuscarora David Cusick's 1825 *History of Six Nations*, Lewis Morgan and Ely S. Parker's *League of the Ho-de-no-sau-nee*, and the Grand River Chief's 1900 account – the material was more than ample. Indeed, the problem faced by the historian was plenitude, not paucity: "from the many sources available we can form a fairly accurate picture of early conditions, and for the period covering the lifetime of Molly Brant and her famous brother the student's difficulty lies in the wealth of available material rather than in its scarcity."[27] File also used contemporary Iroquois knowledge, consulting Mrs. Henry Brant of Tyendinaga about the Brant family's status as chiefs.[28] Yet despite her desire to "form fairly accurate picture[s]," and, of course, please her examiners, File could not resist the lure of Brant's story as that of a heroine, a larger than life figure who had lived in turbulent times and had had thrilling and stirring adventures, a figure with whom her readers (not to mention File herself) might identify on an emotional level. Brant had lived a "life crowded with usefulness and romance and adventure": her time at Carleton Island had been "stirring . . . and the heroine of that tale (once told) would be Molly Brant."[29]

Although the record does not tell us how File viewed her thesis, Duncan McArthur certainly was pleased with her. In a reference letter to the Secretary of the York Township school board, supporting File's application for a position at East York Collegiate, McArthur mentioned that File's "greater maturity of judgment and more extensive experience" had attracted her instructors' attention; even more compelling, though, was her "intense interest in her studies" to which she brought "an active intensely interested mind." Her undergraduate grades were high and her Master's thesis on Molly Brant "represents most extensive research and careful analysis of primary historical materials. She spent the greater part of two summers at the Dominion Archives at Ottawa ... and has produced, I am satisfied, the best and most extensive piece of work dealing with 'Molly Brant.'" McArthur continued:

> I should say that her chief characteristic is an intense, and unbounding interest in her subject. On several occasions I felt it necessary to restrain her from doing an amount of work which I felt her physique, though strong and robust, could not successfully endure. Because of her intensity of

interest in historical studies, she is certain to arouse enthusiasm and loyalty in her pupils. I cannot imagine her teaching a dull lesson in Canadian history. For that reason I have every confidence that she will obtain and hold the affection of her students and that she will be troubled with a minimum degree with the problem of discipline.[30]

McArthur's concern for File's health appears to have been overly paternalistic: it is highly unlikely that he would have expressed similar anxieties for a male student's physical well-being. Yet it was not completely unwarranted, since illness dogged File all her life. Other Queen's professors also wrote letters for File, speaking of her conscientious and thorough approach to her discipline, her capabilities as a historian, and her many abilities – sympathetic while being able to maintain order, her skill at imparting knowledge – as an instructor.[31]

Moreover, at least some members of Tyendinaga wished her well with her work. Mrs. Henry Brant was "thrilled" to hear that File was "delving deeply into the historical treasures" of the archives and glad that she "did not overlook my people, the Six Nations, who (if you will forgive my pride) have a most wonderful history as a nation within a nation ... And after reading the story of Molly Brant does one not feel that she too deserves a place in history, as well as a monument for her loyalty to the British cause which same [monument] should stand in the city of Kingston today."[32] After reading in Kingston's *Whig Standard* that File had received her Master's degree, Clara Hill was moved to write to her, "you cannot imagine how pleased we all were to hear it, and all join in Congratulations to you. You have certainly worked hard and we are real glad that your labour has been crowned with success and you have our best wishes for your future."[33] Even after her thesis had been completed and she had embarked on her teaching career, File continued to interview residents of the Grand River reserve. She discussed the status of the Six Nations and their struggle for sovereignty with Sam Lickers, a Tuscarora chief; Catherine Hill told her about participating in Longhouse ceremonies, her abstention from liquor and alcohol, the honesty of "pagans," and the living she made from fortune telling; Jesse Moses traced the Moses' family genealogy with her; and William Powless explained the problems faced by those who had become enfranchised. "Not one has made good as a white man," Powless concluded, citing the example of "one man who had bought a farm in white territory and is now penniless, a day labourer."[34]

File may well have reread Clara Hill's letter fondly over the years, since she experienced her share of tension and stress during the 1930s and 1940s. Some of this came from her family who, judging from a letter sent to her by her father, were apprehensive about the prospect of File moving up in her profession and away from Napanee. While File was applying for a job in York County, Vandervoort spoke to the chair of the Napanee Collegiate Institute's management committee and felt that a position might be available for her in September. "Considerable less money in Napanee would be more profitable than a greater amount in other places," wrote the Sheriff, who was not above trying to appeal to File's sense of wifely and daughterly responsibility to induce her to stay "home." "I recognize the greater scope in larger centres, but you must also recognize that you are not a girl just starting on her life work, unfortunately you had to lose several years before you could reach out for the larger things, but now that you can reach out and pick your position, don't you think it would be doing a real fine act if you just considered your old dad's wishes and the patient Herb who has been so true through all these years." "Patient Herb" also was a model son-in-law, Vandervoort told his (potentially errant, possibly selfish) daughter, who took his father-in-law for long Saturday drives and spent Sundays with him: both father and husband deserved to have File resume her life in Napanee.[35] While we do not know if the York County Board turned her down, File took up a position at Napanee Collegiate. She may have done so as a result of her family's pressure and the need to secure work during the Depression; however, she probably came to regret it. During the 1930s, File saw her salary cut back twice; she also suffered from illnesses, usually pneumonia, which forced her to take sick leave for which, it seems, she was not paid. Her contract with the Lennox and Addington Board was not renewed in 1941 and File was forced to find teaching work elsewhere. Although W. A. Jennings, the area's school inspector, wrote to File of his "good opinion" of her work "and should any board refer your name to me I shall be glad to speak favorably of what you are doing," that apparently did not sway the Lennox and Addington trustees.[36] File wrote to the Deputy Minister of Education to protest the Board's decision in a letter that highlights the restrictions and strictures imposed by a small town on a married, working woman. The circumstances of her dismissal were humiliating, as she had been called into the school office and told by the secretary that her contract would not be renewed for the fall, a decision that File attributed to her having appealed her unpaid sick leave to the Teachers'

Federation. Although initially resigned to it, File now saw the Board's action as "discourteous" and wanted to have her name cleared. "If you will be good enough to look up the Inspectors' reports on my work I think you will see that they consider me a good teacher. I have never spared myself as far as the school is concerned and much of my ill-health has been brought on by over-work." It was two, relatively new, male trustees who had "been working against" File: one on the grounds of her marriage and the other, "if gossip is correct, because I am not a social asset." Despite widespread social disapproval, though, of married women teachers and assumptions that husbands, not wives, should be breadwinners, File refused to keep the realities of her marriage a secret. "It is I who keep the house going. My husband has had only desultory employment and at less than a living wage. I have kept the house together and most of the time my niece has lived with us and I have provided for her and educated her." By the 1930s Herbert was no longer teaching and instead worked in a canning factory near Desoronto. Insofar as the second charge was concerned – File's lack of social cachet – she offered the following defence: "I live quietly and because of heavy doctors' bills and help I give to others we have to be frugal. Bridge does not appeal to me and my whole desire is to teach well." Even though she had created a garden that was a "little show place" from a bare field and had recently hosted a party in it for sixty guests (proof also that she had recovered from her illness), she asserted: "I will not curry favour. Perhaps it is a mistake, but I feel that a teacher should be judged by her teaching and not her social qualities." Rather than stay in Napanee, then, File applied for a position in Belleville, where the principal of the high school had encouraged her to fight the Board's decision.[37]

It is not likely that File took much comfort from the Deputy Minister's reply. While he thought the Board "was to be criticized" for her dismissal without cause and had found the Inspectors' reports generally "favourable," the latter included some criticisms of her teaching: she talked too much, used "public school methods," and was "apt to deviate too much from the lesson proper." One inspector charged that File did "not stick to [her] text." However, this year the reports found that her "appreciation of the subject [she taught was] above the average and that [she got] good responses from [her] pupils. There is a suggestion, however, in this report that [her] work as a member of the staff has been criticized locally." G. Rogers did not clarify this rather cryptically worded charge and, overall, his advice concerning the Board and any appeal process was not reassuring. File was not likely to gain anything from a Board of Reference and had already stated that she wished to leave Napanee: "so why go through the possibility of public discussion which may affect your getting another job?"[38] File, it seems, took his advice.

After her teaching career ended, File began to reflect on her years at Tyendinaga, a time that she felt was responsible for her lifelong interest in, or, one might say passion for, the history of the Iroquois. "Among the Six Nations" can be read in a number of ways, as both travel narrative and ethnography. Moreover, it also is the history and memory of her exposure to Iroquois beliefs, practices, and values, an exposure that altered her life and thus gives her account elements of a conversion narrative. "Among the Six Nations" can be read both as an account of "what happened" *and* as a meditation mediated by the events that followed her stay on the reserve: her thesis research, her friendships with Aboriginal people, particularly Bernice Loft, and, perhaps, the trials of teaching in places that proved far less congenial than Tyendinaga.

The theme of places encountered – File's entry into unknown territory, the uses of space on Tyendinaga by both File and the Mohawk, their configuration of domestic and community space – runs through File's narrative. For one, these places could surprise, even delight. As File "entered" the unknown terrain of Tyendinaga and began her exploration, she happened upon a landscape almost identical to her own home: "buildings better than the one on the farm met my eye," along with well-cultivated fields, prosperous livestock, and the most modern rural school she had seen. To be sure, she also saw dilapidated buildings and uncultivated fields but even those were in better shape than she had expected.[39] Her destination was a large white house with "shade trees and bright flowers" and "crisp white" curtains, home to a tall, snowy-haired lady with a regal bearing: Mary Maracle or, as File called her, Aunt Mary. "One look into her wise, kind eyes and I had made my decision. I would teach [at] the Central Mohawk School if I could live in her house." However, File had to convince the Maracle family that her boarding with them would not be a burden, as "Aunt Mary" was no longer young and had a very large dairy farm to oversee. "Needless to say," File writes, "I was rapidly changing my opinion of Indians, and my inherited prejudices were vanishing like mist before the morning sun." File managed to persuade the Maracles to take her in temporarily (an arrangement that lasted for six years), partly because of her desperation, partly because of her experience as a farm wife, and in her words, "perhaps, too, it was a beginning of that admiration for each other which has made us such firm friends from that day to this."[40]

File's tale oscillates between several positions vis-à-vis her relationship with the residents of Tyendinaga and non-Aboriginal readers. At times she presents herself as a member of the community. She discusses the Mohawk as "her" people; moreover, the image of the Maracle's house as her "true home" appears at various points in her narrative. "It was, and is a real home to me in every sense of the word. Whenever I am tired or am recovering from an illness, I long for my cheerful room there with its comfortable bed and its three windows, one of them overlooking the bay."[41] In her concluding paragraph, File tells her reader that, although at present she is ill and has written part of her story from a hospital bed, once her doctors let her she is going "to leave the city" and return to "the most restful spot I know on earth, to my own room at Aunt Mary's. There in the peaceful atmosphere of that home, among the people who sympathize instinctively with your every mood, I hope to regain once more a sound mind in a sound body."[42]

While File's appropriation of the Maracle's home as her own bears an uneasy relationship to settler appropriation of Indigenous land, resources, and culture, there may have been more at work in her remembrance of those years. For one, in her direct and prolonged contact with Aboriginal men, women, and children File was unlike the majority of white women, such as Carnochan, engaged in historical writing in the early twentieth century. If they met Aboriginal people face-to-face they did so within the confines of OHS meetings. For the most part, white people's encounters with Aboriginal peoples were imagined, consisting of fantasies of the anonymous stereotypes so disliked by Milton Martin or more romantic meetings with historical figures such as Tecumseh.[43] File, however, moved in and out of intimate and domestic spaces and took part in community events both formal and informal: she entered people's homes, helped prepare the wedding feast for the Maracles' son, nursed the community's sick, and become a godmother to some of Tyendinaga's children.[44] Although to some extent File's position was not unlike that of a missionary, judging by her later relationships with some of the community's families, her adoption into the community, and tributes paid to her when she left Tyendinaga for Queen's it seems that she was viewed with a degree of trust and respect.[45] There are moments in her narrative when she recognizes that the residents of Tyendinaga could not be seen as a people "frozen in time." Not only did the landscape resemble the eastern Ontario farmlands in which she had grown up, "Aunt Mary's" home was a haven of domesticity, with its white curtains and sunny room overlooking the bay, and one of the community's schools was much better than any she had previously seen in rural Ontario.[46] As well, the council built a new council house with a kitchen and dining room "fitted up" by the Ladies' Guild, and File also moved into her new school, "a modern building with all the up-to-date equipment that delights the heart of a teacher." From this building File's pupils came and went, many of them bound for the local high school in Desoronto. "Yet I am repeatedly asked if Indians can learn!" she observed, with no small degree of indignation.[47] None of these elements suggested a community removed from contemporary society, nor were they to be mourned as evidence of the degradation or corruption of Aboriginal culture and society by modernity. For File's readers – and quite likely for the Celia File of the 1920s – these were unexpected Indians in an expected place; the latter, though, was transformed because of the agency of its residents.

In a few places File breaks from her narrative of discovery of both familiar and strange to reflect upon the (at the time unknown to her) history of the Tyendinaga Mohawk and their community; however, more recent history was her central focus. File used her narrative to write a twentieth-century ethnography about the Iroquois, whether concerning the Mohawks' daily behaviour at Tyendinaga or documenting her own observations on the longhouse rituals of the Seneca and Cayuga when she visited the Grand River territory.[48] In this mode, File's position was that of the outsider with privileged and more "authentic" information, whose job was to get the "real" story to other Canadians, the "true narrative" of the Mohawk, as well as to counter the stereotypes that so angered Martin. Time and again she answers an imaginary questioner, explicitly or implicitly. "Her" people are sincere, courteous, and generous; they are not snoops or gossips but welcome people for what they are and ask no questions. Her questioner also asks her "what of Indian's shiftlessness, uncleanliness, cruelty, immorality, and treachery"? File replied by saying she found these qualities but no more than in white society. File then qualifies this statement by reminding her listener: "I am speaking of Indians who are in an advanced state of civilization. To all intents and purposes, their lives are the same, outwardly, as those of their white neighbours. There are good housekeepers and bad housekeepers everywhere, just as there are men who are good managers and good workers, and those who are the reverse." She also admits that she found the "Indians" more callous towards suffering, although such an attitude was "partly due to the patient endurance of pain which no white man would stand."[49] File also points out that any treachery by "the Indian" is no more acute or evident than what has been experienced by Native peoples at the hands of whites: "We may well hang our heads in shame as we look back at our treatment of him. Can we censure him for meeting treachery with treachery, and cruelty with cruelty? Remember, he was fighting with his back to the wall for his home and his lands." Citing the example of century Sir William Johnson and his success in dealing with the so-called "treacherous" Iroquois, a success File attributes to Johnson's honesty, File declares, "it has been my experience that the Indian is more willing to overlook slight injuries than those of my own race. Once deceive an Indian intentionally, however, and you can never again expect him to trust you."[50]

For File, then, the Mohawk of Tyendinaga thus had become "known" to her in ways denied other kinds of Canadians. She herself asks how she managed it, stating "there are teachers on Indian Reserves to-day who have been there much more than six years but are still rank outsiders. They are tolerated, treated with courtesy, but are not accepted and trusted. It is because they have held themselves aloof, have never tried to understand the people among whom they live, have deliberately hugged to their breasts the old, unkind prejudices, the old idea of the superiority of the Anglo-Saxon." All they see on the Reserves is that which does not "happen in a well-ordered Anglo-Saxon community," and they look upon Aboriginal peoples through such a lens of contempt and disapproval. They do not try to "look at it through the eyes of the Indians themselves, nor consider the differences in race and in history."[51] To some extent, as this passage suggests, File herself adopts a stance of moral superiority over such whites, one grounded in her ability to "take on" the norms and subjectivities of Aboriginal people and to become educated in their ways and histories. Theorists of "whiteness" have identified such a stance as forming the moral subjectivity of the enlightened (white) woman or man, who has freed her or himself from the trap of racism, unlike their less enlightened fellow whites.[52] A number of times File calls the Tyendinaga Mohawk "my people," indicating a proprietary attitude towards them.

However, throughout her narrative File points to the many ways she "learned" from the Six Nations; again, the document is also a tale of a partial conversion to Aboriginal ways and values. While she states that it is not "necessary to 'go native'," still "my years among them have left their stamp on me." She tells her audience she learned patience, forbearance, charity, generosity, and hospitality, as well as the fact that material goods do not bring happiness, a lesson that the depression "has since forced home" on the entire world but "I learned it from my Indians by example."[53] It is difficult to know if File's teaching changed as a result of her time on Tyendinaga but she remarks on her pride, joy, and satisfaction in her school. Her pupils, she tells her audience, were much more disciplined, courteous, and respectful than white children; what is more, unlike white children they could be trusted to work independently.[54] File makes it clear that although she had much to give the community, particularly to its children, she too was the beneficiary in this cultural exchange.

She was not, though, untouched by antimodernist assumptions and her own racially inflected perspectives. For one, the notion the Maracles and their community would rejuvenate File and restore her to a healthy state (one that she never seems to have enjoyed) was a construct by no means unique to File; there was a long history of white fantasies that Native peoples' society would relieve the stresses and strains of modernity.[55] She also admits that she found "the Indian inferior to the white man" in some areas; namely, "in the ability to organize and in the development of the acquisitive instinct." Comments about the Mohawk's lack of interest in business, as well as File's characterization of the community as being in "no hurry," showing "no mad rush for material things," suggests that she assumed that Tyendinaga and its residents were removed from the complexities and challenges of 1920s Canadian industrial capitalism and urban modernity. File argues that these "defects" – a lack of acquisitiveness, unconcern for planning – can be attributed to Native history and social organization which, except for a year's food supply, placed no value on saving and hoarding goods:[56] an analysis of Native society that, if she had reflected on her own research or even her other observations, was far from being accurate. The same narrative that argued "racial instincts die hard and are just as slow to develop"[57] also depicted the farm where she boarded as a model of careful business planning and good management, a place where Steve Maracle "owes no small part of his success to Aunt Mary, who is as thrifty as any white woman I know."[58]

It was no accident that File paid special tribute to "Aunt Mary" in the success of the Maracle farms. To be sure, "the Indian" in her narrative is usually masculine: he is "generous" and courteous, no less treacherous than whites, and bad at saving money and organizing matters, all of which can be seen as part of the wider use of a male figure in non-Aboriginal discourse about Aboriginal people. However, File was eager to discuss, defend, and praise the women of Tyendinaga.[59] Indigenous marriage practices had been historically different from those of whites (a distinction brought home to her by her thesis research) but that did not mean they were inferior or immoral. Women who enter into "trial" marriages are not stigmatized by File and "Indian fathers and mothers" love their children and are just as proud of and ambitious for them as are any white parents.[60] File's Mohawk women are domestic beings, good housekeepers who keep three room homes just as clean and happy as ones three times the size. "I do not know of a woman on the Tyendinaga Reserve who is not a good cook," she told her readers.[61] On a number of occasions File mentions the "beauty" of Tyendinaga and the Grand River's women, both certain individuals and as a collective, a beauty both physical and spiritual.[62] In File's narrative, these women work hard at reinforcing community ties and creating homosocial spaces, with their Ladies' Guild, work at wedding feasts, and participation in Longhouse ceremonies.[63] In particular, Mary Maracle exemplifies the numerous virtues and strengths of Iroquois women: she is revered for her wisdom, kindness, serenity, and excellence as a household manager.[64]

While much of these paeans measured Iroquois women by the standards of white, middle-class domesticity and may have been tinged by maternal feminist notions of women's centrality to racial progress, nevertheless File also would have contended with the image of the degraded "squaw drudge," a figure who appears briefly in her thesis, albeit drawn from others' work, as the antithesis of Molly Brant. It is quite likely that she also knew of the stereotype of the drunken, dirty, dissolute, and possibly dangerous Indigenous woman who lacked family and home, one that became part of whites' discourse on Aboriginal people.[65] File's account not only demonstrated more respect for Iroquois women than was usually the case in white Canadian society, it also placed them, their activities, and the spaces they created at the centre of their community. Moreover, while her narrative notes with approval their participation in activities encouraged by Indian agents and missionaries – European-style housekeeping and Ladies' Guilds, for example – it also makes it clear to her readers that women were active in maintaining Iroquois traditions and rituals.

As well as foregrounding the women of Tyendinaga and Six Nations, File also provides us with hints about her own subjectivity as a white woman. File thought of her work on Tyendinaga as an enterprise of benevolence and humanitarianism, not of dominance, and she wrote of having learnt much from the Iroquois. For this teacher, education was not a one-sided process.[66] She also discusses her practice of letting the smaller children take afternoon naps on the cloakroom benches and how one day "the inspector caught me with the tiniest one asleep on my lap one day, the classes tiptoeing up to my desk and reciting almost in whispers for fear of awakening him."[67] File's was an act of kindness, one rarely extended to Aboriginal children in other schools of this period. However, the scenes File recreates of her classroom, that of the "Indian" children joyfully engaged in non-Indigenous education, also had a history, one where white women's benevolence towards children of subaltern groups was intended to rescue and uplift them from their parents' misguided, possibly destructive ways.[68] At one point in her narrative File describes her classroom: the work she did teaching boys and girls to do handicrafts, as well as instructing students on cooking, cleaning up, and public health and hygiene. This passage on her school evokes both missionary accounts of "training" Indigenous children and, too, the child-saving movement of late Victorian and Edwardian Canada, where immigrant and working-class children (and their mothers) were instructed in correct housekeeping.[69]

To be fair, unlike urban moral reformers and child-savers, File did not believe that these children's mothers needed such lessons. Nor, it is worth keeping in mind, had she wanted to go to Tyendinaga: File had not seen herself as a representative of either the missionary or the child-saving cause but, rather, as a woman in need of employment. Nevertheless, the roles File performed (at least in her account) in the community – the teacher of small children, the helper with feasts, the godmother, and the nurse – were accessible to her because of her gender and race. It was as a white woman – and especially as a representative, after all, of the Canadian nation-state – that she had access to the community in an officially defined capacity. This access allowed File to write about the Iroquois as an "authority" in ways that would have been more problematic for Iroquois men and women themselves.

File also notes with some pride that she happens

> to be blessed with dark hair and eyes, and many an Indian girl has skin lighter than mine, as I have often laughingly pointed out as I placed my hand beside hers. This has been a help to me, I know, and I have been asked, not once but many times, and not only by Indians but by white

people who marvel at my sympathy with the idea, but now, especially if it is an Indian who asks, I am sorry I cannot answer in the affirmative; for I know it is the highest compliment he can pay me.[70]

It was because File could not "answer in the affirmative" that she could admit this experience so freely. Having "dark hair and eyes" might permit a degree of fantasy and role-playing akin to that of Grey Owl and other white North Americans who enjoyed, as historian Philip Deloria has argued, "playing Indian."[71] While File might have delighted in the illusion of appearing "more Indian than the Indian," by the time she wrote her memoir she had access to spaces denied the vast majority of Native women: the franchise, two degrees from Queen's, and a history of paid employment within Ontario's secondary schools.

However, if seeing herself as both a member of the Iroquois and, at times, as their benefactor was to File's own intellectual and emotional benefit, the Mohawk of Tyendinaga also recognized that such benefits might be mutual. Their choice of "Loving-hearted" as File's Mohawk name does not appear to have been a coincidence; they had wanted to call her "Good Mother" but felt that the Mohawk name would be too long and unpronounceable by whites.[72] The tributes paid to her by her pupils and their parents on her departure from the Central Mohawk School mention her "kindnesses" and their pride in having "one so talented" as a teacher. "By precept and example you have taught us nothing but good and we will never forget the benefit that you have been to us."[73] Exchanges between File and her Mohawk acquaintances continued after her departure. In 1930 Mrs. Henry Brant wrote to File, thanking her for offering to bring the case of "Gladys" before Dr. Scott when File was in Ottawa. Gladys, the Brant's daughter, was doing well in the second form at school and her mother hoped to keep her there. However, Mrs. Brant wrote: "the need is greater than ever. We managed to pay all expenses last year by robbing ourselves of even the necessaries in order to carry on. But times are harder now and we would be grateful if we could get the Department's aid during the winter months in paying for her board, $3.50 a week … I think it would be a shame to keep her out of school because of lack of funds (but you know how hard our path has been for the last few years). Of course that will not happen if we have to exist on bread and water, so long as she has health to attend." In turn, Mrs. Brant was looking forward to seeing File, was "delighted" to hear from her, and sent her Molly Brant's Mohawk name. "I wish you every success in your thesis, and pray that the compiling of 'The Life of Molly Brant' may succeed beyond your fondest dreams. I am sure you will do excellent work which will be valued historically, as you so richly deserve."[74] File also maintained ties with the Hill family of Tyendinaga, who wrote to her with news of community events and their children's accomplishments in school.[75] But they also asked for File's assistance in their dealings with the Department of Indian Affairs, asking her to write to Ottawa to help them out, as Bob Hill had been ill and was unable to work outdoors in the winter.[76] If settler society's configurations of race and gender, as well as her own "loving heart," led File to play the role of benefactor, then this was a performance involving more than one character, more than one set of motivations, and, as the correspondence suggests, possibly different versions of one script.

Although there is little information regarding the reception of File's paper, John Melling, the Executive Director of Indian-Eskimo Association of Canada (formerly the National Commission on the Indian Canadian), wrote to File in April 1961, congratulating her on "Among the Six Nations." Melling called it "delicate, sensitive, and the most perfect expression of an 'integrated' Canadian that I have read. Time and again, my own Association has tried to insist that 'integration' is not just the process whereby the Indian is touched by the dominant White culture but also the process by which the White is touched by the Indian culture, so that the two blend together in a beautifully harmonious whole. In some of the best written prose that I have had the pleasure of reading for a long time, you have shown this blending to be possible."[77] Perhaps Melling's language of integration and harmonious blending struck a chord with File, with its suggestion that Indigenous-white cooperation, not confrontation, was the desirable approach. There is no evidence to suggest that she saw herself as a political activist. She did not, for example, join in protests against the gendered inequality of the Indian Act, or trace the loss of Aboriginal languages (which she lamented) to the same education system of which she was a part. Nevertheless, she saw herself, and was perceived by some members of the Iroquois, as providing a service to their community: through her work as a teacher, her writing of Iroquois history, and the friendship and support she extended to individuals and families.[78]

Some of her white contemporaries also saw File as a potentially useful intermediary, who might continue to explain Indigenous people for settler society. In 1966 Mrs. G. D. Williams, the editor of *The Intelligencer*'s "Social Department," contacted File. The paper was looking for more local news to "spark" it up and part of that spark, Williams and her publisher felt, might come from Tyendinaga. Recent developments in Indian Affairs had prompted *The Intelligencer* to send a reporter to the reserve; however, Chief John Brant had refused to talk to him "and thus we missed a good story." File, however, "had gained the confidence of the people" and Williams knew she "could get comments from leaders at the Reserve." There were a number of other issues about which the paper hoped File would tackle for their readers. They knew nothing about the system of electing Chiefs and also were very confused about Indian Boards and Associations, since "Kahn-Tineta Horn has added to the confusion, and if there is ever an opportunity to in a non-controversial way discuss the local people's opinion of her, this would make a good story – but a tough one to handle." (Williams was referring to the well-known Mohawk political activist, Kahn-Tineta Horn.) Furthermore, education – a topic that would have been dear to File's heart – would need to be covered. Who went on to high school and post-secondary education? They hoped that she could round these figures out "with comments from the people themselves on the case for and against school integration. When a prominent native son returns for a visit, this would make a good opportunity for a profile."

Tyendinaga, Williams thought, was "unique" in Canada, as it appeared to be the best-educated and self-governed reserve. Could File verify this? "If so, the people of this district are woefully uninformed, and this, I think, is the perfect opportunity to clue them up." While the publisher did not want to "rock the boat" with controversies or exposés, "this is a wonderful chance to do an educational job of presenting the Indians of Tyendinaga to the non-whites around here who have neglected them for so long and are so mis-informed. A small local missionary job, you might say. Indians are hot copy now, and every paper located near a Reserve is milking the Indians for as many inches of copy as possible. This can be turned into a real service to the Indian people if the right person handles the job." But while some news of "Indians" was desirable (and might sell more papers), "of course we must be careful not to pack the paper with Indians every day of the week and get people's backs up," Williams maintained.[79] A few days later Williams thanked her for her clippings and her copy on Melville Hill and the Mohawk Council Meeting, telling her "personally I have never had any difficulty with the Indians" but admitting that she knew only the Hills, Mr. and Mrs. Claus, and Mrs. Lewis. "Perhaps they are the exceptions." She also asked File her opinion of the Claus family's beliefs that

Mohawk children would be best served by being educated apart from whites, feeling that "the Indian child must learn to get along with whites some day – better while young and adaptable than later in life. There must be other factors influencing their opinion." (Despite her desire to educate her white readers about their neighbours, Williams did not mention that the reverse might be true – that whites should learn to get along with Indians.)[80] For the next three years File provided "missionary service," in her editor's words, to area residents. In 1970, though, the paper ended its arrangement with her, as it decided to concentrate on Desoronto and needed an active representative in the area.[81] Celia File's time "among the Six Nations" had, it seemed, come to an end.

To return to File's memoir, though: why was it written in the early 1960s? It may have been prompted by her friendship with Havelock Wallace Robb, the poet, naturalist, public speaker, and admirer of Native people, who lived not far from File at "Abbey Dawn," his five hundred acre bird and game sanctuary west of Gananoque. Robb shared File's interest in Native history and culture: he studied Mohawk, used Native narratives in some of his written work (*Thunderbird*, *Tecumtha*, and *Kayanakonte*), and was adopted by the Iroquois. Robb knew some of the same members of Tyendinaga as File and, over the 1950s and 1960s, he wrote to her frequently about them and his work in Native history and culture. Robb too had his own "conversion" narrative of becoming a champion of Native people, as he told File in 1956 (possibly in response to her query) that "my interest in the Redman was aroused when I was a boy: I saw three Indian women unkindly treated; I saw a peaceful, decent Mohawk unjustly treated, beaten up and knocked to the ground – kicked in the face by a Whiteman! No poet could experience such a thing and remain silent! My life has been my protest."[82] Robb also reminded her of her ties to Tyendinaga and the Mohawk by his use of Mohawk names, both her own and those of others, telling her "Ka-je-je Yoh-sta" (Mrs. Brant) admitted to disagreements between Oshweken, Tyendinaga, and Kahnawake histories and that news of the health of "Ka-noe-rung-ka" (File) had made him "very anxious and distressed."[83]

In addition to Robb's friendship, the difficulties File experienced in her teaching career in the 1940s, as well as her struggles to support her husband and maintain a home while living hundreds of miles away from both, may have underpinned her remembrance of her time at Tyendinaga as one in which she found a "home." It is telling, perhaps, that her narrative is silent about the husband and father that she left in Napanee during those years: "the patient Herb" was written out of File's account, nor does her father figure in it. File, herself a representative of settler society, found a better home on the reserve than that offered by her own kind; similarly, by putting Mary Brant at the centre of the upheavals of the late eighteenth century, File found a "better story" than those narratives of the American Revolution that excluded Brant and the Iroquois.[84] Her foregrounding of "Miss Molly" and her family, the Johnson home, and the households and communal gathering places of Tyendinaga relied on images of domesticity and intimacy to stage, in Antoinette Burton's words, a "drama of remembrance."[85] In File's case, this drama was one of settler society and its colonial history, one written in multiple genres and delivered in multiple instalments. Neither fitting the mould of the colonial missionary nor of the political activist, the spaces File helped create and inhabit were ones in which notions of white women's superiority might be troubled, if not eradicated, both through historical work and the lived experience of being "among the Six Nations." While her writings and experiences were, until recently, forgotten, they left traces of the possibility that relationships between Indigenous and settler women could be registered in a different key.

Chapter Four

"Where Nature had joined hands with man": History, Tourism, and Landscape in Niagara-on-the-Lake

Can one imagine a pleasure more ideal to spend a hot summer's day than lolling under an immense shade tree on a rolling piece of land covered by beautiful green lawns and three-quarters surrounded by water, having a view on one side of gorgeous Lake Ontario and the other the most beautiful and renowned Niagara River, with all sorts of sailing cart passing to and fro, and not a minute of the 24 hours daily without a cool breeze ... In this rich and favored stretch of fruit land, there is no corner so inviting to the seeker after pleasure and health, or to the business man looking for rest and recuperation, as historic and quaint Niagara-on-the-Lake.

In his guide to the town, *Illustrated Niagara-on-the-Lake Canada: Engravings of Some of Her Many Attractions*, John S. Clarke, the newspaper's publisher, could barely contain his excitement (or his adjectives and adverbs). It was "a town where Nature's beauty reigns supreme, that is every year becoming better known to tourists, and better liked as the acquaintance enlarges and improves. Few summer resorts can offer such ease of access, beauty of scenery, or wealth of attraction and historic interest, as can this charming burg, and it therefore sands unrivaled as a Mecca for the tourists."[1] Relying on both enthusiastic prose and a wealth of illustrations, Clarke went on to map out the town's copious attractions: the purity of the atmosphere, its history as Upper Canada's first capital and the site of many War of 1812 battles, local amusements (both sporting and entertainments), its beautiful homes, and the marked peace and security. "Mothers," Clarke promised, "never have any fear regarding the whereabouts or doings of the little ones, as Niagara is one vast playground with no source of danger to encounter."[2]

However, urban dwellers did not have to worry that they were coming to an unsophisticated backwater where they would have to forego their daily amenities. "Niagara-on-the-Lake is thoroughly up to date on civic arrangements, having every modern convenience in the shape of an excellent waterworks system, good drainage, electric light, and ample fire protection. These are the necessities of our modern comfort, and are a great consideration to everyone. The Town Council has a practical knowledge of the requirements of summer tourists, and one will not find himself hedged about by any puritanical and nonsensical by-laws when coming to Niagara."[3] To underscore his point, one of the first pictures in Clarke's guide was a photograph of the town's officials – its mayor, councillors, clerk, and police chief. Those inclined to be nervous about such matters could be reassured by photos of the fire department, water works, lighthouse, and electric light plant.[4]

Clarke may have erred on the side of hyperbole but he would not be the first, or the last, to promote the town by praising its multifaceted nature. While Janet Carnochan worked diligently to educate her fellow residents about the historic riches that surrounded them (and if visitors also were included in these lessons, so much the better), in the late nineteenth and early twentieth century local residents such as Clarke published guidebooks and wrote articles for the press that extolled the area's virtues for tourists. From the mid-nineteenth century on various groups and individuals laboured to produce the town as a tourist attraction and to create for it an identity that managed and married landscape, history, and culture. Niagara-on-the-Lake's tourist attractions were shaped by the efforts of the Niagara Parks Commission (NPC), the Ministry of Tourism, local government, a non-profit cultural organization, and the residents of the area, not merely by the serendipity of its location along the Niagara River and on the shore of Lake Ontario. These various groups both competed and cooperated in the formation of the area's identity, one intended to be distinct from the mass tourism of Niagara Falls and that would position this part of the Niagara Peninsula as a site of significant local, regional, and – for some – national identity. The history of Niagara-on-the-Lake suggests the multiple ways in which notions of "the past" – and tourism's relation to them – were freighted with concerns about the present and hopes for the future.

As American historian Dona Brown argues, "nature alone does not make 'scenery,' and picturesque history alone does not make a quaint tourist destination."[5] Tourists' destinations and the gazes they employ once they reach them have been shaped and directed by more than

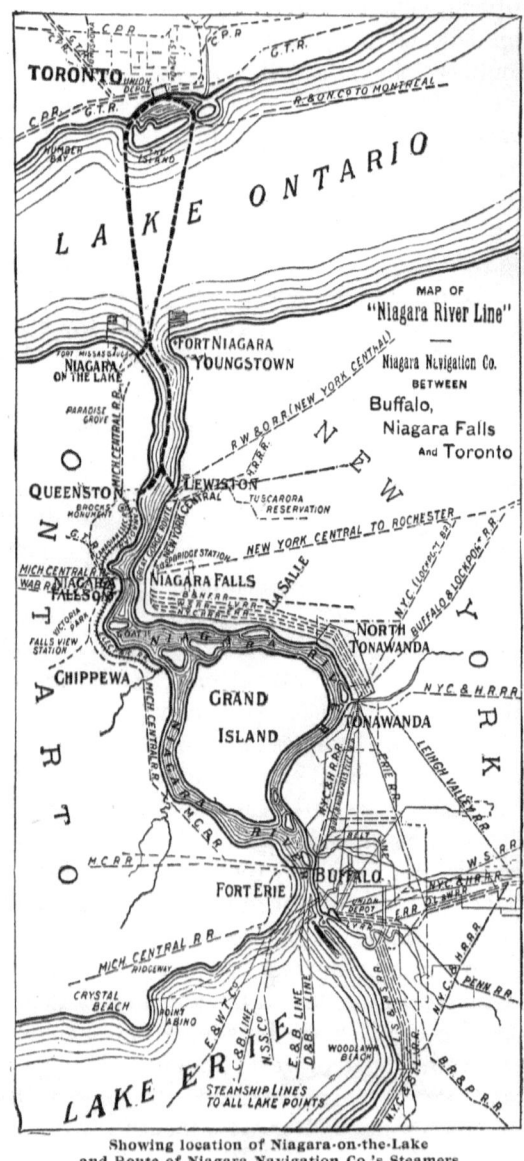

4.1 Putting Niagara-on-the-Lake on the tourist map. John S. Clarke, *Illustrated Niagara-on-the-Lake Canada*. Courtesy Niagara Historical Museum.

4.2 Cover page, Niagara-on-the-Lake tourism brochure, 1897. Courtesy Niagara Historical Museum, 985.4.488.

just individual "choice" or "personal taste." Ideological forces such as romantic ideals of the picturesque and the sublime, antimodern notions of folk culture, and discourses of imperialism and nationalism, combined with either commercial and consumer capitalism or state intervention (or some mixture of both), have played powerful roles in designating and creating certain regions as tourist havens.[6] Some scholars have been interested in tracking and capturing shifting forms of tourist sensibilities, while others have looked at the promotion of certain regions or countries as tourist havens and the effects of tourist industries on these areas.[7] In the Niagara area, Niagara Falls has, understandably, captured the lion's share of both popular and academic historians' attention.[8]

The lure of history in the Niagara Peninsula was not new to the late nineteenth century. Patricia Jasen's work has demonstrated that the War of 1812 battlefields and forts drew a number of visitors, particularly those Americans and Europeans who had been visiting battlefields in their own countries and were interested in the War of 1812 in the Niagara Peninsula. Often motivated ideologically by romantic notions of the sublime, they welcomed the opportunity to be moved by the melancholy of battlegrounds. For these – and many others – the emotional experience of historical tourism was a strong attraction. As well, doomed and tragic heroes fascinated these men and women, a passion that found a ready outlet in the figure of Isaac Brock. His devotion to his people and country, his statesmanship, his gallantry in the war, as well as his reputedly humane treatment of Americans: all of this turned Brock into a very romantic and appealing figure for these visitors. But as Jasen points out, tourists who arrived just after War's end and in the early 1820s had little to guide them in their travels. Except for Brock's monument, few such sites existed, educational plaques had yet to be put up, and only a small number of guidebooks had been written for tourists to consult. Often they had to rely on their own knowledge of the War, as they gazed upon ruined forts and explained their meaning and significance themselves. Others might be guided in their explorations of forts and battlefields by veterans of the War of 1812, who provided them with a combination of partial battle reenactment and oral histories. Their accounts of expeditions to visit Queenston Heights or Lundy's Lane Battleground are full of both the details of the battles fought there and their emotional and sensory dimensions, such as the victors' shouts or the anguished groans of the dying.[9] Yet as the years passed, it became increasingly difficult for tourists to educate themselves about the events of 1812–1815: in addition to the increasingly strong pull of the Falls' commercial enticements, the battlefields and forts fell into ruins and became either less accessible (because of safety) or less identifiable as specific historic sites.

By the 1860s Niagara-on-the-Lake's economy was starting to suffer, so much so that local leaders began to publicly fret over its fate. A number of setbacks, it seems, converged at roughly the same time: county government was moved to St. Catharines, taking with it political clout and the potential to attract investment; the Harbour and Dock Company, which had brought in cross-lake traffic and employment, closed; the British garrison was withdrawn; and the Welland Canal, which increased commercial traffic in the Niagara Peninsula, not only diverted commerce and industry from the town but also made it more difficult to reach.[10] Residents searched for new solutions to boost the town's economy. In 1869, for example, its pharmacist and Mayor Henry Paffard built a new pharmacy modelled on London's Crystal Palace, whose sophistication and elegance made it stand out from the plainer facades and interiors of pharmacies in other small towns in this period. Paffard hoped the pharmacy's architecture and decor would be a tourist attraction; as we shall see, it fulfilled his ambitions, although not quite in the way he had envisioned.

Might other economic alternatives have been considered? Tourism, after all, had not always been the only way of making a living in Niagara and the nearby village of Queenston. Local commentators pointed out that the towns' histories included commercial ventures and small-scale industrial production, particularly from the early to mid-nineteenth century; these enterprises included a number of mills (saw and grist), basket and canning factories, and shipyards. However, the Welland Canal seems to have squashed any hope of their expansion into a major commercial and industrial centre.[11] At least one resident felt that options other than tourism needed to be explored, since the money tourists brought in tended to remain in the hands of hotel and boarding house keepers. Factories – two or three, at least – were needed to promote growth and keep taxes low: "manufactories, more than the number of summer visitors will be the means of a more general circulation of money among the working men and women."[12] However, "No Show for Manufactories," argued J. W., a manufacturer of thirty years, whose article pointed to the impracticality of some resident's expectations that manufacturing would solve Niagara-on-the-Lake's economic slump. Except for basketmaking and canning, a lack of good rail service made it too expensive to bring in raw materials and ship finished products. Since it was impossible to compete with large industrial centres such as Toronto, Hamilton, and Buffalo, why not take advantage of the town's qualities that made it an "ideal summer resort"? It had modern conveniences: electric light, a first-class water system, good fire protection, and "obliging up-to-date merchants to supply the need of visitors with all the necessaries and luxuries of life" and "far more cheaply" than at other summer resorts. Moreover, with its "grand old trees," safe beaches, fishing at the mouth of the Niagara River, and the beautiful lake view, it truly was the "land of milk and honey." Tourists needed to know about all of this. "Invite them to come and spend the summer hours with you, make them feel at home, and as they return to fight the battle of life, renewed in health and strength they will leave that behind them which will enable the merchants and workers of the old town to pass a winter free from care, and wait for the time when they shall return again." Tourism in Niagara might even close political divides. "Let Grit and Tory combine to make everything attractive to strangers, and Niagara shall yet be known as what she truly is, the ideal summer resort of Canada."[13]

Niagara's tourist boosters, unlike their counterparts in other areas (notably Nova Scotia), did not actively attempt to suppress the area's collective memory of industrial and commercial production, although as we shall see they were not eager to recreate this period for tourists' edification. They often invoked these glory days in arguing that the town's economy would benefit from more tourists. The past had shown exactly what, given the right circumstances, Niagara and its environs were capable of achieving. There was no doubt, though, that the conditions of the 1820s and 1830s were gone and would not return. Modern times demanded modern solutions and what could be more modern and forward-thinking than exposing the area's "resources" – its scenery, architecture, and history – to a greater number of tourists, a fast-growing sector within early twentieth-century North America? Tourism, they argued, had already brought some measure of prosperity to Niagara and Queenston; certainly it had worked wonders for Niagara Falls.

Such was the stance taken by F. Winthrop, the Chairman of the town's Finance Committee, who in 1900 publicly urged his fellow residents to pay their back taxes. The town currently was owed $4000 and needed to borrow to make up the balance; incurring interest rates would result in a loss of $240, "which would go a long way towards necessary improvements to bring visitors here and make the place attractive." While other towns might depend on manufacturing, Niagara "is away from any railroad centre and bounded on one side by water, our only dependence is on the tourist traffic and summer residents," Winthrop argued. "How often," he lamented,

> has the remark been made by people in the place, "What do we care for the summer visitors? We have got along very well for the last thirty years without them and I guess we can continue to do so." The man who makes that remark is nothing but an antiquated fossil, and should exhibit himself to the outside world as a freak. How can the storekeeper, hotelkeeper, or professional man spend money in improvements, thereby necessitating the employ of labour from time to time, if he does not get the main part of his profits from the summer residents?

Winthrop called for the town to advertise itself more aggressively: the Pan-American Exposition was coming up and Niagara should be represented there as one of the "prettiest spots in Canada." As well as having a selfish and narrow-minded business sector, Winthrop believed that the town suffered because people confused it with Niagara Falls.[14] Writing under the pen name "Rusticus," one resident believed that conservation was "admirable" but only up to a certain extent: "Let (Niagara) conserve all that remains of the dear old homeland, and adopt all that is essential to the progress of a new world town and it must be ideal."[15] The notion of Niagara as a kind of "sleeping beauty" to be awakened by increased improvements and more visitors is a recurring trope in these writings.

While taxes were important, the town's residents needed to make an effort in other ways. "Something Must be Done," an anonymous citizen complained to the local paper, about the horses and cattle that ran free in the town, particularly around St. Mark's church, the high school, and the summer home of Buffalo's J. K. Barge, sentiments with which the editor fully agreed. "We have conversed with gentlemen who are in the habit of coming here every summer – owning fine residences – and spend thousands of dollars in town annually, and they express regret and say it is almost useless for them to make such extensive improvements on their property when the council takes such little interest in the town's welfare as to allow this state of affairs to exist." Cattle had destroyed the residences of these gentlemen, "as well as to continually deposit a disgusting mass of filth around their premises daily." If "this nuisance is not stopped," these gentlemen saw no choice but to leave, prompting the editor to ask "can it be possible that our citizens would rather have the cows running at random than a yearly influx of tourists? Or can it be that the council have not the moral courage to take a decisive stand on this question. Whichever it may be, unless something is done very soon Niagara-on-the-Lake's popularity as a summer resort will be a thing of the past."[16]

A lack of reliable and frequent transportation, not errant livestock, concerned other writers. "Citizens in favor of good roads" called for a bicycle path between Queenston and Niagara that would serve both local cyclists and tourists. "It is a notorious fact that if the road from here to St. Catharines, particularly that piece in Grantham, were better, we would have ten times the number of wheelmen visiting us." However, as it was not the responsibility of the "Citizens" to choose which roads needed attention, the town could turn its consideration to the Queenston-Niagara Road: "no finer scenery or fairer field for wheeling exists than the river bank from here to Queenston Heights. No seven miles of road or rather by path is in as good condition to start on to make cheaply and expeditiously a model."[17] "What Niagara Needs," stated an "Ex-Councillor," was better train service: it was clearly "absurd" to think that economic matters would improve with only "the monopoly road" to enter and exit town in the summer, a situation that American visitors asked the "Ex-Councillor" about constantly.[18] Percy Beale believed the solution would be a trolley that would link the town to Buffalo, an extension of the existing line that would "revive the town" – a necessity because "without our American visitors our municipal and business finances would be small indeed." There was no time to waste, Beale warned: "fresh and popular summer resorts are coming to the front all around us, and we are nowhere in comparison." Lest anyone think he was exaggerating the dire need for such a line, Beale pointed out that recently he had travelled to Niagara from Toronto, a trip that began at 7:30 a.m. and ended at 6:30 p.m. "Rapid transit indeed!"[19]

In response to local businesses and individuals lobbying, rail companies and steamship lines occasionally attempted to improve their service to the area. In the early 1900s the Niagara and Port Dalhousie Rail Road ran a train from Port Dalhousie, in St. Catharines' north end, to Niagara to serve the area's fruit growers and the town.[20] Although it is not likely that the amount of traffic satisfied tourist promoters, lake-going steamers, often with Indigenous names (the *Chippewa*, the *Cayuga*), docked at Niagara-on-the-Lake; their passengers might spend some time in the town before making their way to the Falls. Furthermore, much to the satisfaction of the cyclists (a group that also included "the young ladies," excited by the prospect of "early morning spins"[21]) three months after the "Citizens" called for its completion the bicycle path between Queenston and Niagara was almost done, a development that would please "devotees of the wheel, [who] will not go to any place where they cannot have pleasant runs out whenever the spell overtakes them."[22]

While residents fretted that tourists either were not arriving in sufficient numbers or that they would cease to do so in the future, in the early twentieth century it appears their fears were somewhat misplaced. While their numbers are impossible to pin down (particularly without a local Chamber of Commerce, which was not established until 1949[23]), tourists left their mark on Niagara, not just within the pages of the local newspaper but also on the physical landscape. The predominant form of tourism was practiced by the "summer folk," the well-to-do Americans (and a few Canadians) who built large homes in

4.3 Deck of the *Chippewa*, c. 1890s. One of the most luxurious of the lake steamers, the *Chippewa* was 311 feet long and included a 192-foot salon. Courtesy Niagara Historical Museum.

the village and along the River Road between Niagara and Queenston and their less wealthy counterparts who rented summer cottages in Niagara township's Chautauqua area.[24] For those who could not stay the entire summer, the town's well-appointed hotels – the Queen's Royal, the Chautauqua, the Riverside, and the Oban – catered to guests from the Niagara area, southern Ontario, Montreal, and American cities such as Buffalo, Chicago, New York, and Portland.[25]

These visitors came for a variety of reasons, for to be a tourist to this area (then and now) meant, as Clarke had pointed out, that one's experiences were not organized around one particular site but instead were shaped by multiple sensations and activities. Different, yet overlapping, forms of tourism existed: landscape viewing, whether of the Niagara River, Lake Ontario, the Escarpment, or of the surrounding farms' fruit orchards; the tourism of rest and relaxation from urban life

4.4 "Sweet Memories" of Niagara-on-the-Lake on board the *Cayuga*, c. 1913. The *Cayuga* held just under 2000 passengers and a crew of 75. Built in 1906, she took over 15 million passengers across the lake until 1957. Courtesy Niagara Historical Museum.

that sojourns in the spacious houses, the large hotels, or the cottages of Chautauqua might bring; and historical and educational tourism, in which knowledge of the past could be attained by visits to the Niagara Historical Museum, historical landmarks such as Brock's Monument or Butler's Burying Ground, and leisurely walks around Niagara-on-the-Lake itself to view examples of "historic" architecture (after the town was rebuilt in the 1810s and 1820s, much of it was not disturbed or significantly altered). An annual summer army camp in Niagara-on-the-Lake, while not officially designated a "tourist site," also brought in hundreds – sometimes thousands – of army officials and soldiers (one of them being Milton Martin), all of whom had to be provisioned by local businesses. In turn, the soldiers provided entertainment for both residents and tourists.[26]

History, Tourism, and Landscape   123

4.5 Postcard of Michigan Central Railroad train at Queen Street station, 1923. The building on the left is today's Prince of Wales hotel. Courtesy Niagara Historical Museum.

None of these activities, of course, were discrete entities. Those who wrote to the local paper about their experiences spoke not just of the range of pleasures offered by Niagara-on-the-Lake and Queenston, they also penned paeans to the area's harmonious "nature" that united all these delights (and urged friends and relatives to pass on these sentiments).[27] Moreover, for middle- and upper-class tourists, the primary consumers of Niagara and Queenston's tourism, spending leisure time in this area was not a frivolous enterprise. Instead, it could be a type of self-improvement, an opportunity to become immersed in Canadian history by simply moving through the local landscape. The anonymous author of "Chautauqua Breezes," for example, was eager to quash any suspicion of hedonism that might be attached to a Niagara vacation. Although something was "in the air of this delightful place that produces such a feeling of calmness and contentment," the town and surrounding area were immersed in reminders of Canadian history. The anonymous author writes:

4.6 The "Summer Folk": Lansing House, 284 Queen St, Niagara-on-the-Lake (now Lakewinds B&B), originally built in 1899 by Watts Sherman Lansing, Buffalo and Niagara. Photograph by Paul Jenkins.

> There is floating in the air of Niagara and its environs memories of bygone days. Memories that will never fade away from Canada's patriotic sons, [of their] ... noble exploits and hardy endurance of the defenders of the Empire, who in 1812, counted not their lives dear that they might hand down to their descendants the country that was their heritage, and to this day this Canada, 'the brightest gem in the British crown,' and is ours to hold intact to hand down to our descendants ... Then what more fitting place for Canadians than Niagara and its district (with its magnificent orchards and fruit farms) to spend their vacation, where love of nature and love of country is in the very air we breathe, and among whose dwellers you imbibe the very spirit of contentment.[28]

The presence of the Chautauqua grounds and assembly in Niagara Township, on the western edge of town, underpinned such claims to moral uplift. Organized independently from the New York circuit but resembling it in its emphasis on education and "wholesome" entertainments, in the 1880s and 1890s the Chautauqua held conferences on such themes as "the deepening of spiritual life" and attracted tourists to the Chautauqua and Lakeside Hotels, which also featured beaches, tennis courts, and other forms of recreation.[29]

The Chautauqua Hotel and its surrounding cottages were designed to appeal to a broader, somewhat less well-off group of tourists than those who patronized the other hotels or owned summer homes. Nevertheless, tourist promoters concurred that tourism in Niagara was "genteel," marked by decorous bourgeois entertainments and

History, Tourism, and Landscape 125

4.7 Souvenir postcard of the Queen's Royal Hotel. Courtesy Niagara Historical Museum.

recreation. Sports such as swimming, tennis, lawn bowling, croquet and golf played a large role in advertisements, both textual and visual, for the town. An upcoming lawn tennis tournament in late August 1896, hosted at the Queen's Royal Hotel, for example, promised to bring players from the United States; it also featured a concert at which Miss Beverly Robinson, the daughter of Toronto lawyer and businessmen John Beverley Robinson and granddaughter of the province's attorney general, would sing. Miss Robinson, the organizers were proud to note, was en route to an international tour with Emma Albani, the Italian-Canadian opera star. As well as sports and singing, the festivities also promised a "calico cotillion" and musicale, to be followed by a ball and prize-giving.[30]

The hotels also hosted bicycle "tourneys" or gymkhanas that, as Phillip Gordon Mackintosh has argued, subordinated athletic feats to displays of bourgeois order and decorum.[31] The 1896 "tourney" held at Queen's Royal opened with a grand marshal and fire brigade

4.8 Queen's Royal Rotunda, c. 1890s. Courtesy Niagara Historical Museum.

4.9 Dining in style, Queen's Royal Hotel, c. 1890s. Courtesy Niagara Historical Museum.

4.10 Niagara Assembly/Canadian Chautauqua, c. 1880s. Courtesy Niagara Historical Museum.

members wearing red shirts and white caps, carrying red Japanese parasols and riding bicycles decorated with red flags; furthermore, they were followed by a tandem bicycle sporting white and pink dahlias with asparagus ferns. The rest of the parade consisted of teams: riders from Gus Fleischmann's Buffalo-based company who rode under arches made up of heliotropes, asters, roses, and carnations; twelve cyclists from Queen's Royal sported golden road, poppies, sweet peas, sunflowers, and ribbons; while Chautauqua's entry included gladiolas and a Union Jack.[32] The summer of 1900, wrote the local paper's editor, "promises to be a banner season here. A large number of the first people in Washington, St. Louis, Baltimore and other American cities are enjoying this most beautiful of climates and resorts." The town would provide them with many sporting events, both as spectators and participants, such as a yacht regatta, provincial lawn bowling championships, an international tennis tournament, and the third annual bicycle gymkhana.[33] The town's two golf courses, laid out by residents Charles Hunter and J. Geale Dickson at Fort George Course in 1877 and at Fort Mississauga a year later, were particularly well used; the Fort George Course saw a number of competitions,

4.11 Selling historic Niagara. *Niagara Advance*, June 1919.

including International Tournaments held in 1895 and 1902. For at least one local businessman, golf was crucial to the town's ability to draw in visitors. During the First World War, with members of the Canadian Expeditionary Force camped on the courses, Queen's Royal Hotel owner Henry Winnett wrote to the town's mayor to complain about the lack of activities for his guests. Winnett believed that Niagara-on-the-Lake would "never ... be anything but a summer resort and without good golf it won't amount to a 'hill of beans.'"[34]

Yacht regattas, lawn bowling, and the bicycle "tourneys" presented an image of tourists and residents (summer and full-time) engaged in polite, well-mannered entertainments; they also, as pictorial evidence suggests, might appeal to members of both sexes. Although the phrase "New Woman" is notable from its absence in the local press, bicycling, swimming, tennis, and golf were all sports that drew their fair share of female participants, both in the town itself and from elsewhere.[35] Both men and women belonged to the Golf Club, although women tended to play mostly on the Fort Mississauga course. Although newspaper editorials tended to dwell on the opportunities afforded by middle-class men by Niagara's soothing atmosphere, clearly middle-class women were active participants in those spaces created by tourism, just as in

4.12 The army comes to Niagara-on-the-Lake, c. 1914. Courtesy Niagara Historical Museum.

urban spaces they had become increasingly visible in department stores, theatres, art galleries, and museums.[36]

As well, it was no secret that hotelkeepers and local boosters hoped that Americans would constitute a significant part of the clientele. Although the War of 1812 was increasingly becoming a significant part of the town's historical memory – and, as we shall see, would become even more so once levels of the state became involved – everyone, it seemed, wanted to welcome the Americans. At the very least, they were encouraged to behave as though they did. "This year," Clarke wrote to *The Times* in 1900, "we have been favored with a large number of tourists principally from the southern and northern States and we urge an intelligent effort not only to retain but largely increase this business ... We agree our summer business is our most valued and paying one."[37] Plans to restore Fort George by the Niagara Golf Club touched a nationalist nerve, according to *The Times*. Club members proposed to rebuild and restore the buildings, mark its graves, trim the grass and root out weeds, and open it up to tourists and sightseers as well as golfers. However, "some soreheads are kicking," a group that included writers to *The Globe and Mail* argued, while they raised "an absurd cry of

View from Fort Mississauga, showing part of C. E. F. Camp and Niagara River, Niagara-on-the-Lake, Canada.

4.13 The CEF Camp, First World War.

desecration of Canadian relics" that ignored the ruins, weeds, and "predatory bovines [that] now wander at their own sweet will through the bastions" (the writer also pointed to the similar state of Navy Hall, which had been "modernized" into a stable and was permeated with an air of "wreck, ruin, and abandonment"). Those who had been "shouting themselves hoarse in Toronto should think twice before using phrases such as "'desecrated' by Americans." While the club membership might be made up largely of the latter, "at least they show more true regard for our old historical landmarks than we as Canadians have done ourselves."[38] For those who wished to attract paying visitors, the rupture in Niagara's history created by its having been burnt in 1813 could be consigned to the past, lodged safely in the Museum and the Historical Society's publications.

Much of the public discourse around tourism came from those civic leaders or businessmen with a direct interest in promoting Niagara's pastoral and historic charms: it is much harder to find the opinions and perspectives of other local residents from this period, particularly those with seasonal employment in hotels, restaurants, shops, and the golf

History, Tourism, and Landscape   131

club.³⁹ However, in 1981 the Museum and town library organized the collection and preservation of oral histories, conducted with those who either had grown up in the town or arrived in Niagara in the 1920s. Many of these "reminiscences" thus covered the interwar years, a period when tourism began to decline; however, the interviewees' memories provide glimpses of relationships between "the summer folk" and those whose fortunes might have depended on them. Daisy Elliot, who took up residence in the town after her marriage in 1925, recalled that many wealthy Americans came to Niagara in the summer "but the local people weren't bothered by this summer influx"; moreover, as a boy her husband had found work caddying for them. Jeanette Webster believed "the Americans who had summer homes here, were to a large extent a part of the town." Kitty Walsh, who arrived in Niagara as a five-year-old child with her widowed mother, was more ambivalent about American summer residents, as she suggested "at one point people began to resent them because they paid poor wages and they refused to work for them. But some of them were very nice people especially the Greiners who had a big house on John St. and the

132   Creating Colonial Pasts

4.14 Chautauqua assembly. This YMCA group came from both Canada and the United States. Courtesy Niagara Historical Museum.

Wettlaufers. Mrs. Wettlauffer once invited all the people from town to a big party." Young local men who worked in the tourist industry might find prospective – albeit potentially clandestine, given class differences – dates among the daughters of wealthy hotel guests. Long-time resident Glen Bishop, who worked as a golf caddy, ticket seller at the local movie theatre, and Queen's Royal bellhop fondly remembered those "millionaires' daughters" with whom he spent time at the park or the show.

One well-off American family, the Rands, had left a clear impression on the residents' memories (not to mention the town's landscape with their estate, "Randwood"). Elliott thought of the Rands as "very friendly people," while Walsh's memories of "Mr. Rand" included his demanding behaviour at the gas station: he would pull up, blow his horn, and refuse to get out of his car. "I thought he was too demanding. But the Rand girls were lovely and not a bit snooty." For his part, Bishop recalled "the Rands [have] done more good for the town and paid

4.15 Ladies' Lawn Bowling Club. The club was located close to the Queen's Royal Hotel. Courtesy Niagara Historical Museum.

higher taxes than any other family" (he also paid tribute to "the genius" of Calvin Rand, one of the founders of the Shaw Festival).[40]

But summer, the time when "all our friends came from Toronto and Buffalo," ended. "Then the last boat pulled away from the dock at the end of the season, [and] we'd resign ourselves to a Fall and Winter of desolation almost."[41] Such a sense of "desolation" also started to set into the town in the early 1930s, as the residents felt the Depression's inroads more keenly. In the 1920s the Queen's Royal, the most prominent and elite of the town's hotels, had already faced financial troubles. In 1922 the president of the Queen's Royal, W. Goffat, asked the NPC if they would be interested in purchasing the property and provided the Commission with the following inventory: seven acres, over twelve thousand feet of lake frontage, one hundred bedrooms, a dining room that sat three hundred, three annexes with sixty-six additional beds and bathrooms, a casino designed for three hundred patrons, three bath houses, tennis courts, and a boat house. Although the Commission's chair, William Ellis, expressed an interest in the property, nothing

4.16 Caddies, Niagara Golf Club, 1902. Courtesy Niagara Historical Museum.

appears to have come of it.⁴² By 1934, the hotel having closed and its furniture and fittings auctioned off, the town took possession of the property in lieu of back taxes.⁴³

Over the next few years letters to the editor and articles debated the property's future. Should the land on which it had stood be turned into a park and the rest divided into building lots, proposed J. Musson? Perhaps the town might "forgive" taxes (except for school taxes) on the homes valued over $5000, since all would benefit from "this class of person?"⁴⁴ W. D. Caskey agreed that a park would be an excellent use of the property, unpopular though this might be with local taxpayers. No other site could give residents and tourists access to the waterfront in quite the same way, he thought. "The appreciation of its attractiveness is shown by the willingness of wealthy people to spend large sums on building beautiful homes here." This might be the town's last chance to save the site for its residents, Caskey argued. Moreover, Niagara was unlikely to be anything other than a residential and tourist spot, so it

4.17 "Randwood," c. 1940. The home was bought by George F. Rand in 1905, who changed its name from Woodlawn to Randwood. Courtesy Niagara Historical Museum.

was wise to sacrifice immediate revenue for future needs.[45] Council member D. A. R. Rodgers, however, felt that the best approach would be to divide the property into building lots so that the town might reap the tax benefits; residents' interests could be protected by restricting the height of hedges and fences. "I would make no allowance for any part of it to be a park," the thrifty-minded Rodgers opined, "because all parks are luxuries, built by towns and cities as they prosper and become congested. I know of no park that has brought prosperity, and many that have decreased the value of the surrounding property." There were other spots that could be developed as "bathing beaches," he believed, and cited the Niagara Parks Commission's (NPC) work with the Mississauga Reserve. "Charity begins at home," thought Rodgers. "Why should the town spend money on giving a beach to outsiders who don't spend much money (if they spent anything) and who might create a great deal of annoyance. The foundation of what business the town has rests on the desire of our summer visitors and residents for quietness."[46]

While the town decided to turn the property into a public park, that did not quell the debate. In July 1936 William Kirby wrote to the town paper expressing his concern about rumours that it would be sold to an "outside interest for a paltry sum." The park, Kirby argued, was part of the townsfolk's "great heritage," an opinion that had been confirmed recently at a well-attended public meeting, where the people had made it clear that they wanted "this property made over to them and kept as a fine, clean, well-appointed recreation ground for themselves and their children and their guests who come to our midst. Not a playground of the hurdy-gurdy type – that was never entertained. They desired it as a suitable place to bathe and properly supervised by some person the town can well employ as, say, a life guard, in the summer. We can vision a beauty spot there where the people can enjoy the beach, which is Providence's inheritance to our recipients."[47] A week later the paper's editor added his voice to the debate, calling for the property to remain public: in this case, for the benefit of private enterprise. Those homeowners who rented rooms or their entire house to tourists during the summer months – a "lengthy list," the editor reminded his readers – would see a steep decline in their business, and thus in their ability to pay their property taxes, if the beach were to be closed. "Summer residents" also had told the editor that they would stop coming if the Queen's beach were to pass into private hands.[48]

Debates over the ownership, access to, and use of public space, whether of Queen's Royal Park or of historic sites, continued into the summer of 1936. According to the paper, two hundred and seven businessmen signed a petition to the town council calling for the Queen's Royal site to be kept as a park. If the town sold the park for development, they claimed, it would lose its greatest asset, "A few years ago industries were discouraged that would have located here. The cry then was that this was a natural summer resort and keep it as such. Today the council was shutting off the waterfront and doing away with its main asset as a summer resort. The industries were lost and the summer resort business would be lost also." While the chairman of the finances committee, Mr. Greaves, asked how the town would pay its debts, as it already owned a number of properties whose owners had defaulted on their taxes, Joseph Mulholland could not understand why the "people's representatives" were "virtually giving away" the waterfront. Citing the case of Mississauga Beach (the Chautauqua grounds, which the town had acquired), where the town had sold off waterfront lots but had "retained dozens of lots back of that which would be useless except for what you see going on there now, the building of the cheapest sort of cabins. Visitors have refused to come back because of the way beach activities were being shut off. Why you can't hold a wiener roast at the foot of Queen Street because the regulations in effect said you had to be off the beach by 11 p.m.!"[49] In the same month, "what value picnics?" the editor wondered. Apparently some residents had raised objections to tourists holding picnics; not, the editor believed, to make them feel unwelcome per se but instead out of the belief that picnics did not generate revenue and only ran up the town's expenses. Such a belief did not take into account the perishable refreshments that might be bought in the town, not to mention their "word-of-mouth" effect on long-term prosperity. "They bring publicity to the town; friend passes the word on to friend" – with the result that picnickers returned for a few weeks, perhaps even for a few months.[50] "Progress" agreed, believing that while it was certainly desirable and worthwhile to try to attract manufacturing, few had come forward to do so; in the meantime the town had proved itself attractive to short- and long-term visitors and should continue to do so.[51]

It was not just the potential transfer of public assets to private hands – with the subsequent, and somewhat ironic, threat to private enterprise – that worried residents. Some were not so sure that the summer folk would continue to come even if Queen's Royal Park remained open, as the question of transportation to Niagara was a sore spot. Canada Steamship Lines, the *Advance*'s editor complained, did not advertise its trips to the town, unlike its promotion of runs to Queenston and Port Dalhousie. "If our town had not attractions for the holiday visitors we would have felt differently about it, but it has many, which we need not detail here ... You would be surprised at the number of people who cross the lake on CSL boats, who believe that they see Niagara-on-the-Lake when the boat ties up for a few minutes at the wharf." The editor had "heard of people" who had happened to disembark "and who have been surprised at the beauty and attractiveness of this town, of which one cannot see a particle from the wharf."[52] Two years later this was still a problem. Damage by ice that spring to the Niagara wharf meant that CSL boats would bypass Niagara, dock at Queenston, and run a bus between the two towns for those who wished to visit the former. This was not appealing, argued the author: CSL was giving the town a "raw deal" ("nothing" would have been better, he grumbled) and several businessmen thought they should be connected by boat to Port Dalhousie. A number of residents had asked the town council to urge CSL to put Niagara back on their route: if it were properly advertised, its "historic sites and museums, military camp and parks" had the potential to draw in large numbers of tourists from Toronto.[53]

Tensions over space were not, of course, unique to Niagara-on-the-Lake, as other resort towns that developed in the nineteenth and into the twentieth century felt them.[54] Niagara appears to have had, of course, the misfortune of seeing the number of visitors decline just as the Depression set in. While the Depression does not seem to have been the sole cause of residents' anxieties about the "summer folk," the spectre of the municipality being saddled with large amounts of unpaid taxes in the 1930s, no industrial or commercial tax base, and no firm promise of help from other levels of government must not have allayed residents' fears that holding on to properties such as Queen's Royal would do nothing but send their own taxes soaring. Moreover, at times tensions over which kind of tourists were considered desirable also erupted. When in 1937 G. R. Warren, "of Niagara Falls," the paper noted, attempted to build tourist cabins on his Niagara Boulevard lot (close to the Mississauga Beach area), he was met with a "storm of protest." Warren's application for a permit resulted in a special town council meeting, at which both councillors and residents of the area spoke out against his plans. "Respectable" houses of "good appearance" and "decent summer homes" – those that presently existed and might be owned by either locals or summer residents – were juxtaposed against the "cheap ... tourist huts and false log cabins" of Warren's plans. The town came in for some blame, as a number of speakers castigated it for allowing small, inexpensive lots to be sold instead of those of "higher prices to people who would have [built] better class homes." "Do you want this place to be another Port Dalhousie or Coney Island," asked Mr. Ackermann, "or do you want it to be seen as beautiful, restful old Niagara?"[55]

While clearly class prejudices and concerns fueled the opposition to Warren's plans, his being from Niagara Falls probably sharpened these feelings and gave them focus. Tourist promoters' and a number of residents' desires that the area develop a more "elevated" and bourgeois tone distinct from the populist appeal of the Falls – not to mention the latter's racial heterogeneity – were always implicit in discussions that focused on the need to cultivate taste and dignity in Niagara's tourism.

This comparison may have been so apparent to contemporaries that there was no need to mention Niagara Falls by name; they may also have wished to avoid stirring up further controversy. Ackermann may well have chosen other locations as examples of "undesirable" tourist sites to avoid creating bad feeling.

If transportation by boat and rail seemed to residents to be less than adequate, it was the NPC's work on the River Road during the late 1920s and early 1930s that improved the physical links between Niagara-on-the-Lake and Queenston and demonstrated a new degree of state interest in the area as a site of historical interest. The NPC's extension of the Parkway was not the first sign of its presence in Queenston. The Commission owned the park at the Heights in which both Brock's and Laura Secord's monuments stood. Before the 1920s it had worked to ensure that Queenston Heights' Park maintain a respectable, wholesome image through the regulation of concession booths, amusements, placement of cab stands, and the behaviour of both tourists and the Commission's staff.[56] All these endeavours, of course, were not unique to Queenston Heights, for as Karen Dubinsky has argued the NPC also ran Queen Victoria Park in the Falls in a similar manner.[57] But the Commission's work on the roadway to Niagara-on-the-Lake increased its ability to manage and shape the tourist landscape, since as part of this work it expropriated various properties along the road and river. By doing so the NPC was not only able to turn the road into a spacious boulevard, one with large, grassy verges and plenty of trees, it was also able to control the appearances of many riverside properties and establish a number of historical landmarks.[58] The overall effect was that of a gateway into Niagara-on-the-Lake that mingled the pastoral with the historic, themes the NPC had worked to create in Queenston. As well, running alongside the parkway was the Niagara River. With the American villages of Lewiston and Youngstown and the restored Fort Niagara clearly seen on the opposite bank, the river view was more than just a continuation of the scenic backdrop. It also might remind the visitor (who may very well have been from the US) of both the two countries' shared history and of Canada's determination to maintain a separate historical – and thus national – identity, since the Parkway circled around Fort George and ended at Navy Hall.

On a practical level, the Niagara Parkway was also designed to draw more tourists from Niagara Falls northward so they might discover the refined delights of Niagara-on-the-Lake. J. Musson, the Mayor of Niagara-on-the-Lake, urged the NPC to complete the road as fast as possible. Driving conditions between Queenston and the town were, he claimed, "unspeakable" and his council "entertain[ed] the view that it is, owing to the national and international travel upon it, a work coming entirely within the sphere of your Commission."[59] These "improvements" occurred as vacationers in eastern North America increasingly opted for automobile rather than rail travel, with a corresponding decline in the fate of the large hotels, such as Queen's Royal, that had been many rail passengers' destinations.[60] (In Niagara, of course, residents were sceptical about whether the rail company had ever served the town adequately.)

The Commission's activities were greeted with mixed reactions. As well as Musson, Queenston and Niagara officials welcomed the Commission's involvement in "improvements," particularly for road construction.[61] Yet not all local officials viewed the Commission without reservation. At times the Niagara Township Council took action to prevent the NPC from expanding its control over the area, both around Queenston Heights and along the Parkway.[62] Some of the residents whose properties were being expropriated were happy to sell portions of their lands to the NPC, particularly during the Depression. Others, however, resented the Commission's perceived intransigence, either over the fact of expropriation or, more commonly, the prices offered for their properties.[63]

One of the battles fought by the Commission was over the placement of newspaper boxes along the roadside. The NPC believed that these boxes were eyesores; it argued that many were badly constructed or not maintained, had been painted in a variety of bright colours, and were clustered around regular mail boxes, thus adding to the visual clutter along the Parkway. However, it was not just that they were unsightly. They also carried (at least in the Commission's eyes) blatant commercial advertising since the paper's name was painted in bold letters on each box. In attempting to rid the parkway of the curse of newspaper boxes, the NPC called on the offices of the Postmaster General and the Deputy Minister of Highways. It also contacted the owners of the offending receptacles: *Niagara Falls Gazette*, *St. Catharines Standard*, the *Hamilton Spectator*, *Mail and Empire*, *Buffalo Evening News*, and the *Globe*. H. W. Anderson at the *Globe* reassured Jackson that his paper "was anxious to do nothing to disfigure the appearance of the roadways, particularly those along the parkway under your jurisdiction. [We know] your own keen interest in preserving the charm and beauty of the Park surroundings." Two weeks later, though, the NPC's

Supervising Engineer, Major James Bond, informed the Deputy Minister of Highways, R. M. Smith, "in spite of my keeping a close watch [*The Globe* was] able to erect between twenty and thirty boxes between inspection trips."[64]

Once the road extensions were complete, the Commission undertook a number of projects in Niagara-on-the-Lake, such as supervising the construction of a sea wall along Lake Ontario.[65] It had already assumed some responsibility for Butler's Burying Ground; in 1909 it purchased the two-acre plot on the outskirts of Niagara-on-the-Lake.[66] As the Historic Sites and Monuments Board placed a number of markers in Niagara-on-the-Lake and along the parkway (and in other spots), the NPC was asked to take responsibility for their maintenance.[67] But the most highly visible manifestation of the NPC's presence in the town, and probably their major contribution to historical tourism in it, was the restoration of Fort George.

Of course, the Commission was certainly not the first to notice the presence of historic sites in the town, undertake their preservation, and designate the area one of "history." As we have seen, Niagara's history was a significant part of local boosters' promotion of the town, used to remind visitors of its national significance and its educational value. Equally importantly, since the 1890s the Niagara Historical Society (NHS), led by Janet Carnochan, had lobbied various levels of government for the preservation of Forts George and Mississauga, Navy Hall, and the "ordnance lands," a large open expanse on the edge of town owned by the Department of National Defence (DND).[68] Yet so far as the NHS was concerned, little had been done to prevent these buildings and sites from rapid deterioration. Indeed, the NPC's correspondence files contain numerous requests from local historians and politicians that the Commission take over the Forts and Navy Hall. Fort Mississauga in particular was the object of a huge amount of concern. Located on the town's golf course, open to curious tourists and their children, and said to be literally falling apart, for many concerned citizens it was the site of numerous imagined accidents and maiming; its sorry physical state also represented a distressing lack of concern for Canadian history.[69]

Fort George, however, was a different bundle of mortar and bricks; the NPC understood it to be a historical landmark, a symbol of loyalty to Britain, and a potential tourist attraction. Not only did the restoration promise to fulfil all three conditions, it also began in 1937 when the town was searching for work for those residents on relief and was more than happy to draw upon the Commission's funds. Relief workers had been used to build the sea wall and, judging by correspondence between the NPC, the Department of Labour, and municipal officials, few had any qualms about using this kind of labour in the service of patriotic pride.[70] Yet the Fort's restoration was hardly an answer to the municipality's prayers that indigent workers might be taken off their hands. The contractor, Brennan Paving Company of Hamilton, argued that the project called for skilled trades, such as stonemasons, and such workers were not to be found on Niagara-on-the-Lake's rolls. Seventy-three men were employed at the start of construction but only twenty-four were on the direct relief rolls.[71] However, this proportion appears to have increased and, once work began on log structures at the Fort, the company reported to Thomas McQueston, "we have found workmen in the Niagara district who have proven themselves very adept at log construction. These men are not from our paving organization but are the men that we have secured through the Employment Agencies and who were on relief." Eighty-five percent of the men employed on the project were from the rolls, a practice that would continue if McQueston gave Brennan Paving the tender for the log buildings.[72] Relations between Brennan Paving and the Commission during the process were far from harmonious; the work, though, was completed in 1940 and the Fort was unofficially opened to visitors.[73] After the war, Fort George began to attract a growing number of schoolchildren, as principals and teachers targeted it as a suitable site for field trips.[74]

By the end of the Second World War, therefore, various levels of government were involved in shaping both the historical and the tourist landscapes of Niagara-on-the-Lake and Queenston. The monuments at Queenston Heights, the markers along the parkway (such as the stone laid at Brown's Point, the spot where Brock supposedly rallied the York Volunteers to fight at Queenston Heights), Butler's Burying Ground, and Fort George were all reminders to both residents and visitors of Canadian loyalty to Britain (regarding, for example, the arrival of the Loyalists and the War of 1812). While such a theme would seem obvious, almost "natural," given the NPC's choice of sites to protect and restore, it is worth pointing out that the Commission carried out this work in ways that reinforced certain aspects of the landmarks' history and downplayed others. The period chosen for Fort George's reconstruction, for example, was that of its original state as built by John Simcoe in the 1790s, not the structure put up by American troops in 1813 after they had destroyed much of the original building. This incarnation of the Fort was, according to the NPC's historian Ronald Way, "never actually attacked and had few historical attractions for Canadians."[75] The NPC's decision not to restore Fort Mississauga was partly based on its lack of any stirring military history during the war, as it was built in 1814–15 on a site that offered a greater command of the river's mouth.[76] Once Fort George was opened as a tourist site, it was (and continues to be) marketed primarily as a material reminder of the War, although those events occupied a very brief part of the building's history.[77]

Concepts of Canadian national identity were also woven through these commemorations of imperial ties. Such discourses were not new, of course, nor were they entirely the creation of the state's officials; they were, however, given financial support and legitimation during decades when it was feared that Canadians were becoming too American.[78] At opening ceremonies, on inscriptions, and on guided tours the visitor was reassured that he or she was not looking at simply outposts of empire but, rather, at the Canadian nation in embryo.[79] A very easy way of making this teleological connection, of course, was to point out that both the Loyalists and the War of 1812 were important and central assertions of Canadian difference from their American neighbours. Yet such a stance was far from uncomplicated. Just as tourist promoters and local politicians worried that the town needed to attract the "summer folk," the need for American tourists – and their dollars – made it difficult, if not impossible, to assert national identity without some qualifications. These commentators would go on to declare their friendship for the folks across the river who were now "good neighbours," ones who were both geographically close but who now might also own property in the town. Guests from "across the river" also were invited when the NPC unveiled a monument or opened a building; they were reminded of the peaceful, "undefended" border that had existed for over a century.[80]

Forts, monuments to wartime heroes, and military graveyards were not only about loyalty to the nation and empire; as well, such sites also commemorated national identity and the past in a militaristic and masculinist fashion. To be sure, the Queenston Heights memorial to Laura Secord demonstrated that female patriotism had existed and was remembered. After the war, with the acquisition and restoration of MacFarland House on the Parkway (chosen because it had been a British battery and hospital for both sides during 1812), scenes of recreated colonial domesticity would be added to the historical landscape. Its parlour, kitchen, and bed chambers reminded tourists of women's historical presence, a domestication of the site that newspaper reporters seized on eagerly, with photographs of young women exploring the home, carrying out domestic tasks, entertaining one another, and, interestingly, reclining on a four-poster bed.[81] The one anomaly in the NPC's collection of battlefields and barracks was the Mackenzie House in Queenston, which the NPC purchased and renovated during the 1930s to commemorate the struggle for British democracy in Upper Canada.[82] Before the 1950s, though, the NPC generally chose to focus on military deeds and structures that were presented, for the most part, as the province of men.[83] Not just any men, either: while the "gallant militia" and British soldiers were not forgotten, it was the officers whose way of life was recreated in Fort George's furnished quarters – those who presided in the area – who were celebrated.

This formation of the past also had a racial component, inscribing the deeds of white Upper Canadians as being worthy of commemoration. The NPC records do not suggest that the area's Coloured Corps received much, if any, attention from government officials. While it is less clear just how – or if – Aboriginal people, as Loyalists, members of Butler's Rangers, and Britain's allies in the War of 1812, were depicted for tourist audiences, at least one observer of 1950 ceremonies to honour Brock and the soldiers of 1812 was less than pleased. Writing to *The Globe*, C. N. A. Ireson of Toronto claimed that there had been no mention of "Brigadier Tecumseh or Captain Brant ... Indian allies were most completely ignored and their descendants could take such an omission as an affront to the red race of Canada." Pointing to the textbooks' history of the Iroquois' support for the British, Ireson argued:

> the white man's gratitude must be short-lived, when a government-sponsored ceremony cuts the Indians dead at an international ceremony of an event in which they were so conspicuous. Any one who saw the Six Nations' Indian pageant and the costumes in use on their reserve near Brantford last year could not help but wonder who neglected to take advantage of such a wealth of readily available pageant material to add more colour to the Fort George ceremony, and to honour the Indian people who have spilled so much of their blood in the defence of Canada in all wars, including the last one. Let us hope such a glaring omission of our red U.E.L.s will not occur again at similar historic ceremonies.[84]

Other aspects of Niagara and Queenston's past, ones that Janet Carnochan had worked so diligently to research – the formation of a small yet visible African-Canadian community, industrial and commercial expansion after the War of 1812, the formation of civic society and the social realm – were ignored or downplayed in favour of a historical landscape marked by military structures and artefacts, a landscape that was reinforced by the presence of the military camp in the town.[85]

Yet making these choices would be granting the NPC too much power to argue that it simply imposed itself upon unwilling residents. To be sure, once the Commission decided to involve itself in a project, it waged a considerable amount of political and financial clout. But the Commission's correspondence files provide abundant evidence of its determination to limit itself to certain projects, a determination manifested in the face of considerable demand from the community that it expand its scope. From the early 1900s to the 1950s the NPC received numerous requests from individual owners, historical societies and their supporters, and local politicians to purchase or be a partner in the restoration or support of various sites, such as the Queen's Royal Hotel, the Niagara-on-the-Lake Historical Museum, the Field House, Upper Canadian merchant Alexander Hamilton's Queenston home (Willowbank), the Secord homestead in Queenston, and, as previously mentioned, Fort Mississauga. Without fail NPC officials would respond that they had discussed such matters at a board meeting but could not, at present, afford these properties.[86]

At times Niagara politicians, entrepreneurs, and residents invited the Commission to buy property in Niagara-on-the-Lake. In the summer of 1926 Musson and R. B. Haley, a real estate broker from Toronto, visited Phillip Ellis, the NPC chair, in an attempt to pique his interest in the Mississauga Beach area as a spot for (presumably) an NPC park. Haley then wrote to him shortly afterwards to inform him "some 100s of motorists from the U.S. and elsewhere have already been making this property a terminus of their outings because of the bathing facilities enjoyed," and that Haley's company, meanwhile, was receiving many inquiries from people from Buffalo who were interested in buying lots. He also pointed out that Mr. Gaby, of the Ontario Hydro Commission, had put up a summer home in the area and that before his company sold any more sites they wanted to know if the NPC was interested. The reference to Gaby's home was probably intended to awaken Ellis's interest and demonstrate that this was an eminently respectable location for the NPC, since Ellis had been the Chairman of the Toronto Hydro Electric Power Commission. Haley also reminded the NPC that the main thoroughfare, Shakespeare Avenue, ran through a "fine oak grove" that continued to the south edge of the property. Had his timing been slightly different, Haley might have included the NPC among his customers. The board, however, turned him down, pointing out that they were presently involved in buying property along the River Road and could not afford to purchase the Chautauqua lots.[87]

Haley's request, though, received more serious consideration than that of Miss Onslow, who contacted the Commission in 1947 concerning a parcel of DND land on the west side of town. Since the military took over this property, she wrote, it had been "disgracefully neglected" and she proposed that the NPC buy it and turn it into a provincial park that would provide information about the province and would include a bird sanctuary, community centre, entertainment hall, cafeteria, chapel, and "up-to-date bathing facilities for all." Her vision for the site included not just tourist attractions but also local residents who, she claimed, could be induced to plant memorial trees "to those who have lived in the district for years and helped in humble ways to improve it." She also foresaw the site becoming a war memorial, albeit a very practical one; the land not used in the park could be divided into five-acre lots and sold as cooperative farms to veterans and anyone else interested in the venture. The Commission, however, summarily dismissed Onslow's plans for the land and its future, and the General Manager, Maxim Gray, informed her that as the property belonged to the DND his board was uninterested.[88]

Members of the public also saw the NPC as a keeper of historical artefacts. After the restoration of Fort George, the Commission regularly received requests to either receive donated materials or, even more commonly, purchase them. These goods included household items – furniture, textiles, china, cutlery, and silverware – and military souvenirs such as armaments, medals, busts of Brock and Tecumseh, and uniforms.[89] Occasionally collectors of Aboriginal beadwork approached the NPC but their offers to sell these artefacts were turned down.[90] These offers, for Aboriginal and non-Aboriginal goods, were often accompanied by the suggestion that their owners' only alternative was to sell to American dealers; thus, of course, the NPC would be gaining valuable historical objects and performing a national service. The owner of the Field house, Dr. G. T. Field of Chase, Michigan, offered the most unusual deal. The eighty-six year old doctor first contacted the Commission in 1941; he had heard that the NPC "contemplates buying this old house and turning it into an historical museum." Having no heirs, he was considering leaving his estate to either the NPC or the Historical Society, "which I suppose are only one." "As evidence of my faith in Canada and the desire to help what I can I will tell you I have bought $2100 Canadian Government Bonds and contemplate buying more." He was not a rich man, he warned the NPC, but was homesick for the land of his birth and wanted to return. Field's letter was first sent to Mackenzie King whose office forwarded it to the Commission; the general manager, Ellison Kaumeyer, replied that he would like to meet him and discuss matters further. Yet further contact with Field proved that he had more than a simple donation in mind. The following year, he offered to improve the building's museum and art gallery to which he would donate his collection of family portraits, furniture, a library that included a variety of books, and, most notably, an assortment of taxidermy specimens (elk, deer, moose and buffalo heads). All these goods would come in exchange for a position as a librarian and caretaker "with a small salary." The Commission responded cautiously, telling Field they were interested but could not do anything for the duration of the war.[91]

The Commission usually refused to buy the materials offered by Field and his like, telling the would-be vendors that they accepted donations but had neither the funds nor, in the case of the stuffed animals, suitable display space. Such may have been the situation but in the case of the Servos family's home, Palatine Hill, and its collection of heirlooms, the NPC's dealings seem to have been less than honourable. From 1931 until the end of the decade Mrs. M. E. Servos-Snider, one of the last family members to live in Palatine Hill on Lakeshore Road, invited – one might say beseeched – the NPC to buy the property and its contents. Commission members, including Way, inspected the home but decided they could not afford Servos-Snider's price, although the NPC suggested in its internal correspondence that it might purchase a few items.[92] However, upon hearing in 1938 that Servos-Snider had died, commission member C. B. Lindsey suggested to Kaumeyer that they should get in touch with her executors to negotiate some purchases.[93] Their attempts at bargain hunting were quashed, though, when Kaumeyer's letter to Louis Blake Duff, a local newspaper editor and historian, was returned with a note scribbled on the bottom: "Mrs Snider of Palatine Hill is not late. In fact I saw her dancing a polka three nights ago. Late people do not do that."[94] After Servos-Snider's death in 1942, the Commission negotiated with her heirs to "obtain" a number of "pioneer articles" for the Fort George museum.[95] Subsequent publicity for the Fort's opening featured the "rare museum pieces" from Palatine Hill and the Servos family.[96]

The Commission was, it should be noted, accused of far greater unethical (at times, illegal) dealings by a number of parties, from Mitchell Hepburn's Liberals to New Democratic opposition members during the 1970s.[97] Servos-Snider's asking prices may have been grossly inflated, although that is almost impossible to determine. What emerges, though, from the records of these decades are conflicting interpretations of the Commission's role as a purchaser and preserver of the area's past. Local residents, organizations, and politicians constantly appealed to the NPC to intervene in the appearance of the local landscape by keeping historical properties and materials from either passing into the hands of developers or simply falling down. The Commission, however, had fairly firm ideas and an apparently stricter budget and, despite such opportunism, it usually declined to assist. It was interested in putting resources into certain markers, particularly (although not exclusively) those associated with the War of 1812; for the rest, it preferred that private enterprise or another level of government take responsibility. While levels of the federal and provincial state were certainly engaged in shaping the area's landscape, they often lagged behind local organizations in their response to tourism and demands for historical preservation and restoration. Far from simply imposing its visions on recalcitrant residents, the state often proved itself incapable or unwilling to meet certain groups' expectations and demands.

In the immediate aftermath of the Second World War, the future of Niagara-on-the-Lake came under increased scrutiny. "Niagara Preserved and Restored," a report prepared by the Niagara Post-War Planning Commission's Historical Section, examined the options that the town might explore. The Commission, which included both Niagara and Toronto residents, was sensitive to accusations of sentimentality or ancestor-worship for its own sake; consequently, it began by arguing, "the only valid motive for restoration or preservation of an old thing is the desire to make it serve the present and the future."[98] It then went on to place the town in the larger context of North American historical tourism, pointing out that while Europe might suffer from a "surfeit of ancient things" (the past "weighs too heavily on such lands and prevents their people from laying hold on the future," as in the case of Mussolini's Italy), on this side of the Atlantic "we have been inclined to swing too far in the other direction, to worship the perpetual changes inherent in a continental policy of progress at all costs."[99] In the United States, the best example of restoration had been Virginia's Williamsburg: "one of the greatest restoration projects ever carried out, not only on account of its size and scale but because of its historical and artistic importance and because of the spirit of scientific accuracy which has animated it."[100] Williamsburg, however, "represents a period and a local culture of unusual refinement and interest," one not experienced by Canada during the eighteenth or, indeed, any other century. Yet the same kinds of influences that formed colonial Virginia made their way north, the writers believed, shaping a certain type of architecture, literary style, and legal and governmental structures.[101] "A few traces" of "this great formative influence" remained in the Maritimes, Quebec, and Ontario, but were fast disappearing. No better evidence of "the cultural values inherent in [Canada] of the British colonial influence" could be found than at Niagara, a place where Loyalist settlers, "men and women of British stock," could follow John Graves Simcoe's well-ordered plan for a stable, highly organized society that replicated the tidiness of eighteenth-century Britain: including, it should be noted, its "clean cut class distinctions."[102]

While Niagara-on-the-Lake had managed to preserve many of its early nineteenth-century buildings, it was singled out not just for its architecture. Instead, the authors of the report saw its future as a "cultural centre" that would instruct historians, artists, architects, and the general public; the latter group could be presented with "the entertainment and educational opportunities inherent in a re-creation of aspects of life in another period of history." However, while Williamsburg was an important influence, it should not be copied slavishly. "Our aim is not to transform the Town of Niagara completely and turn it into some sort of a museum town, but simply to bring out, embellish and intensify the attractions which the place already possesses ... here you may see and understand certain valuable aspects of a past that has disappeared from sight elsewhere, things of great interest which are unique." The report went on to argue that the natural beauty of Niagara, its "superb trees and gardens," while, "strictly speaking irrelevant to the matters of restoration and preservation," would still be a "powerful influence."[103] In furthering their aims, they called for a lengthy list of activities to be undertaken, such as the preservation and restoration of buildings, changes to zoning regulations, and the beautification of sidewalks and boulevards. The report also requested the formation of institutions such as a Research Library, a House of Art, and summer schools, as well as the establishment of historical pageants, dramatic entertainments, musical festivals, opera, and ballet. Furthermore, merchants on the town's main commercial strip could be persuaded to modify their store fronts: "the object of these modifications would be to give Queen Street more of an old world atmosphere and also a degree of uniformity which would greatly increase its attractiveness." Of course, such a plan would only be effective if all property-owners participated but the report's authors believed, given the finances, they would cooperate.[104] A new hotel and restaurant were also among the town's "most urgent needs"; the authors hoped that an old hotel might be reconstructed to meet modern standards while "retain[ing] its essential charm."[105]

Who, though, was expected to undertake and pay for all these improvements? Williamsburg had been financed by the Rockefeller Foundation and no such benefactor could be sighted on Niagara-on-the-Lake's horizon; better, too, that a public body be in charge of this work. The report ended with the hope that the NPC, the provincial government, and the Dominion government would cooperate and thus prevent the town's "fine buildings" from vanishing. Yet while the provincial Ministry of Tourism and the federal Department of Northern and Indian Affairs expressed interest in Niagara-on-the-Lake's preservation, it is debatable whether they wanted the job of restoring "historic Niagara."[106]

At least one local couple, though, were eager to promote the town's history. Florence and Trellie LeDoux, who ran the town's marina and small-boat rentals, decided in 1950 to publish a historical booklet and map of Niagara and to conduct guided tours. The LeDouxes were "Developing Fine Tourist Service for Niagara," proclaimed the *Niagara Advance*. Both residents and tourists could buy their map and booklet; the guided tours would start from the "attractive booth of log cabin style" that Trellie built at the corner of King Street and Simcoe Park. "It is believed that this service being provided by Mr. and Mrs. LeDoux will be of considerable value to the town by way of boosting tourist business."[107] Their map was in many ways closer to Carnochan's vision of the town and may well have been based on her research. It included military sites but also located the town's first newspaper offices, churches, the Masonic hall, hotels and inns, the library, and schools. Florence's *Sketches of Niagara* fleshed out the map and provided more detail about its featured sites; it also, though, provided paragraphs that detailed Aboriginal history (including "Indian Kidnappings"), the early Jesuits, the Loyalist arrival, and narratives of the town's "runaway slaves."[108] The frontispiece to the 1955 edition of the brochure featured an Indigenous (possibly Iroquois or Ojibwa) man, wearing a buckskin tunic, leggings, and moccasins, sporting two feathers in his hair, and proffering what appears to be a calumet, or peace-pipe, shaking the hand of a white male Scout leader, dressed in full Scout uniform (the Scouts were holding an international jamboree on the town's commons). Lest anyone miss the point of this friendly meeting, the book's subtitle "*Where Yesterday Meets Today*," would clarify matters: here was an imaginary Indian that might be found in, for many white tourists at least, an unexpected space.

Just how many tourists availed themselves of the LeDoux's services, or bought the book and map, is unclear but the couple continued their interest in the town's history and its commercial potential. In 1973 Florence bought and restored the Angel Inn, which she ran until the late 1980s, incorporating the ghost story of British soldier Captain Swazye, killed in its cellars in the War of 1812 by American officers, as a colourful (and long-lasting) tourist draw.[109]

The Ministry of Tourism, though, began to demonstrate more interest in Niagara-on-the-Lake and Queenston during the early 1960s.[110] Much of the interest in spending ministry resources on Niagara was expressed not by the Minister, James Auld, but by officials within the department and archivists who pointed out to Auld in 1964 that Niagara-on-the-Lake "is potentially one of the best historical and tourist development projects that the government could undertake."[111] Two years later D. F. McOuat, the provincial archivist, and Peter Klopchic, the Director of the Travel Research Bureau, prepared a lengthy report on "The Historical Significance of Niagara and its Potential as a Tourist Attraction." McOuat and Klopchic argued that "there is probably no community in Ontario which possesses greater historical significance or greater potential for historical development than Niagara," an assessment based not just on the Loyalist presence or the War of 1812 but because of its status as the first capital of Upper Canada and the number of provincial "firsts" established there: the printing press, newspaper, brick building, Agricultural Society, jail, public library, and organized volunteer fire brigade. Moreover, the town's "comparative lack of commercial development" had resulted in the preservation of many early buildings, leaving it with "many fine remaining private homes that constitute Niagara's greatest historical heritage." While "the potential of history is frequently not recognized ... in recent years there has been an increasing interest which the forthcoming centennial has strengthened." They also cited a survey conducted by the Canadian Government Travel Bureau in which 44.8 percent of visitors

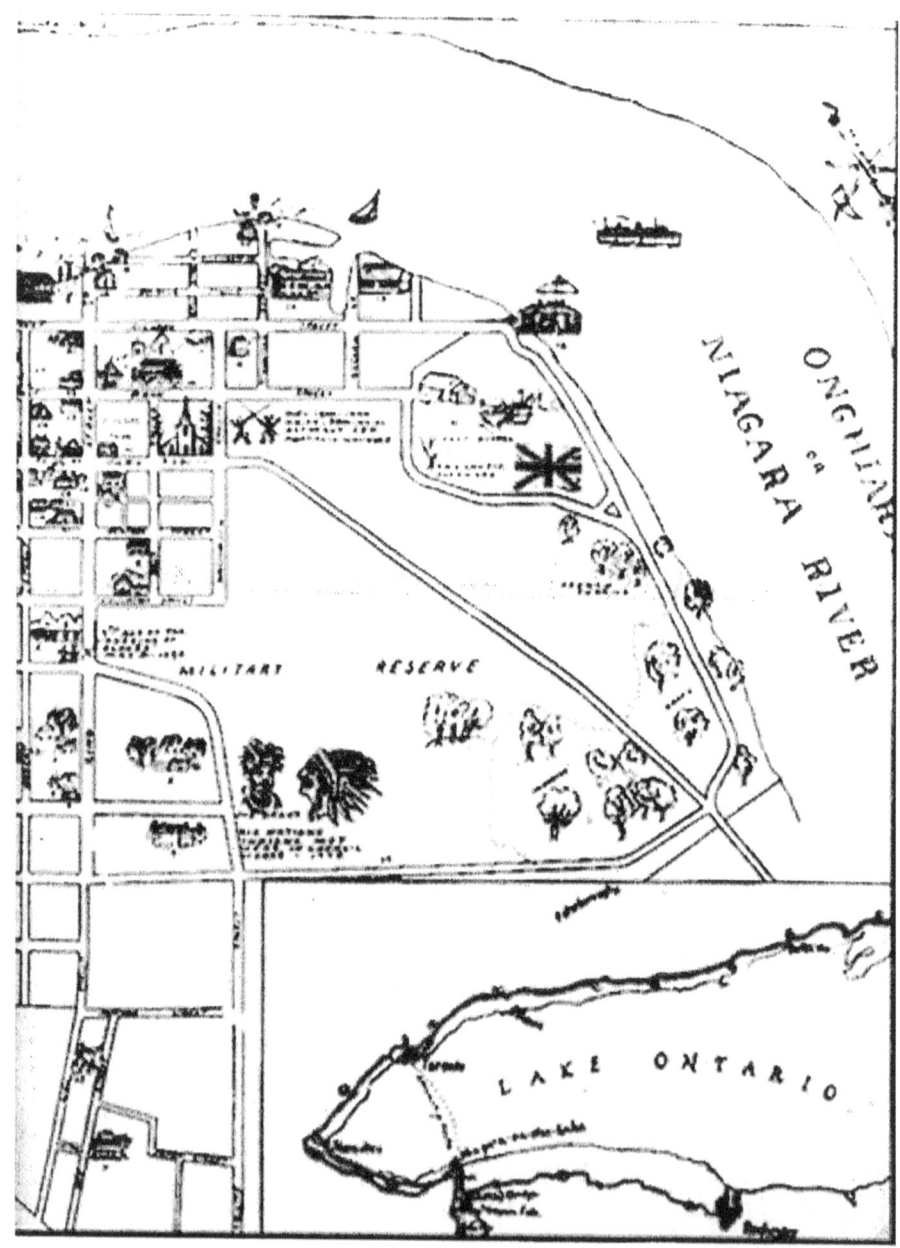

4.18 (above)Tourist map of the 1950s and (opposite) detail of the map, Florence and Trellie LeDoux.

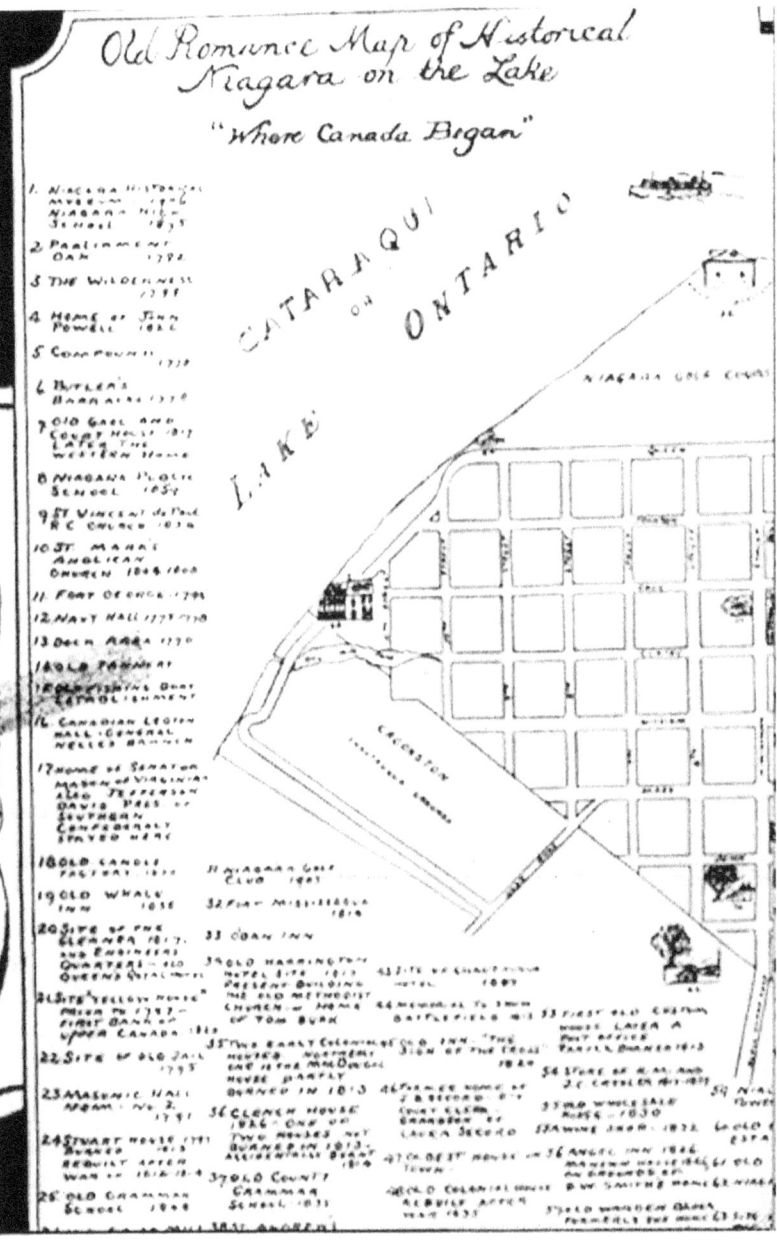

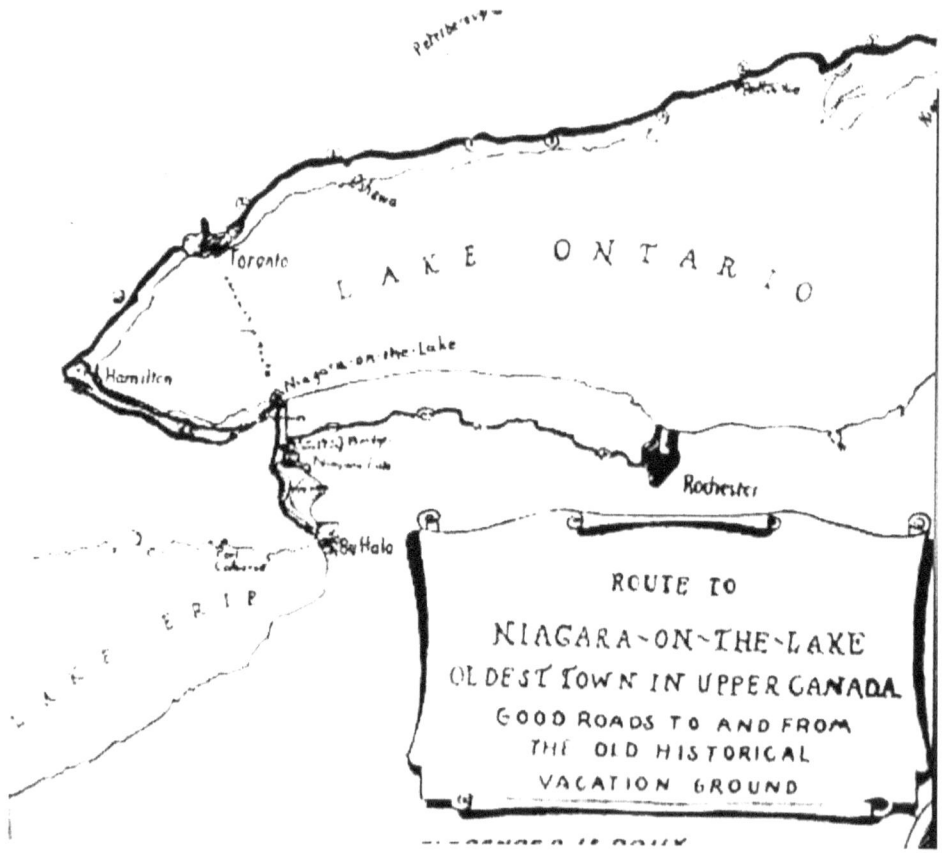

4.19 The tourist route of the 1950s, Florence and Trellie LeDoux.

expressed an interest in historic sites; it was clear to McOuat and Klopchic, then, that "any centre with major historical assets would be well advised to preserve and exploit its history." Niagara also had the advantages of proximity to the United States, good highway connections, and a link to the Falls by the "eight mile scenic drive" along the River. "The Niagara region is fortunate that much of its early and colourful history is to a great extent also the history of the U.S. and should be of exceptional interest to American visitors."

To arouse such interest, the "central core" must be preserved through a mixture of zoning, public acquisitions of buildings "of outstanding

4.20 Niagara's history in the 1950s, Florence LeDoux, 1955.

historic nature" (with the proviso that the public would be charged for admission and eventually the site would become self supporting), and "special arrangements with private owners," the report suggested. It went on to recommend:

> Whatever main historic area is ultimately decided upon every effort should be made to preserve the remaining historic buildings and to prevent the intrusion of high rise occupancy structures, incongruously modern stores, and other buildings screened off by trees or other landscaping, priority might be given to the removal of overhead wiring, merchants and home owners encouraged to renovate in accordance with nineteenth-century practice and so on. Perhaps special street lighting, period signing, special arrangements for parking and other measures could be carried out by the municipality. Restriction in the main historic area need not prevent different development programs elsewhere in the community.

Historic homes were not enough, though. Niagara-on-the-Lake "urgently needed" a new marina, "specialty shops," "attractive tourist establishments and restaurants," and an "expanded summer theatre." If all these elements were put in place and properly advertised "there is not the slightest doubt that this town could become one of most successful tourist towns in Ontario."[112] J. A. Macdonald, Assistant Deputy Minister of Northern and Indian Affairs, expressed similar sentiments at the federal level. Writing to W. H. Cranston, the Co-Chairman of the Ontario Archaeological and Historic Sites Advisory Board, Macdonald pointed out that his department wanted to develop "a comprehensive, historically authentic, effective and exciting restoration and interpretation program to cover the early history of the Niagara-on-the-Lake and Niagara Falls area with special emphasis on the War of 1812." There was a certain urgency to his plans since the Shaw Festival's artistic director, Paxton Whitehead, was eagerly searching for a site for a new theatre and was interested in federally owned lands.

While civil servants were writing memos to each other, the Niagara Foundation (NF), a voluntary group made up of a number of prominent residents, formed in 1962 to protect the town's "unique historic architectural character." The Foundation asked that, as local government was being reviewed, Niagara-on-the-Lake be treated as a separate entity, much like Ottawa's National Capital Commission. Local-level "modifications" had to be made to accommodate growth while simultaneously protecting "certain valuable qualities" presently offered by the town. They did not provide a detailed outline for the achievement of these goals but argued that there was more to "the development of regional government of this area than the purely physical problems of providing and administering such necessities as water, roads, schools, sewers, housing, and buildings."[113] This was not the first – nor would it be the last – time that the Foundation would make its case for Niagara's preservation. The Foundation, in tandem with the Ontario College of Pharmacy (OCP), also played a key role in lobbying the province to support the restoration of Field's, the town's mid-nineteenth-century apothecary building. They secured a grant from the Ministry of Tourism to buy the pharmacy and then turn it over to the OCP, who, in turn, would oversee its restoration.[114] However, the Ministry moved at an overly leisurely pace in advancing the funds and, on at least one occasion, the NF withdrew their offer to the province. Wool expressed the members' level of frustration, writing to Auld that to say that the patience of a few Directors is exhausted is putting mildly ... I understand we are criticized for the unsightly appearance of the building on the main street of the Town ... Here we are the first capital of Upper Canada and we get no more consideration than the most recent municipality of "so and so." I'll grant you that there is some flowery talk on our local heritage but talk is cheap and it produces nothing. I personally find it inconceivable that nowhere in the coffers of the government of the richest province in Canada can we find the funds to undertake a project which no reasonable taxpayer should question as to value in relation to the importance of what is involved.[115]

Matters were eventually resolved, with the newly created Ontario Heritage Foundation (OHF) taking over the building, and the Niagara Apothecary opened 27 May 1971. A smiling Fern Guindon, Auld's successor, members of the Foundation, and James McNulty from the Department of Northern and Indian Affairs happily posed for the *Advance*'s camera.[116] As Paul Litt has pointed out, though, Henry Paffard's vision of a modern building that would stand out from its contemporaries was lost in the process of restoration and interpretation. Today's tourists seem to be oblivious to Paffard's concepts of modernity and progress and instead see the Apothecary as representative of a generic and quaint "small-town" Victorian Ontario.[117]

Yet although the Apothecary's was somewhat of a success story, Auld's perceptions of the province's role in historical tourism were telling. At an early stage in the Apothecary negotiations the Minister had told James Allan, the provincial Treasurer, that while "there can be no doubt that the preservation of the original area of Niagara-on-the-Lake and the restoration of some of the early buildings within this area would be a major historical attraction ... I don't think the province should become involved in any undertakings of Niagara-on-the-Lake, but I do think that some financial encouragement should be given. As you know, a number of the citizens there are presently restoring, correctly, their own homes, and the congregation of the Anglican Church have [sic] done a magnificent job in its restoration."[118] While making a "one-shot" grant to the NF was acceptable to Auld, sustained provincial control of private properties – or even many other public buildings – was not. In many ways Auld's attitude resembled the NPC's measured approach to preservation. However, like the Commission, the Ministry was confronted with local residents and others concerned with Niagara's

4.21 "History" meets development in the 1970s ... *Niagara Advance* 9 August 1973.

fate. Correspondence to the Minister, newspaper editorials, and letters to the various editors spoke of the potential of Niagara-on-the-Lake, the need to act swiftly before its "history" was desecrated and destroyed by development, and the hope held out by sites such as Quebec City.[119] Auld was also confronted with the indefatigable lobbying of Robert Welch, the area's MPP, who wrote innumerable memos and letters on behalf of the town's preservation and urged Auld to take action so that both the area and the province might reap the benefits of the increased tourist trade that would result from "Niagara conserved."[120]

4.22 ... and then is pressed into the service of the hotel and restaurant industry. It is not clear what "dining in the colonial style of Upper Canada" entailed. *Niagara Advance* 9 August 1973.

To be sure, not all agreed that the town would automatically gain from such provincial undertakings as the OHF's purchase of private property. Municipal politicians, for example, objected to the Foundation's non-profit and therefore tax-exempt status. George Voth, the town's Treasurer, pointed out to Auld that, while the entire province benefited from restoration, the community was left to absorb the loss of revenue. "As our area, one of the oldest in Ontario could, in the future, be adversely affected by numerous acquisitions by the foundation we must express concern." Voth was advised by Auld not to worry unduly, since it was unlikely that the OHF would be acquiring the private homes that comprised the bulk of Niagara-on-the-Lake's historic properties. He was also reminded that in 1968 the council had passed a resolution agreeing that the tax loss would be outweighed by the advantages: "the restoration of this beautiful and unique historic site will be a source of pride and educational benefit to residents of the Niagara area. Undoubtedly it will greatly enhance the town's attraction to tourists and visitors and the support and stimulus to business and industry thereby provided."[121] The Ministry of Tourism and the Ontario Heritage Foundation were not the only bodies that local businesses approached for assistance in preservation and restoration. In 1971, for example, the provincial Ministry of Trade and Development loaned Newark Hotels (the company that owned the Prince of Wales Hotel) $2600 to renovate its premises; the money went towards a new dining room, outdoor beer garden, eleven more bedrooms, and the refurbishment of the men's beverage room to accommodate women (the hotel also had been used to accommodate officers in both world wars).[122]

Perhaps the most significant development in the town's history of post-war tourism, though, was the founding of the Shaw Festival. Begun in 1962 through the efforts of Calvin Rand and Brian Doherty, a former Toronto lawyer, playwright, and theatrical entrepreneur who had moved to Niagara and was also active in the Niagara Historical Society, throughout the 1960s the Festival grew from a small, two-week season of *Candida* and *Don Juan in Hell* to just over two months of performances of Shaw's *The Doctor's Dilemma* and *Back to Methuselah*, as well Ferenc Molnár's *The Guardsmen*.[123] By the end of the decade the Festival's artistic director, senior administrators, and Board of Directors felt that a larger venue was needed, a decision that produced lively, at times acrimonious, public debate, as well as some highly publicized anonymous attacks on the theatre.

Theatre in Niagara was not a new phenomenon. Productions at the Royal George Theatre, built before the First World War, had entertained both residents and soldiers from the camp and continued to do so once the venue became a movie theatre in the interwar decades.[124] In August 1948 Eileen Parsons announced that her summer theatre school season had ended that year but would return the following summer. Parsons's school offered classes in acting, speech, and "theatre background"; it ended its term with two productions, one of which was Edward Percy and Reginald Denham's 1940 psychological thriller *Ladies in Retirement*.[125] Furthermore, there were those who welcomed the Festival, believing that it would bring employment and more tourists and would do so in a way that would add, not detract, from the kind of "genteel" tourism enjoyed by Niagara earlier in the century. Such was the attitude of an editorial that wished the Festival all the best for its 1969 season, with the hopes that the "youth" who came to see performances would behave themselves, that local businessmen would make "special efforts" to "provide visitors to Niagara with extra service following a most pleasant welcome," and that residents would "make every effort to lay out the red carpet for our visitors."[126]

The ensuing controversies over "the Shaw," as residents came to dub the Festival, were complicated, underpinned by a number of different concerns and attitudes towards the theatre's presence. One issue became particularly contentious: that of the Festival's expansion and future location. While Ottawa had offered it land for a new theatre on the site of Butler's Barracks (the Commons), a prospect that "delighted" Board President Calvin Rand, others stated that the new site was going to be the golf course at Fort Mississauga, a prospect that saw the majority of the women on the theatre's Board resign and drew protests from within the town, Buffalo, and Toronto.[127] Although promises that the Commons, not the golf course, was indeed the future site calmed matters down, two years later suggestions that the theatre might expand its rented space by building onto the town hall (or Courthouse) provoked a flurry of letters to the editor. A group of "ratepayers" were concerned that the building's foundation would be damaged, that the library – "a more important cultural value (with more) potential than the theatre" – would suffer, and that the Shaw would take up too much space for too long a period.[128] Mrs. Grant Worthington, a tourist and Festival patron, urged Niagara to not "spoil the charm" of the town's downtown, arguing "you need a Mirvish with imagination, not another O"Keefe or Stratford."[129] (Worthington was referring to Toronto entrepreneur and theatrical impresario Ed Mirvish.) Others concurred: Jack Buchanan, for example, believed that while the theatre could take "some credit" for tourism's growth, less then 10 percent of the town's visitors were theatre

4.23 Theatre for patriotism, *Kathleen Mavourneen*, March 1915. Courtesy Niagara Historical Museum.

4.24 *Rural Matinee*, Capt. John D. Shawe, c. 1950. Shawe's painting depicts a winter matinee at the Brock theatre. A retired army captain (and former circus stunt rider), Shawe and his wife Marguerite moved to Niagara-on-the-Lake in 1945. Courtesy Niagara Historical Museum 2003.0100.001.

patrons. Moving its location to the outskirts of town, then, would mean those who came for "historical attractions" would not be greeted by parking congestion.[130] Barbara Casselman, though, reminded residents that Shaw had brought jobs (either directly or as spin-offs), good theatre had an "educational value," and that nobody had objected to "all the visitors who come for Fort George" and other events. Casselman only wished that she had $5000 to donate to the Festival.[131]

There were those who had little use for Shaw, though. A group of self-identified "senior citizens" decried the province's grant of $250,000 to the Festival, arguing that it did not necessarily benefit all Ontario citizens and certainly not all the residents of Niagara-on-the-Lake. Shaw was "taking over" the Town Hall, they complained, its ticket prices were beyond the reach of seniors' budgets, and the practice of stopping the Town Hall clock (placed in the nearby cenotaph) during performances was a "desecration" of a memorial to its wartime dead, one not to be interfered with "and especially by such a frivolous thing as any group of theatrical people's wishes."[132] The festival also had to contend with its request to be exempt from municipal taxes, which apparently had raised the ire of two local councillors. Taking out a page in the *Advance*, the Board of Directors reminded residents no other major, professional, and non-profit theatre in Canada (Stratford, Lindsay, Winnipeg, Charlottetown, Vancouver) paid property taxes; the Ontario Arts Council and the Canada Council supported all major arts organizations; of the $1450 municipal grant given to Shaw, $1350 went back to the town in the form of rent for the Court House space (as well as utility bills and the janitor's salary); ticket prices, like university tuition, were kept low through grants and thus the Festival remained accessible; and there were enough small parking lots nearby to support the theatre's audience. Moreover, the Board felt it necessary to address George Bernard Shaw's politics directly: obviously someone had raised objections. As the Board wrote,

> There is no need to go into the irrelevant remarks about Shaw being a Marxist or Communist. It is enough to say that most people know that Shaw was a socialist ... socialism is clearly different from Marxism or Communism, and that political beliefs anyway do not effect an artist's talents and achievements. Most of Shaw's plays dealt with social injustices of the day, not socialism. *Major Barbara* and *Arms and the Man* are strong indictments of war and the armaments race. While there are good capitalists on the Shaw Festival board, they are sophisticated enough to know that one of the world's greatest playwrights is worthy of a festival of his plays and is worthy of the support of the capitalists of the 1970s.[133]

Presumably one of those "good capitalists" was the Chairman of the Board, Calvin Rand.

Attacks on the Festival took a much nastier and personal tone later in the year, as a twelve-page anonymous letter was sent to town residents and the newspaper. The letter stated, "we can show you how through your tax dollar how *YOU* support the *Shaw Festival*, its plays, its people, and its parties. Read ahead, get the facts, then decide." Postmarked from Niagara Falls, New York, it set out a very detailed indictment of the Festival's Board, artistic director, and senior administrators, charging they were corrupt and nepotistic, wasted money, and either were from elsewhere or did not live year-round in Niagara. It also accused Shaw himself of being a Communist – "no free enterprise for him, no hard work to sustain yourself, like those who presently act out his plays, he did not believe in working for living" – and an atheist. Those responsible for the Festival were not only parasites who took advantage of taxpayers' dollars to line their pockets with high salaries and indulge themselves with expensive trips and lavish parties, they also were immoral (alcoholism was a charge frequently repeated in the letter).[134] The actors and the production staff were "of course, only seasonal and temporary employees. They are a very uninhibited group. Many are said to be homosexuals (which is now legal and, we guess, acceptable) and they say the use of drugs and alcohol increased sharply with their arrival."

Moreover, the Festival's treatment of its acting and directing apprentices came in for a lengthy, quite vituperative paragraph in which it was depicted as keeping them drugged (to the point of collapse and addiction) to withstand the seventy-two hour work week they were expected to put in, work that usually featured little more than sweeping floors and collecting garbage, despite the training grants Shaw supposedly received to teach its apprentices. Its abuse of these "young people" was contrasted with the lax hours kept by senior staff. Worst, though, was the local council and mayor who, from the anonymous author's perspective, acquiesced to Shaw's demands and wasted the town's revenues; one councillor was accused of taking bribes from the theatre. The letter ended with a set of demands, including that the theatre (if allowed to stay) build on federal property; pay full taxes; take no grants, provincial or federal; purchase goods and services locally; ensure its permanent employees maintained permanent residences in town; provide separate entertainment facilities for its actors and production staff; publish an annual audited statement of its expenses, including salaries; and submit its productions to a committee composed of the Council and "our religious leaders." A handwritten, shortened version of the letter, which was signed "A Mennonite," was sent to the *Niagara Advance* and published on its front page, 21 January 1971, accompanied by an editorial disavowing such sentiments and conduct as "disgraceful" and stating, moreover, that this was most certainly not the work of any

Mennonite congregation.[135] Subsequent letters to the editor protested the letter writer's methods and, to some extent, his or her sentiments, while one resident wrote to deny that he had been its author.[136]

However, resentment of the theatre erupted publicly at a council meeting in March 1971. George Howse presented the council with a twelve-hundred-signature petition that protested the Festival's tax-exempt status and the proposed Court House addition. Citing overcrowding and parking problems in the downtown area, Howse called for its relocation on the five-acre Commons lot. "Why," asked Howse, "should we and our friends have to subsidize theatre-goers from Buffalo and other places?" Other members of the delegation focused on the question of taxes, feeling that exempting Shaw and not groups such as the Canadian Legion was both unfair and would result in downtown residents paying even heavier taxes for poorer municipal service. The theme of "the Shaw" as an outside force receiving unfair advantages came up in these submissions, as did the image of the theatre's employees disturbing residents by their "off-stage antics."[137]

Were these simply small-town tempests in very small teapots, fueled by a fear of change and a dislike of outsiders? To some extent, yes. But in this case, animosity towards the unknown was underpinned by the suspicion that those employed in the performing arts did not, in fact, "work," interlaced with a dose of homophobia, and culminating in a disdain for government-subsided art that appears to have been rooted in a degree of anti-intellectualism. Furthermore, local concerns over taxes were, as we have seen, ones that stretched back to at least the interwar decades: "who would pay?" was a cry with its own particular history. Nor would this be the last outburst of anger towards the Festival.[138] Nevertheless, Shaw's expansion to a seven-month, three-theatre season, its contributions to the local economy, and the growth of a larger and more permanent workforce that began to live year-round in the town in the 1980s and 1990s, mitigated, if not completely eradicated, local hostility to its presence.

Today a visitor to Niagara-on-the-Lake is offered souvenirs and experiences that reflect either the town's "Loyalist" or "British" heritage, evoke memories of its Edwardian heyday as a charming summer resort, or by their cost and aura of cultural capital (which may have little or nothing to do with the town's history) remind their holders that they are not strolling the strip of Niagara-on-the-Lake's disreputable – and better-known – older sibling: Clifton Hill in Niagara Falls. Controversies continue to erupt over the use of space and conceptions of

History, Tourism, and Landscape 167

WE CAN SHOW YOU HOW THROUGH YOUR TAX DOLLAR HOW <u>YOU</u> SUPPORT THE SHAW FESTIVAL, ITS PLAYS, ITS PEOPLE, AND ITS PARTIES. READ AHEAD, GET THE FACTS, THEN DECIDE.

Postmarked N.Fall, N.Y. Oct 7/70

4.25 Front page of the "Poison Pen Letter," courtesy Archives of Ontario.

168 Creating Colonial Pasts

4.26 The "Poison Pen Letter" hits the front page. *Niagara Advance* 21 January 1971.

the town's historical and cultural landscape. From 2008 until 2010, conflicts over a proposed new summer concert venue on the town's western edge made their way into the local and, at times, national and international press.[139] As well, although tourists from outside of North America can be seen and heard in the town, the need to attract American visitors is an ongoing concern for those businesses and organizations whose livelihoods depend on tourism, a group that includes, of course, the Shaw Festival.[140]

We cannot, of course, really "know" what Janet Carnochan would make of her home today, although it is interesting to speculate about her possible reactions to twenty-first-century Niagara-on-the-Lake. It is likely that she would be appalled by the commercial imperatives that at times have shaped local government's decisions and be dismayed by Queen Street (its main street) in July and August, thronged with

4.27 Twenty-first-century tourism, Niagara-on-the-Lake, 2 September 2011. Photo Credit Paul Jenkins.

4.28 Twenty-first-century tourism, Niagara-on-the-Lake, 2 September 2011. The Royal George Theatre is the white building in the background.

tourists seeking out "cute shops," ice cream, and fudge, and who may well know little or nothing about the town's past. Moreover, Carnochan's late Victorian Presbyterian sensibilities probably would not approve of a theatre dedicated not to the Chautauqua's religious sensibilities but, rather, to the legacy of an avowed agnostic. To be sure, though, she might well have approved of George Bernard Shaw's teetotalism! Yet the pragmatism that allowed Carnochan to accomplish much of her work might also lead her to appreciate that some degree of historic preservation took place precisely because of the need to bring in tourists. She also would be delighted, I would like to think, that her beloved Museum and Historical Society are presently thriving, particularly in the context of the 1812 bicentennial commemorative activities.

What does appear clear, though, is that any narrative of the town's history must be situated in the complex interplay between larger economic, social, political, and cultural developments and the town's particular characteristics and specificities. Neither isolated from modernity, as some of its supporters – and detractors – liked to claim, nor simply reflecting more abstract developments, Janet Carnochan's "historic town" demonstrates the multilayered and complicated ways in which constructs of the past have their own histories, ones that intermingle rationality and pragmatism with emotion and desire.

Conclusion

"Mending the Threads of the Past"

In his exploration of the "crooked line" forged between social and cultural history in the late twentieth century, the British-born historian of Germany Geoff Eley stresses the intensity with which his generation of scholars, those Marxists and feminists who came of age during the exhilarating days of the 1960s and 1970s, brought to the study of history. "History mattered," Eley writes, but not in straightforward or predictable ways. "How exactly the past gets remembered (and forgotten)," he argues, "how it gets worked into arresting images and coherent stories, how its gets ordered into reliable explanations, how it gets pulled and pummeled into reasons for acting, how it gets celebrated and disavowed, suppressed and imagined – all have tremendous consequences for how the future might be shaped."[1]

While Janet Carnochan, Elliott Moses, Milton Martin, Celia B. File, and Niagara's heritage and tourist promoters ostensibly had little in common with Eley's central cast of characters – academic luminaries with international scholarly reputations – they too were deeply convinced of history's importance, its immediacy and relevance for distinct events, individuals, and, in particular, places in southern Ontario. Janet Carnochan believed passionately in the need to anchor the Niagara landscape in the past, one that she believed was all around her and her fellow-townsfolk, to be found in buildings, street names, landmarks such as the Forts and the "Parliament Oak," gravestones, and, of course, documents and material culture. While historical research had its own particular set of moral imperatives for Carnochan – memorializing a past marked by parliamentary and voluntary institutions, Christian principles, and the upholding of British liberty – it also had the power to make sense of, give meaning to, and celebrate a particular place, her home town.

For their part, Elliott Moses and Milton Martin saw the past as a way of addressing present misconceptions of their people, a means of thinking about Indigenous futures in a settler society that all too often insisted on relegating them to a past that had been – so far as non-Indigenous Canadians were concerned – irretrievably and irrevocably lost. History embodied multiple, sometimes entangled, forms of desire and held a range of meaning for these Mohawk men. At times the history of the Six Nations was something to celebrate, replete with narratives of Indigenous men's dedication to their community and to the Crown; it also, though, could be a narrative of betrayal, deceit, and oppression, personified by the Indian Act and those who framed and enforced it. As well, Moses and Martin depicted the Grand River territory, past and present, as a place of both refuge and regeneration for the Six Nations; at the same time, though, they also spoke of those places where Indigenous people historically were not welcome and pointed to the range of restrictions on Indigenous mobility in contemporary Canadian society.

Celia B. File's dedication to the past took multiple, albeit interrelated forms: honouring Mary Brant's contributions to the creation of British North America, restoring her heroism and bravery to the historical record; earning herself professional legitimacy and better employment; attempting to ensure that the nineteenth- and early twentieth-century histories of the Iroquois people in southern Ontario was not forgotten; and, finally, remembering her own part, in a memoir marked by wistfulness and yearning, in Indigenous-white relations in the more recent past. Like Carnochan, File's historical work, moreover, celebrated a place (in her case Tyendinaga) that held potent and poignant memories for her. Unlike Carnochan, though, File's place had become distant, perhaps even alien, when she wrote her memoir: a tinge of nostalgia for people, place, and time hangs over "Among the Six Nations," a sentiment that is not so apparent in *History of Niagara*.

Although the Niagara heritage and tourist promoters whose activities are the subject of chapter 4 were motivated by visions of a place whose past, in tandem with its "natural" beauty and modern attractions, was on display for commodification, it would be unwise to assume that civic pride in the area's history did not underpin their actions. To be sure, some were more interested in the economic benefits tourism might bring to the town: if historical sites and buildings served that function then so much the better, although such markers of the past must not be allowed to impede commercial progress. However, the ranks of tourist promoters also included those who saw the relationship differently. By bringing in increased municipal revenues, tourism could help protect the town's historical landscape and, they hoped, it would attract the kind of tourist who would share residents' appreciation for Niagara's past. The question of who occupied the role of "history's defender" in Niagara was, I would argue, never as clear-cut as narratives of "historic preservationists" dedicated to a pure vision of the past versus commercially motivated tourist promoters might suggest.

A longing for history was not, of course, innocent of or unmarked by power. The individuals and organizations in this book occupied a range of positions in their relationship to influence and power, the institutions, structures, and practices that shaped late nineteenth- and twentieth-century Canadian society. For one, different concepts of gender relations created different kinds of narratives, ones that emphasized some aspects of the past and downplayed others. Moses, as we have seen, was ambivalent about Iroquois women's role in the past, while Carnochan and File worked hard to create narratives that featured women as important historical actors. Moreover, gender relations and their intersection with those of race played a role in shaping the kinds of historical work these men and women could engage in. While it is unlikely that Janet Carnochan aspired to a career in the university history departments that were forming during her lifetime – she probably would have found their focus on documents and "high politics" arid and uninspiring – nevertheless in all likelihood her gender, coupled with the need to support herself and her aging parents, would have made it impossible for her to realize a career as a "professional" historian. Celia File, who achieved a degree of academic distinction and recognition, may have been seen as "less serious" a scholar because of her age, gender, marital status, and, in particular, her insistence on putting an Indigenous woman and her history at the centre of her historical scholarship. Yet despite their marginalization from certain circles of academic influence and their origins in rural and small-town Ontario, both women had access to levels of education and training that made it possible for them to pursue history as a vocation in ways that others (particularly the Indigenous women that so intrigued File) could not, or at least not in the same way. Moreover, while they might have lacked the visibility and public influence of, for example, David Boyle (in Carnochan's case) or Duncan McArthur (in File's), nevertheless during their lifetimes these women were not entirely without public profiles or the ability to shape southern Ontarians' conceptions of the past.

Carnochan and, in particular, File were also the beneficiaries of changes to white, middle-class women's status and capacity for mobility outside the home, although (as chapter 1 has noted) Carnochan occupied a less visible relationship to first-wave feminism than some of her contemporaries, while File does not appear to have been involved in any substantial manner in the campaign for suffrage.

In contrast, gender and race were configured differently for Elliott Moses and Milton Martin, albeit in no less complicated ways. As white women Carnochan and File saw themselves become enfranchised at both the federal and provincial level of government; Moses, though, could not vote until 1960. For his part, Martin's choice to become enfranchised came with a cost – the loss of his official status as an Indian. Moreover, while both men obtained formal education and occupied positions of public visibility, influence and, for different audiences, respect, other Indigenous men (and women) did not have the same access to public platforms or to those journalists who sought out Moses's and Martin's opinions and critiques of both Indigenous and settler society. In offering their thoughts, opinions, and historical analyses, both men did so as "civilized Indian men" and as such probably satisfied at least some white audiences' fantasies that assimilation had been a success. Yet although Moses and Martin might have agreed with their audiences on some aspects of the issue – and indeed appeared to have very self-consciously cultivated just such an image at times – such a position was far from being secure, nor did taking it up lead to predictable outcomes. As we have seen with Moses, his representativeness might have been questioned by other Indigenous people, while Martin used his position and prominence to launch pointed attacks on settler society's racism and, in particular, stereotyping of his people's history.

In turn, although the promoters of heritage and tourism in Niagara were undoubtedly more politically and socially privileged than, for example, Elliott Moses, they were keenly aware that their small-town status and the contingencies of the town's history had left them vulnerable to being marginalized, lagging behind the benefits of southern Ontario's late nineteenth- and, especially, twentieth-century modernity (particularly in the area of transportation). Living in such proximity to Niagara Falls also meant being very cognizant that the town lacked the visibility – if also the problems – of its neighbour: the need to compete for tourist dollars played no small role in debates over the town's future. However, the need to protect and promote historic sites, buildings, and artefacts also entered into these debates, for despite the presence of wealthy tourists at the turn of the century there was never enough capital for heritage activists to feel secure that Niagara's historic treasures would be given their due. Furthermore, various levels of government did little to provide such reassurance: the restoration of Fort George came out of the exigencies of the Depression, while the Niagara Parks Commission proved wanting, in the eyes of at least some residents, in its refusal to buy items or property deemed valuable but endangered.

An understanding of power and its relation to the past shaped these historians' work in other ways. As we have seen, narratives of war, diplomacy, empire, and the creation of the Canadian nation were never entirely absent from historians' understandings of history: witness the place of the American Revolution, the Loyalist influx, the War of 1812, and the creation of "Canada," events and processes that underpin much of the historical writing in which these individuals were engaged. Moreover, a number of those who appear in this book were involved in the larger-scale commemorations of province, nation, and empire that historians have explored: Carnochan was a prominent member of the Ontario Historical Society during her lifetime, for example. However, for these men and women creating histories in particular places also meant engaging with and seeing empires and nation-states not just as abstractions, their creations and conflicts disembodied processes, but, rather, as entities that could only truly be understood at the level of the local place and the embodied individual. This did not mean jettisoning the frameworks of the British Empire or the Dominion of Canada: it did, though, mean appreciating them more acutely, by trying to understand how Mary Brant coped with the vicissitudes of the American Revolution as both diplomat *and* mother; how the women (and at times men) of Niagara endured wartime invasion and privation, the loss of home, hearth, and family; or how settler society's need to assimilate Indigenous people resulted in the damaging representations that Ontario's children confronted on a daily basis in their school texts. Yet the history of a place was more than these political, military, and diplomatic narratives. It could be found in the school, the church, the voluntary organization, the local historical association and library, and the landscape, all of which might hold historical meaning and significance.

In imbuing particular places with discrete historical meanings, we also have seen how these men and women also explored questions of their own subjectivities: some in ways quite obvious (Martin, Moses, and File), others in a more subtle, yet telling, manner (Carnochan, the

Niagara residents of the last chapter). Yet this imaginary traffic was not one-way: just as history might help reaffirm one's sense of self, it also provided a means of moving beyond it, perhaps even temporarily transcending that self, its limitations and its failures. Dwelling on the pleasures of Tyendinaga in the 1920s and the home it offered her might help File forget, for a time, the struggles she had faced both personally and professionally; Molly Brant's enterprise in the face of the tumult of the late eighteenth century could remind her to bolster her own courage in the face of familial pressures to keep her own intellectual and professional desires in check. For Elliott Moses, Delaware history might, perhaps, help assuage some of the ambivalence he felt about being an "assimilated Indian," one who nevertheless took pride in certain aspects of his Indigenous heritage, both vis-à-vis settler society and the relatively more politically powerful Iroquois community in which he lived.

To be sure, the notion of history as a kind of escape and refuge from the present is, of course, not new, nor does using history in such a way necessarily end in results benign for either one's conception of the past or actions in the present. Yet it is worth considering, I think, the types of emotional and moral sustenance that engaging with the past might offer individuals as they struggled with the vicissitudes of their lives, ones that for many in this book were far from easy. Seeing a "better story" in the past might result in a different kind of engagement with the present and create new aspirations that might be realized in the future. No less than Eley's counterparts, these men and women understood that remembering the past had consequences.

Notes

Introduction

1 My research on these relationships has been published in "Private Lives and Public Performances: Aboriginal Women in a Settler Society, Ontario, Canada, 1920s–1960s," *Journal of Colonialism and Colonial History: Special issue, Colonialism in Settler Societies* 4, no. 3 (2003): 1–16; "Performing for 'Imperial Eyes': Bernice Loft and Ethel Brant Monture, Ontario, 1930s–1960s," in *Contact Zones: Aboriginal and Settler Women in Canada's Colonial Past*, eds. Myra Rutherdale and Katharine Pickles (Vancouver: University of British Columbia Press, 2005), 67–89.
2 For work that seeks to redress this problem, see Peter Baskerville, *Sites of Power: a Concise History of Ontario* (Don Mills, ON: Oxford University Press, 2005).
3 The phrase is Philip J. Deloria's. I am greatly indebted to his perceptive and very witty book, *Indians in Unexpected Places*, both for its empirical evidence of Native Americans' presence in multiple locations where they were not supposed to be and for his invaluable insights into the meaning and significance of those appearances. *Indians in Unexpected Places* (Lawrence, Kansas: University Press of Kansas, 2004).
4 For example, J. R. Miller, *Compact, Contract, Covenant: Aboriginal Treaty-Making in Canada* (Toronto: University of Toronto Press, 2009); J. R. Miller, *Shinkgwauk's Vision: A History of Native Residential Schools* (Toronto: University of Toronto Press, 1996); John S. Milloy, *A National Crime: The Canadian Government and the Residential School System, 1879 to 1986* (Winnipeg: University of Manitoba Press); Robin Jarvis Brownlie, *A Fatherly Eye: Indian Agents, Government Power, and Aboriginal Resistance in Ontario, 1918–1939* (Don Mills, ON: Oxford University Press, 2003).

5 David Glassberg, *Sense of History: The Place of the Past in American Life* (Amherst, MA: University of Massachusetts Press, 2001), 8.
6 This is a rapidly-growing field. See Alan Gordon, *Making Public Pasts: The Contested Terrain of Montreal's Public Memories, 1891–1930* (Montreal and Kingston: McGill-Queen's University Press, 2001); Ian McKay, *The Quest of the Folk: Antimodernism and Cultural Selection in Twentieth-Century Nova Scotia*, 2nd ed. (Montreal and Kingston: McGill-Queen's University Press, 2008); Gordon, Alan, *The Hero and the Historians: Historiography and the Uses of Jacques Cartier* (Vancouver: University of British Columbia Press, 2010); Patrice Groulx, *Pièges de la mémoire: Dollard des Ormeaux, les Amérindiens et nous* (Hull, Québec: Vents d'Ouest, 1998); Robert Cupido, "Appropriating the Past: Pageants, Politics, and the Diamond Jubilee of Confederation," *Journal of the Canadian Historical Association Journal of the Canadian Historical Association/Revue de la Société historique du Canada* New Series 9 (1998): 155–86; Norman Knowles, *Inventing the Loyalists: The Ontario Loyalist Tradition and the Creation of Usable Pasts* (Toronto: University of Toronto Press, 1997); Greg Marquis, "Celebrating Champlain in the Loyalist City: Saint John, 1904–10," *Acadiensis* 33, no. 2 (Spring 2004): 27–43; H.V. Nelles, *The Art of Nation-Building: Spectacle and Pageantry at Quebec's Tercentenary* (Toronto: University of Toronto Press, 1999); Brian S. Osborne, "Constructing Landscapes of Power: The George Etienne Cartier Monument, Montreal," *Journal of Historical Geography* 24, no. 4 (1998): 431–58; Peter E. Pope, *The Many Landfalls of John Cabot* (Toronto: University of Toronto Press, 1997); Ronald Rudin, *Founding Fathers: The Celebration of Champlain and Laval in the Streets of Quebec, 1878–1908* (Toronto: University of Toronto Press, 2003).
7 James S. Opp and John Walsh, eds., *Placing Memory and Remembering Place in Canada* (Vancouver: University of British Columbia Press, 2010).
8 Although see Alison Norman, "'A highly favoured people': The Planter Narrative and the 1928 Grand Historic Pageant of Kentville, Nova Scotia," *Acadiensis* 38, no. 2 (Summer/Autumn 2009): 116–40; Françoise Noël, "Old Home Week Celebrations as Tourism Promotion and Commemoration: North Bay, Ontario, 1925 and 1935," *Urban History Review* 37, no. 1 (Fall 2008): 35–46; and a number of the chapters in Opp and Walsh, eds., *Placing Memory*.
9 For example, Antoinette Burton, ed., *Archive Stories: Facts, Fictions, and the Writing of History* (Durham: Duke University Press, 2005); Ann Laura Stoler, *Along the Archival Grain: Epistemic Anxieties and Colonial Common Sense* (Princeton, NJ: Princeton University Press, 2009); Terry Cook, "The Archive(s) Is a Foreign Country: Historians, Archivists, and the Changing Archival Landscape," *Canadian Historical Review* 90, no. 3 (September 2009): 497–534.

10 Elizabeth Furniss's *The Burden of History: Colonialism and the Frontier Myth in a Rural Canadian Community* explores the development and implications of such myths in the late twentieth-century context (Vancouver: University of British Columbia Press, 1999). The prevalence of smaller museums in British North America is discussed in Lynne Teather, *The Royal Ontario Museum: a prehistory, 1830–1914* (Toronto: Canada University Press, 2005). See also Lynne Teather, "'Delighting the Eye and Mending the Heart': Canadian Proprietary Museums of the Early Nineteenth Century," *Ontario History* 94, no. 1 (2002): 49–78; Mary Tivy, "Dreams and Nightmares: Changing Visions of the Past at Doon Pioneer Village," *Ontario History* 94, no. 1 (2002): 79–100. As historian William J. Turkel has argued, "place" itself can be read as an archive. William J. Turkel, *The Archive of Place: Unearthing the Pasts of the Chilcotin Plateau* (Vancouver: University of British Columbia Press, 2007).
11 For Creighton, see McKay, *The Quest of the Folk*; for Cruikshank, see C. J. Taylor, *Negotiating the Past: The Making of Canada's National Historic Parks and Sites* (Montreal and Kingston: McGill-Queen's University Press, 1990); for Skelton, see Terry Crowley, *Marriage of Minds: Isabel and Oscar Skelton Reinventing Canada* (Toronto: University of Toronto Press, 2003).
12 Susan Crane, "Writing the Individual Back into Collective Memory," *American Historical Review* 102, no. 5 (December 1997): 1372–85.
13 Most work that discusses schools and teaching has either focused on textbooks or contemporary debates over students' knowledge and the teaching of history in the schools. For example, Ken Osborne, "'Our History Syllabus Has Us Gasping': History in Canadian Schools – Past, Present, and Future," *Canadian Historical Review* 81, no. 3 (September 2000): 404–35; Peter Seixas, ed., *Theorizing Historical Consciousness* (Toronto: University of Toronto Press, 2004); Ruth W. Sandwell, ed., *To the Past: History Education, Public Memory, and Citizenship in Canada* (Toronto: University of Toronto Press, 2006); Jocelyn Létourneau, *A History for the Future: Rewriting Memory and Identity in Quebec* (Montreal and Kingston: McGill-Queen's University Press, 2004). In the Canadian historiography, the role of teachers as "public historians" is an unexplored topic, as is that of students' historic participation as an audience for historic sites and museums. Billie Melman's *The Culture of History: English Uses of the Past 1800–1953* explores aspects of the latter. (Oxford: Oxford University Press, 2006).
14 Guy Beiner, *Remembering the Year of the French: Irish Folk History and Social Memory* (Madison: University of Wisconsin Press, 2007); Marla M. Miller and Anne Digan Lanning, "'Common Parlors': Women and the Recreation of Community Identity in Deerfield, Massachusetts, 1870–1920," *Gender and History* 6, no. 3 (November 1994): 435–55.

15 Historians have been grappling with their own subjectivities and the reasons why they study the people, places, events, and processes that they do. For a review of relatively recent work in this area, see Susan Crane, "Historical Subjectivity: a Review Essay," *The Journal of Modern History* 78, no. 2 (June 2006): 434–56; and also "Round Table: Self and Subject," *Journal of American History* 89, no. 1 (June 2002): 17–53. The historians who participated in the round table were Richard White, Karen Halttunen, Philip J. Deloria, Jacquelyn Dowd Hall, John Demos, Laurel Thatcher Ulrich, and Michael O'Brien.

1 Janet Carnochan's Historical Town

1 Henry J. Morgan, "Carnochan, Miss Janet," in *Canadian Men and Women of the Time: A Handbook of Canadian Biography of Living Characters*, 2nd ed. (Toronto: William Briggs, 1912), 159–60 and 202; John L. Field, *Janet Carnochan* (Toronto: Fitzhenry and Whiteside, 1985); 5; Cecilia Morgan, "Janet Carnochan," *Dictionary of Canadian Biography, Vol. 15* (Toronto: University of Toronto Press, 2005). Fellow member of the Ontario and Niagara Historical Societies, Elizabeth Thompson, collected a number of Carnochan's obituaries. See, for example, "Miss Janet Carnochan Dies at Niagara-on-the-Lake at Age of 87," 2 April 1926; "Foundress of the Historical Society," *St. Catharines Standard*, n.d.; "Janet Carnochan," *The Globe* 17 April 1926; "Historical Figure is Lost to Canada," *Mail and Empire* 1 April 1926. All of these obituaries were found at Archives of Ontario (hereafter cited as AO), MU5440, Series D, Box 21, Ontario Historical Society (hereafter cited as OHS) Thompson Scrap Book.
2 Francis Drake Smith, "Miss Janet Carnochan. A Sketch and an Appreciation," *Canadian Magazine* 38, no. 3 (January 1912): 293–7; Field, *Janet Carnochan*, 6. For a discussion of the feminization of the public-school teaching workforce in nineteenth-century Ontario, see Marta Danylewycz and Alison Prentice, "Teachers' Work: Changing Patterns and Perceptions in the Emerging School Systems of 19th and Early 20th Century Central Canada," *Labour/Le Travail* 17 (Spring 1986): 59–80.
3 Smith, "Miss Janet Carnochan," 294; John Carnochan to Janet Carnochan, 18 March 1862 and Janet Carnochan to John Carnochan, 19 June 1868, Vault Box 147, File 993.067.08-15, Carnochan Papers, Niagara Museum; Field, *Janet Carnochan*, 6.
4 See, for example, Marjory MacMurchy, "Representative Women: Miss Janet Carnochan," 26 November 1910, OHS Thompson Scrap Book; and also "A Happy Birthday," n.d., OHS Thompson Scrap Book.

5 Janet Carnochan, *Shipwrecked on Sable Island, 1879*, edited by John L. Field (Niagara: Niagara Historical Society, 1986), Pamphlet #44; Smith, "Miss Janet Carnochan," 297.
6 Smith, "Miss Janet Carnochan," 295.
7 Ibid. See also Field, *Janet Carnochan*, 43–5.
8 Carnochan, "Two Frontier Churches," 2 July 1890, Vault Box 38, 993.5.078, Carnochan Papers, Niagara Museum. This paper was read before the Canadian Institute at their meeting in Niagara-on-the-Lake.
9 Niagara Historical Society Minute Books, 1895–1909, 1909–1923, 1923–1952, MS193, Appendix F, Reels 6 and 7; see also Niagara Museum, Carnochan Papers, Vault Box 37 989.5.505.a.b.c.
10 For a collection of Carnochan's newspaper columns, see the OHS Thompson Scrap Book.
11 "A Museum for Niagara's Relics," *Niagara Times* n.d., circa 1903, OHS Thompson Scrap Book; "Memorial Hall's Informal Opening," *St Catharines Daily Standard*, 2? March 1907, OHS Thompson Scrap Book; "Memorial Hall Formally Opened," 5 June 1907, OHS Thompson Scrap Book; NHS Minute Books, 1899–1907. See also Field, *Janet Carnochan*, 36–42.
12 Her relationship with the OHS is discussed in Gerald Killan, *Preserving Ontario's Heritage: A History of the OHS* (Ontario Historical Society, 1976), 21–2, 132–5; Drake, "Miss Janet Carnochan," 295; Field, *Janet Carnochan*, 53–5. See also OHS Correspondence, 1898–1925, MU5422-29, Boxes 1–10, Series C, AO.
13 Reviews of this book are in Vault Box 38, 993.123, Carnochan Papers, Niagara Museum.
14 Killan, *Preserving Ontario's Heritage*, 132–5; Janet Carnochan to George Ross, n.d. and Janet Carnochan, "A Plea for the Commons," *The Globe*, n.d. January 1919, Vault Box 37 989.5.444.a.b. and 989.5.514, Carnochan Papers, Niagara Historical Museum; Janet Carnochan, "Military Reserve at Niagara," 28 June 1905, OHS Thompson Scrap Book; Janet Carnochan to James Coyne, 31 December 1901, Box 1, MU5422, Series C, OHS Correspondence, AO.
15 For discussions of these organizations and individuals, see Killan, *Preserving Ontario's Heritage*; Norman Knowles, *Inventing the Loyalists: The Ontario Loyalist Tradition and the Creation of Usable Pasts* (Toronto: University of Toronto Press, 1997); Colin M. Coates and Cecilia Morgan, *Heroines and History: Representations of Madeleine de Verchères and Laura Secord* (Toronto: University of Toronto Press, 2002); Cecilia Morgan, "History, Nation, and Empire: Gender and Southern Ontario Historical Societies, 1890–1920s," *Canadian Historical Review* 82, no. 3 (September 2001): 491–528.

16 Janet Carnochan, "Women in Canadian Literature," paper read at the Annual Convention of the Ontario Education Association, April 1887, Vault Box 38, 993.5.070, Niagara Museum, Carnochan Papers. See also her biography of Emma Currie, untitled manuscript, 20 September 1913, Janet Carnochan Scrapbooks, Box 2, Women's Literary Club Records, Special Collections, Brock University.

17 "Minutes of the Niagara Historical Society (NHS) Meeting," 12 March 1917, *Niagara Historical Society Minute Books* 1895–1964, Appendix F, Reel 7, MS193, p. 183, AO; "Janet Carnochan, "Ms of Speech: 'First Years of Canadian Woman's Rights Movement,'" File 989.5.459, Vault Box 37, Niagara Historical Museum, Carnochan Papers.

18 "Fifth Annual Report of the Niagara Historical Society (NHS)," 20 October 1900, *Niagara Historical Society Minute Books* 1895–1964, Appendix F, Reel 6, MS193, AO.

19 "Eighth Annual Report of the Niagara Historical Society (NHS)," 13 October 1903, *Niagara Historical Society Minute Books* 1895–1964, Appendix F, Reel 6, MS193, AO.

20 "A Museum for Niagara's Relics," *Niagara Advance*, n.d. 1903; "Memorial Hall's Informal Opening," *The Daily Standard*, 27 March 1907; "Memorial Hall Formally Opened," *The News*, 5 June 1907.

21 "Memorial Hall's Informal Opening," *The Daily Standard*.

22 Laurel Thatcher Ulrich, *The Age of Homespun: Objects and Stories in the Creation of an American Myth* (New York: Vintage Books, 2001).

23 "Catalogue of Articles in Memorial Hall," (Niagara-on-the-Lake: Niagara Historical Society, 1911), 29-30, accessed 31 January 2011, http://www.niagarahistorical.museum/media/NHS24A%20Catalogue%20of%20Articles%20in%20Memorial%20Hall.pdf.

24 Ibid., 26.
25 Ibid., 26–7.
26 Ibid., 22. 34, 54, 53, 51, 9, 28.
27 Ibid., 20, 8, 6.
28 Ibid., 31.
29 Ibid., 14. A sickle used by Riley in 1812 was part of the case displaying agricultural implements (65).
30 Ibid., 30.
31 Ibid., 127, 18, 42, 13, 49, 54.
32 Ibid., 54, 22, 55–6, 31, 3, 13, 23, 24, 30, 41 48, 50, 54, 57–8, 59, 22, 60, 24–5.
33 Ibid., 24–5.
34 Carnochan to David Boyle, 16 June 1902, OHS Correspondence 1898–1903, Box 3, Series C, MU5422, AO.

35 Michelle Hamilton, *Collections and Objections: Aboriginal Material Culture in Southern Ontario* (Montreal and Kingston: McGill-Queen's University Press, 2010), 117.
36 "Twelfth Annual Report," 13 October 1906, *NHS Minute Books* 1895–1964, Appendix F, Reel 6, MS193, AO.
37 "Catalogue of Articles in Memorial Hall," 23–4.
38 The Patriotic Young Ladies of York are discussed in Cecilia Morgan, *Public Men and Virtuous Women: the Gendered Languages of Religion and Politics in Upper Canada 1791–1850* (Toronto: University of Toronto Press, 1996), 38–40.
39 "Catalogue of Articles in Memorial Hall," 9, 33, 53, 28, 65–6.
40 "Historical No. 246," 13 February 1911, *Scrap Album of the OHS*, Box 21, Series D, MU5438, AO.
41 Accessions Registers, 1896–1945, *NHS Minute Books*.
42 "Catalogue of Articles in Memorial Hall," 4–5.
43 Ibid., 17–18. Along with that of his aide John MacDonnell, Isaac Brock's body was reinterred in 1824 at the base of the first Brock monument at Queenston Heights. After it was damaged in an explosion in 1840, the monument was rebuilt; Brock was given another funeral in 1853 upon the completion of its reconstruction.
44 Ibid., 6, 18.
45 Ibid., 1, 6–7, 18–19.
46 Ibid., 43.
47 Ibid., 47.
48 Hamilton, *Collections and Objections*, 74.
49 "Minutes of the Niagara Historical Society (NHS) Meeting," 27 October 1943, *Niagara Historical Society Minute Books* 1895–1964, Appendix F, Reel 6, MS193, AO.
50 Ibid., 5 December 1927.
51 Elizabeth Thompson to Andrew Hunter, 22 September 1927, File 1 1927, OHS Correspondence, Series C, MU5430 1927–28, AO.
52 Thompson's complaints bring to mind Carolyn Steedman's witty and perceptive contemplation of dust and the archives. See her *Dust: The Archive and Cultural History* (New Brunswick, NJ: Rutgers University Press, 2001).
53 Thompson to Hunter, 22 September 1927, File 1 1927, OHS Correspondence.
54 John L. Field, *Janet Carnochan* (Markham, ON: Fitzhenry and Whiteside, 1985), 42.
55 "Niagara's Tourist Attractions," *Niagara Advance*, 12 June 1919; Isabel B. Macdonald, "Old Niagara: A Garden of Historical Treasures," *The Globe*, 21 November 1908.

56 "Executive Committee Report," 14 October 1954, *Niagara Historical Society Minute Books* 1895–1964, Vol. 4.
57 Janet Carnochan, "An Evolution of a Historic Room," (Niagara-on-the-Lake: Niagara Historical Society #5, 1913–14), 18, accessed 31 January 2011, http://www.niagarahistorical.museum/media/NHS5Old%20Time%20Sermon,%20Mrs.%20Rouseaux%20&%20Historic%20Homes.pdf.
58 This is a large body of scholarship. For some particularly pertinent work, see Gerald Killan, *David Boyle: From Artisan to Archaeologist* (Toronto: University of Toronto Press, 1983); Donald A. Wright, "W. D. Lighthall and David Ross McCord: Anti-modernism and English-Canadian Imperialism, 1880s–1918," *Journal of Canadian Studies/Revue d'études canadiennes* 32, no. 2 (Été 1997 Summer): 134–54; Kathryn Harvey, "Location, Location, Location: David Ross McCord and the Makings of Canadian History," *Journal of the Canadian Historical Association/Revue de la Société historique du Canada* 19, no.1 (2008): 57–82; Steven Conn, *Museums and American Intellectual Life, 1876–1926* (Chicago: University of Chicago Press, 1998).
59 Carnochan, "An Evolution of a Historic Room," 1.
60 Carnochan, "An Evolution of a Historic Room," 24.
61 Niagara writer, historian, and customs collector William Kirby also published a history of the town, *Annals of Niagara* (Niagara: no publisher, 1896). Kirby's history, however, focused primarily on exploration, military, and political history and was not as all-encompassing as Carnochan's.
62 Janet Carnochan, *History of Niagara* (St Catharines: Oakhill Publishing, 2001), 1. First edition 1914.
63 Ibid., 117, 128, 131, 141–5.
64 The phrase is from Bonnie Smith, *The Gender of History: Men, Women, and Historical Practice* (Cambridge, MA: Harvard University Press, 1998), 149.
65 For nineteenth-century academic historians' worship of documents and disdain for other sources, see Smith, "The Practice of Scientific History," chap. 4 in *The Gender of History*.
66 Field, *Janet Carnochan*, 51. He concedes, though, that this was a not uncommon practice for historians such as Carnochan.
67 Carnochan, *History of Niagara*, 17–18.
68 Ibid., 80, 61–5.
69 For the growing obsession with sources and bibliography in university-based history, see Bonnie Smith, *The Gender of History: Men, Women, and Historical Practice*.
70 Antoinette Burton, "Introduction: Archive Fever, Archive Stories," in *Archive Stories*, ed. Burton, (Durham: Duke University Press, 2006), 1–24; Smith, "The Birth of the Amateur," chap. 2 in *The Gender of History*.

71 Carnochan, *History of Niagara*, 20–1.
72 The uses of Longfellow's poem in Canada are discussed in Ian McKay and Robin Bates, *In the Province of History: The Making of the Public Past in Twentieth-Century Nova Scotia* (Montreal and Kingston: McGill-Queen's University Press, 2010), 71–129; also Monica Macdonald, "Railway Tourism in the 'Land of Evangeline,' 1882–1946," *Acadiensis* 35, no. 1 (Autumn 2005): 158–80.
73 Carnochan, *History of Niagara*, 135.
74 Ian McKay, "Helen Creighton and the Rise of Folklore," chap. 2 in *The Quest of the Folk: Antimodernism and Cultural Selection in Twentieth-Century Nova Scotia* (Montreal and Kingston: McGill-Queen's University Press, 1994); McKay and Bates, "Down the Twisting Path of Destiny: The Impossible Liberalism of Thomas Raddall," chap. 4 in *In the Province of History*.
75 Carnochan, *History of Niagara*, 4–5.
76 McKay, *Quest of the Folk*, 94–6, 119–24.
77 Carnochan, *History of Niagara*, 5.
78 Ibid., 314.
79 Ibid., 35.
80 Ibid., 34.
81 Ibid., 35.
82 Ibid.
83 Ibid., 36.
84 Ibid., 84.
85 Ibid., 128.
86 Ibid., 129.
87 Ibid., 106.
88 Ibid., 21–3.
89 Ibid., 34.
90 Ibid., 318–19, 160.
91 Ibid., 130, 132, 68, 92, 164, 217, 225, 243, 260, 286–8.
92 Ibid., 238.
93 Ibid., 141.
94 Ibid., 208–9.
95 Ibid., 210.
96 Ibid., 245.
97 Ibid., 15.
98 Ibid., 107.
99 Ibid., 117–18.
100 Ibid., 132.

101 Ibid., 177.
102 The feminine attributes attributed to memory by University of Toronto historian W. S. Wallace are discussed in Coates and Morgan, *Heroines and History*, 158–63. See also Smith, "The Practices of Scientific History," and "Men and Facts," chaps. 4 and 5 in *The Gender of History*.
103 Coates and Morgan, *Heroines and History*, 161. For "child-saver" Maria Rye, see Joy Parr, "Maria Rye," *Dictionary of Canadian Biography Vol. XIII* (Toronto: University of Toronto Press, 1994), accessed 2 April 2011, http://www.biographi.ca/009004-119.01-e.php?&id_nbr=7046&interval=15&&PHPSESSID=hc9ggegt828p8mufuj8p5s9b03.
104 Coates and Morgan, *Heroines and History*, 3.
105 Barbara Graymont, KOÑ WATSIÃ TSIAIÉÑ NI (Gonwatsijayenni/Mary Brant), *Dictionary of Canadian Biography Vol. IX* (Toronto: University of Toronto Press, 1979), accessed 2 May 2011, http://www.biographi.ca/009004-119.01-e.php?&id_nbr=1991&&PHPSESSID=je13umq8sno3v7c8pf8qs41rl0; Gretchen Green, "Molly Brant, Catherine Brant, and Their Daughters: A Study in Cultural Acculturation," *Ontario History* 81, no. 3 (September 1989): 235–50.
106 Carnochan, *History of Niagara*, 142.
107 Ibid., 183–4, 245.
108 Ibid., 127, 246–7; also 198.
109 Green, "Molly Brant, Catherine Brant, and Their Daughters."
110 Ibid., 186–7.
111 Ibid., 191.
112 Ibid., 192.
113 Ibid., 194–5.
114 Ibid., 198–9.
115 For Ontarians' fascination with Tecumseh, see Guy St-Denis, *Tecumseh's Bones* (Montreal and Kingston: McGill-Queen's University Press, 2005).
116 Ibid., 200.
117 Ibid., 199–200. As Steven Conn has pointed out, Indigenous Americans' rhetoric, including that of Tecumseh, was much admired in the early nineteenth century. See his *History's Shadow: Native Americans and Historical Consciousness in the 19th Century* (Chicago: University of Chicago Press, 2004), 82–93.
118 St-Denis, *Tecumseh's Bones*, 199.
119 Ibid., 22, 35.
120 Ibid., 44.
121 Ibid., 196–7.
122 Morgan, "History, Nation, and Empire."

123 Carnochan, *History of Niagara*, 206–7.
124 Ibid., 203.
125 Ibid., 204–5.
126 Ibid., 206. In their *Slavery and Freedom in Niagara*, historians Michael Power and Nancy Butler suggest that the children of the community were able to use higher levels of education than those afforded their parents to leave the town for better jobs. (Niagara-on-the-Lake: Niagara Historical Society, 1993), 57.
127 Carnochan did discuss the arrival in Niagara of Irish immigrants fleeing the 1847 Famine in her "Emigrants of 1847 in Niagara," *Niagara Historical Society Pamphlet 31* (Niagara-on-the-Lake: Niagara Historical Society, n.d.).
128 Janet Carnochan to John Carnochan, 19 June 1868, Vault Box 74, Niagara Historical Society Museum.
129 Barbara McDonald to Janet Carnochan, 8 May 1882, Vault Box 38, Niagara Historical Society Museum.
130 "Carnochan, Miss Janet," *Women of Canada: Their Life and Work* (Ottawa: National Council of Women of Canada, 1900), 207; Francis Drake Smith, "Miss Janet Carnochan. A Sketch and an Appreciation," *Canadian Magazine* (January 1912): 293–7; Marjorie, "Representative Women: Miss Janet Carnochan," 26 November 1910; Elizabeth C. Ascher, "Miss Janet Carnochan, the Well-Known Niagara Historian and Teacher Will Receive Many Felicitations From 1000s of Friends and Admirers," 12 November 1921; Marjorie MacMurchy, "Leading Women Educationists. Canadian Women as Teachers Are Taking Large Place in the Making of Dominion," *Toronto Star Weekly*, 7 October 1911; Helen Ball, "Miss Janet Carnochan a Canadian Historian. Why It Was a Courteous and Appropriate Act When the Toronto Teachers Named Their IODE Chapter After Her," *Toronto Daily News*, 18 April 1914; Margaret Lillie Hart, "Canada's Woman Historian. Miss Janet Carnochan, NOTL, Collector of Priceless Facts and Traditions Concerning Our Country," *Toronto Sunday World*, 6 April 1913. All clippings are from the *OHS Scrap Album: First Canadian Historical Exhibition*, Box 19, Series D, MU5438, AO.
131 Smith, "Miss Janet Carnochan," 293.
132 Ball, "Miss Janet Carnochan a Canadian Historian."
133 "A Memorable Event," June 1921, *Ontario Historical Society Scrap Album*, MU5483, Series D, Box 19, OHS Fonds, AO.
134 "Janet Carnochan. Niagara's First Citizen Called Home,"; "Miss Carnochan Built Her Own Monument, More Appropriate Than Any of Bronze; And It Should Be Permanently Preserved," *Mail and Empire* 10 April 1926; "Janet Carnochan obituary," *The Globe* 17 April 1926;

"Historical Figure is Lost to Canada," *Mail and Empire*, 1 April 1926. All clippings are from the *OHS Scrap Album First Canadian Historical Exhibition*.

135 "Memorial to Historian. Memory of Miss Janet Carnochan is to be perpetuated," 19 March 1927, *OHS Scrap Album First Canadian Historical Exhibition*; "100th Birthday of Writer Celebrated. Memory of Janet Carnochan Was at Large Gathering on Tuesday Evening," *Niagara Advance* 16 November 1939, Janet Carnochan Scrapbook, Box 2, Women's Literary Club of St. Catharines Fonds, Brock University Special Collections; Frances Phelps, "Founded Historical Society. Janet Carnochan Compiled Much of Area's Early History," *St. Catharines Standard*, 29 June 1955, Janet Carnochan Scrapbook, Box 2, Women's Literary Club of St. Catharines Fonds, Brock University Special Collections; John Field, "Teacher, historian writer. Janet Carnochan made a valuable contribution," *Niagara Advance Historical Issue*, 1978, 4–5, Janet Carnochan Scrapbook, Box 2, Women's Literary Club of St. Catharines Fonds, Brock University Special Collections; Carol Alaimo, "Niagara's Janet Carnochan. History may have passed her by but Ontario will finally honor her," *St. Catharines Standard* 30 May 1984, Janet Carnochan Scrapbook, Box 2, Women's Literary Club of St. Catharines Fonds, Brock University Special Collections. In 1995 local rose breeder, Palatine Roses, produced a white hybrid tea rose named after Carnochan, see http://www.palatineroses.com/rose/janet-carnochan-garden-rose-hybrid-tea-white-near-white-or-white-blend/, accessed 16 August 2011. As well, on the 100th anniversary of Memorial Hall's opening, 4 June was declared "Janet Carnochan Day" in Niagara-on-the-Lake; admission to the museum is free on that day.
136 Carnochan, "An Evolution of a Historical Room."
137 Smith's *The Gender of History* discusses the development of the image of the ideal historian as the lone scholar. See also Donald A. Wright, "Gender and the Professionalization of History in English Canada Before 1960," *Canadian Historical Review* 81, no. 1 (March 2000): 29–67.
138 Melman, *The Culture of History*, 324.

2 History and the Six Nations

1 "Epitome of Chief Deh-ka-nen-ra-neh's Speech," *OHS Report* (Ontario Historical Society, 1899), 41. In this chapter I have used "Six Nations" rather than Haudenosaunee, since the individuals and community used the former term during this period.

2 Gerald Killan, *Preserving Ontario's Heritage: A History of the Ontario Historical Society* (Toronto: Love Press, 1976), 43, 48–9; *OHS Report* (Ontario Historical Society, 1898), 28–9. This was not the first time that the Six Nations had pointed to their historical legacy. Seth Newhouse's (Onondaga) history was prepared in the 1870s. See Sally M. Weaver, "The Iroquois: The Consolidation of the Grand River Reserve," in *Aboriginal Ontario: Historical Perspectives on the First Nations*, eds. Edward S. Rogers and Donald B. Smith (Toronto: Dundurn Press, 1994), 207.
3 *OHS Report* (Ontario Historical Society, 1911), 47–8.
4 *OHS Report* (Ontario Historical Society, 1898), 42.
5 Michelle A. Hamilton, *Collections and Objections: Aboriginal Material Culture in Southern Ontario* (Montreal and Kingston: McGill-Queen's University Press, 2010).
6 Robert F. Berkhofer, Jr., *The White Man's Indian* (New York: Random House, 1979); Daniel Francis, *The Imaginary Indian: The Image of the Indian in Canadian Culture* (Vancouver: Arsenal Pulp Press, 1992); Philip J. Deloria, *Playing Indian* (New Haven: Yale University Press, 1998); Paige Raibmon, *Authentic Indians: Episodes of Encounter From the Late-Nineteenth-Century Northwest Coast* (Durham: Duke University Press, 2005); H. V. Nelles, *The Art of Nation-Building: Pageantry and Spectacle at Quebec's Tercentenary* (Toronto: University of Toronto Press, 1999); Norman Knowles, *Inventing the Loyalists: The Ontario Loyalist Tradition and the Creation of Usable Pasts* (Toronto: University of Toronto Press, 1997); Peter Geller, "'Hudson's Bay Company Indians': Images of Native People and the Red River Pageant, 1920," in *Dressing in Feathers: The Construction of the Indian in American Popular Culture*, ed. S. Elizabeth Bird (Boulder, CO: Westview Press, 1996), page numbers; Kathryn McPherson, "Carving Out a Past: The Canadian Nurses' Association War Memorial," *Histoire sociale/Social History* XXIX, no. 58 (November 1996): 418–29.
7 Nelles, *The Art of Nation-Building*, 172–81; Geller. "Hudson's Bay Company Indians," 68–73; Knowles, *Inventing the Loyalists*, 123–5; Raibmon. "Theatres of Contact: the Kwakwaka'wakw at the Fair," chap. 3 in *Authentic Indians*.
8 "Indian Folk School 'Unqualified Success,'" *The London Free Press*, 22 March 1964.
9 Sally M. Weaver, "The Iroquois: The Consolidation of the Grand River Reserve in the Mid-Nineteenth Century, 1847–1875," and "The Iroquois: The Grand River Reserve in the Late Nineteenth and Early Twentieth Centuries, 1875–1945," in *Aboriginal Ontario*.

10 Weaver, "The Iroquois: The Consolidation of the Grand River Reserve"; Carl Benn, *The Iroquois in the War of 1812* (Toronto: University of Toronto Press, 1998), 19.
11 Weaver, "The Iroquois: The Consolidation of the Grand River Reserve," 182.
12 Gerald Killan, *David Boyle: From Artisan to Archaeologist* (Toronto: University of Toronto Press, 1985), 180–6; Michelle Hamilton, *Collections and Objections*.
13 *OHS Report* (Ontario Historical Society, 1911): 44–7.
14 Ibid., 43.
15 For John Ojijatekah Brant-Sero, see Penny Petrone, *Dictionary of Canadian Biography, Vol. 14* (Toronto: University of Toronto Press, 1998), 137–9; Cecilia Morgan, "'A Wigwam to Westminster': Performing Mohawk Identity in Imperial Britain, 1890s–1900s," *Gender and History* 25, no. 2 (August 2003): 319–41.
16 Killan, *Preserving Ontario's Past*, 44. See also Hamilton, *Collections and Objections*, 127–9. While I agree with Hamilton that the Six Nations were motivated by a desire for political support, I would also suggest that a desire that settler society be educated about their history also played a role.
17 Asa R. Hill, "The Historical Position of the Six Nations," *OHS Papers* 19 (1922): 103–9. 103–4, 106.
18 See Coates and Morgan, *Heroines and History: Representations of Madeleine de Verchères and Laura Secord*, 146–9.
19 I have made this argument about Mohawk performer and historian Ethel Brant Monture; see "Performing for 'Imperial Eyes': Bernice Loft and Ethel Brant Monture, Ontario, 1930s–1960s," in *Contact Zones: Aboriginal and Settler Women in Canada's Colonial Past*, eds. Myra Rutherdale and Katharine Pickles (Vancouver: University of British Columbia Press, 2005).
20 For a very insightful discussion of this perspective as it pertained to commemoration and historical preservation, see Andrew Nurse, "'But Now Things Have Changed': Marius Barbeau and the Politics of Amerindian Identity," *Ethnohistory* 48, no. 3 (Summer 2001): 433–72.
21 James Opp and John C. Walsh, introduction to *Placing Memory and Remembering Place in Canada* (Vancouver: University of British Columbia Press, 2010), 4.
22 Weaver, "The Iroquois: The Grand River Reserve," 245–8.
23 *Minute Book 1*, Brant Historical Society Records (hereafter cited as BHSR), 9 February 1911.
24 Ibid., 14 March 1918. In 1917 the Brant Historical Society (hereafter cited as BHS) struck a committee to get more pictures of Pauline Johnson into

Notes to pages 64–71 193

Aboriginal schools and to set up a prize for the best essay on "Indian life and history on the reserve," see *Minute Book 1*,10 May 1917.
25 *Minute Book 1*, BHSR, 18 January 1934, 11 December 1913, 13 March 1914, 3 February 1917, 18 September 1929, 20 May 20 and 10 June 1931, 4 July and 5 October 1933, 20 April 1937.
26 *Minute Book 1*, BHSR, 20 March 1935, 21 November 1939; *Minute Book 2*, BHSR, 18 March 1941, 19 November, 1947.
27 *Minute Book 1*, BHSR, 26 January 1937; *Minute Book 2*, BHSR, 18 March 1941, 22 January 1943.
28 See, for example, Hilton Hill, "Ancient Customs of the Six Nations Indians," 1 May 1944; *Minute Book 2*, BHSR.
29 "Pageant Presented in Connection With the Celebration, by the Six Nations, of the Sir William Johnson Bi-Centennial, May 24, 1938," File 9, 'Memoranda 1928–70,' MG30, C169, Vol. 1, Elliott Moses Files, Library and Archives Canada (hereafter cited as LAC); "Seventh Annual Pageant at Ohnedagowah (Great Pine) Forest Theatre, Six Nations," August 1955, File 3, Box 7, p. 12–20, Kathleen Coburn Papers, Victoria University Library.
30 Anne McClintock, *Imperial Leather: Race, Gender and Sexuality in the Colonial Contest* (London: Routledge, 1994), 40–2.
31 "Indian Folk School 'Unqualified Success,'" *The London Free Press*, 22 March 22 1964.
32 *Minute Book 1*, BHSR, 12 January 1931.
33 *Minute Book 2*, BHSR, 21 January 1951.
34 Jean Waldie, *Brant County: The Story of Its People, Vols. 1 and II* (Brantford: BHS, 1984, 1985). In many ways Waldie resembled Carnochan in her devotion to historical research and the writing of her community's history.
35 Opp and Walsh, "Introduction," 2.
36 Morgan, "Performing for 'Imperial Eyes': Bernice Loft and Ethel Brant Monture, Ontario, 1930s–1960s."
37 This biographical sketch of Moses is from the Finding Aid, MG30, C169, Elliott Moses Files, LAC. See also "Seventy-Five Years of Progress of the Six Nations of the Grand River," Elliott Moses's address to the Waterloo Historical Society's annual meeting, 22 October 1968, Vol. 1, File 1, Elliott Moses Papers, Articles by Elliott Moses, 1957–1975.
38 "Mayors Entertained at Rotary-Civic Luncheon. Elliott Moses of the Six Nations Gave an Eloquent Address. Indians Present," *Brantford Expositor* 5 March 1937, Vol. 2, File 4, Elliott Moses Papers, "Scrapbook, 1936–41."
39 See Vol. 1, File 1, Articles by Elliott Moses, 1957–1975, Elliott Moses Papers.
40 Ibid.
41 Ibid.

42 Ibid.
43 Ibid.
44 Alison Norman's PhD dissertation points to the work of Iroquois teachers, many of whom were women, on Six Nations. See "Race, Gender and Colonialism: Public Life among the Six Nations of Grand River, 1899–1939" (PhD dissertation, University of Toronto, 2010).
45 Moses, "Seventy-Five Years of Progress."
46 "Time," Vol. 1, File 1, Articles by Elliott Moses, 1957–1975, Elliott Moses Papers.
47 "Indian Not Chief, Frost Informed," File 13, Elliott Moses Papers.
48 Moses, "Conflicting Views on Indian Reserves," December, 1960, Vol. 2, File 4, Elliott Moses Papers, Scrapbook, 1936–41. "Big White Owl" was probably Delaware author Jasper Hill.
49 "Not Quite White, 'Against Indian Integration,'" *Brantford Expositor*. The author was probably reacting to a speech Moses had just delivered to the city's Kiwanis club, "Indian Act Retards Progress." See also "Reservation As Refuge From Rat Race," *The Cayuga*; "Two Indians Clash Over Social Views"; E. P. Garlow, "A Band Chief's View," *Brantford Expositor*. Clippings from Vol. 1, File 12, Speeches, 1966–9.
50 See, for example, Penny Petrone, ed., "Walk in our moccasins," chap. 5 in *First People, First Voices* (Toronto: University of Toronto Press, 1991).
51 Thanks to Michael Ripmeester for reminding me of this very important point. Peter Jones (Kahwewaquonaby), *History of the Ojebway Indians* (London: A. W. Bennett, 1861); George Copway (Kahgegagahbowh), *The Traditional History and Characteristics Sketches of the Ojibway Nation* (London: Charles Gilpin, 1851).
52 See *Minute Book 1*, BHS, 24 January 1935 and n.d. January 1944; *Minute Book 2*, BHS 16 March 1948, 20 May 1953, and 19 May 1954.
53 "Pageant Presented in Connection With the Celebration, by the Six Nations, of the Sir William Johnson Bi-Centennial," 24 May 1938.
54 Moses, "A Short History of the Chapel of the Delawares," Vol. 1, File 1, Elliott Moses Papers, Articles by Elliott Moses; "Moses, Delaware Story," Vol. 1, File 4, Elliott Moses Papers; *Lenape-English Dictionary*, 1899, Vol. 2, File 7, Elliott Moses Papers.
55 Nathan Montour, "The Life Story of My Grandparents," Vol. 2, File 8, Elliott Moses Papers.
56 Al Chandler, "Delaware Mask Returned After a Century," *Brantford Expositor* 30 January 1955.
57 Elliott Moses, "Historical sketch of the introduction of the elective system of council on the Six Nations reservation in the year 1924," Vol. 1, File 1, Elliott Moses Papers, Articles by Elliott Moses.

58 Ibid.
59 See Josiah Hill, Secretary, Six Nations Council, "Summons to Witness," March 10, 1908, Vol. 1, File 7, Elliott Moses Papers, Legal Papers, 1840–1908. See also Nelson Moses, "To the Chiefs," File 5, Elected Chiefs, 1894–1917.
60 Elliott Moses, "Historical sketch of the introduction of the elective system."
61 See J. R. Miller, *Shingwauk's Dream: A History of Native Residential Schools* (Toronto: University of Toronto Press, 1996).
62 Elliott Moses, "The Long House People," Vol. 1, File 12, Elliott Moses Papers, Speeches, 1966–9.
63 Welby Davis, "A Protest," *Brantford Expositor*, Vol. 1, File 12, Elliott Moses Papers, Speeches 1966–9; "Indian Mother to Resist Banishment Order," "Historian's Daughter Ejected: Claims Indian Ouster Vote Passed by Majority of One," *Brantford Expositor*, Vol. 1, File 13, Elliott Moses Papers, Clippings 1888–1930.
64 Arif Dirlik, *Postmodernity's Histories: The Past as Legacy and Project* (Lanham, Maryland: Rowan and Littlefield, 2000), xii, 217.
65 For a discussion of enfranchisement, see Robin Jarvis Brownlie, *A Fatherly Eye: Indian Agents, Government Power, and Aboriginal Resistance in Ontario, 1918–1939* (Don Mills, ON. and New York: Oxford University Press, 2003), 39–40, 137–41, 149.
66 "Indian School Principal Heads 4th Inf. Brigade," *Globe and Mail* 8 December 1939; "Indian Officer Appointed York County Magistrate," *Toronto Telegram* 22 November 1944; Gordon Sinclair, "Indian Colonel Regrets Brigade Has Lost Kilts," *Toronto Daily Star* 13 December 1939; "Full-Blooded Indian Named To Command 13th Brigade," 24 June 1940. All articles from Oliver Milton Martin File, Woodland Cultural Centre (hereafter cited as WCC).
67 "New York County Magistrate and Wife," *The Evening Telegram* 23 November 1944; see also "'School for Parents' Urged by York's New Magistrate," *The Globe and Mail* 24 November 1944; "Magistrate Martin Dies at 65," *The Globe and Mail* 19 December 1957; "York Magistrate Brig. Martin Dies," *Toronto Telegram* 18 December 1957. All articles from Oliver Milton Martin File, WCC.
68 "Indian School Principal Heads 4th Inf. Brigade."
69 For example, "Colonel O. M. Martin Will Command 4th Infantry Brigade. Brilliant Soldier-Principal of Danforth Public School Honoured by Appointment," Oliver Milton Martin File, WCC; "York Magistrate Brig. Martin Dies"; "Magistrate Martin Dies at 65."
70 "Oliver Milton Martin," 18 December 1957, Oliver Milton Martin File, WCC.
71 "Magistrate Martin Dies at 65."

72 Sinclair, "Indian Colonel Regrets Brigade Has Lost Kilts."
73 Ibid.
74 "York Magistrate Brig. Martin Dies."
75 "Indian Teacher is Resentful. Denies Red Man Originally Primitive as Stated," Vol. 2, File 2, Elliott Moses papers, Scrapbook 1918–1937. It is likely that his speech was given in the 1930s.
76 "Premier Gets Head-Dress, But Mrs Hepburn Has Indian Name," Vol. 2, File 2, Elliott Moses papers, Scrapbook 1918–1937. The ceremony may have been held in 1935, one year after Hepburn's election; articles from 1936 and 1937 in Moses's papers cover the Premier's appearances alongside members of the Six Nations.
77 Oliver Milton Martin, "The Indians of Canada, Part I," *The Canadian Friend* 47, no. 8 (January 1951): 4–6.
78 Ibid., 5.
79 Ibid., 6.
80 Oliver Milton Martin, "The Indians of Canada, Part II," *The Canadian Friend* 47, no. 9 (February 1951): 3–5.
81 Heidi Bohaker and Franca Iacovetta, "Making Aboriginal People 'Immigrants Too': A Comparison of Citizenship Programs for Newcomers and Indigenous Peoples in Postwar Canada, 1940s–1960s" *Canadian Historical Review* 90, no. 3 (September 2009): 427–61.
82 Martin, unpublished and untitled paper, p. 9–10, Oliver Milton Martin File, WCC.
83 Ibid., 11.
84 Ibid., 14, 18.
85 Ibid., 15–19.
86 Ibid., 19, 38–40, 41.
87 Ibid., 32.
88 Ibid., 32–6, 37.
89 Ibid., 42.
90 Ibid., 43.
91 Ibid., 43–5.
92 Ibid., 46.
93 Ibid., 47.
94 Ibid., 48.
95 Philip J. Deloria, *Indians in Unexpected Places*, 230.
96 Cecilia Morgan, "A Wigwam to Westminster"; Donald B. Smith, "Frederick Ogilvie Loft," *Dictionary of Canadian Biography Vol. XVI* (Toronto: University of Toronto Press), accessed 11 March 2011, http://www.biographi.ca/009004-119.01-e.php?&id_nbr=8419&interval=15&&P

HPSESSID=06euoln11b2f4jjo19p278s131ee; Deloria, *Indians in Unexpected Places*, 87.
97 Deloria, *Indians in Unexpected Places*, 230.
98 The former is typified by Pierre Nora's work in *Realms of Memory: Rethinking the French Past*, Vols. 1–3 ed. and forward Lawrence D. Kritzman, trans. Arthur Goldhammer (New York: Columbia University Press, 1996–1998), the latter by work such as Gastón Gordillo, *Landscape of Devils: Tensions of Place and Memory in the Argentinean Chaco* (Durham, NC and London: Duke University Press, 2004).

3 Celia B. File and the Politics of Memory

1 "Biographical Sketch," prepared by Jennifer Bunting, Finding Aid, Celia File Papers, Lennox and Addington Historical Society (hereafter cited as LAHS); "File, Mrs. H. C.," Alumni Files, Box 14, Series II, Coll. 3736.16, Queen's University Archives (hereafter cited as QUA); "Celia File, Gardening Columnist," *Napanee Beaver*, 15 September 1973.
2 "Golden Wedding 1958," and "Mr. and Mrs. Herbert File Mark Golden Anniversary," *The Post-Express*, 7 August 1958, Celia File Papers, File 5.33, Box 5, LAHS.
3 "Biographical Sketch."
4 Duncan MacArthur to Celia File, "Queen's University," 8 October 1929, Celia File Papers, Box 2, LAHS.
5 "Life of Molly Brant," n.d., Molly Brant Collection: miscellaneous, QUA, 5, 20–1; see also Mrs. Celia B. File, M.A., (Teacher), Napanee, compiled by, "Material re: Molly Brant and her children," MU2098, Ontario Archives. This material – transcribed portions of manuscripts, handwritten notes, and an article from *The Canadian Magazine* – was donated by File 30 June 1933.
6 "Kanoerohnkwa"/Mrs Celia B. File, "Among the Six Nations," Elliott Moses Papers, Memoranda 1928–70, MG30 C169, LAC, p. 7.
7 *Queen's Review*, May 1934, Celia B. File Fonds, File 1, Box, 1, Coll. 3053, QUA.
8 "Biographical Sketch."
9 Ibid.; n.d., "Fire Destroys Largest Building in Oil Springs," *Windsor Daily Star* 10 February 1945, Celia B. File Fonds, File 3.9, Box 5, QUA; Herbert File to Celia File, 11 February 1945, Celia B. File Fonds, File 5.25, Correspondence 1934–45, QUA.
10 "Biographical Sketch."
11 Ibid.

12 File to Havelock and Edith Robb, 3 and 26 March 1960 28 January 1962, 22 February 1964, Celia B. File Fonds, Robb Correspondence, File 1, Box 1, QUA.
13 "Life of Molly Brant," 15.
14 Ibid., 59.
15 Ibid., 87–8.
16 Ibid., 93–4.
17 Ibid., 108.
18 Ibid., 27.
19 Ibid.
20 Ibid., 30.
21 Ibid., 65, 71, 101.
22 For example, William Renwick Riddell, "Was Molly Brant Married?," *Ontario Historical Society Papers and Records* 19 (1922): 147–57.
23 "Life of Molly Brant," 59, 12.
24 Ibid., 27, 32–3.
25 Ibid., 42.
26 Ibid., 28–9.
27 Ibid., 6.
28 Ibid., 20–1.
29 Ibid., 113.
30 Duncan McArthur to the Secretary of the School Board, York Township, 11 March 1931, Celia B. File Fonds, File 3.12, QUA.
31 A. E. Prince, 10 March 1931, James A. Roy, 10 March 1931, and Henry Alexander, 10 March 1931, Celia File Papers, File 3, Box 3, LAHS. No recipients were listed on the letters: presumably they were given to File to use when applying to positions.
32 Mrs. Henry A. Brant to File, 19 August 1929, Celia File Papers, File 5.24, Correspondence 1923–34, Box 5, LAHS.
33 Clara Hill to File, 12 October 1930, Celia File Papers, File 5.24, Correspondence 1923–34, Box 5, LAHS.
34 Interview notes with Sam Lickers, Oshweken, n.d. August 1933, and with Catherine Hill, 13 August 1933, Celia File Papers, File 73, Box 1, LAHS; Interview notes with Jesse Moses, Oshweken, 10 August 1933, Celia File Papers, File 99, Box 1, LAHS; Interview notes with William Powless, n.d. 1933, Celia File Papers, File 100, Box 1, LAHS.
35 C. W. Vandervoort to File, 25 February 1931, Celia File papers, File 5.24, Correspondence 1923–34, Box 5, LAHS.
36 W. A. Jennings to File, 28 June 1941, Celia File Papers, File 5.25, Correspondence 1934–41, Box 5, LAHS.

37 File to G. Rogers, "Communications re: Teaching in Lennox and Addington," 28 June 1941, Celia File Papers, File 3.10 Box 3, LAHS.
38 G. Rogers to File, 2 July 1941, Celia File Papers, File 5.25, Correspondence 1934–41, Box 5, LAHS.
39 Kanoerohnkwa/File, "Among the Six Nations," 1.
40 Ibid., 3.
41 Ibid.
42 Ibid., 11.
43 Cecilia Morgan, "History, Nation, Empire: Gender and the Work of Southern Ontario Historical Societies, 1890–1920s," *Canadian Historical Review* 82, no. 3 (September 2001): 491–528.
44 Kanoerohnkwa/File, "Among the Six Nations," 6.
45 For example, Myra Rutherdale, *Women and the White Man's God: Gender and Race in the Canadian Mission Field* (Vancouver: University of British Columbia Press, 2002).
46 Kanoerohnkwa/File, "Among the Six Nations," 1.
47 Ibid., 6.
48 Ibid., 7–11.
49 Ibid., 4.
50 Ibid., 5.
51 Ibid., 4.
52 This is quite a large body of scholarship. For example, Vron Ware, *Beyond the Pale: White Women, Racism, and History* (London: Verso, 1992); Jane Haggis, "White women and colonialism: towards a non-recuperative history," in *Gender and Imperialism*, ed. Clare Midgley (Manchester: Manchester University Press, 1998), 45–75; Anna Cole, Victoria Haskins, and Fiona Paisley, eds., *Uncommon Ground: White Women in Aboriginal History* (Canberra: Aboriginal Studies Press, 2005); Fiona Paisley, *Loving Protection? Australian Feminism and Aboriginal Women's Rights 1919–1939* (Melbourne: Melbourne University Press, 2000).
53 Kanoerohnkwa/File, "Among the Six Nations," 4.
54 Ibid., 6.
55 Patricia Jasen, *Wild Things: Nature, Culture, and Tourism in Ontario 1790–1914* (Toronto: University of Toronto Press, 1995).
56 Kanoerohnkwa/File, "Among the Six Nations," 5–6.
57 Ibid., 6.
58 Ibid.
59 See, for example, S. Elizabeth Bird, "Introduction: Constructing the Indian, 1830s–1990s," in her *Dressing in Feathers: the Construction of the Indian in Popular Culture* (Boulder, Colorado: Westview Press, 1996).

60 Kanoerohnkwa/File, "Among the Six Nations," 5.
61 Ibid., 4.
62 Ibid., 4, 9.
63 Ibid., 4, 6, 8–10.
64 Ibid., 4.
65 Sarah Carter, *Capturing Women: The Manipulation of Cultural Imagery in Canada's Prairie West* (Montreal and Kingston: McGill-Queen's University Press, 1997); Coates and Morgan "Lessons in Loyalty: Children's Texts and Readers," in *Heroines and History*, 164–94.
66 Kanoerohnkwa/ File, "Among the Six Nations," 4.
67 Ibid., 6–7.
68 Haggis, "White women and colonialism: towards a non-recuperative history."
69 Anna Davin, "Imperialism and Motherhood," in *Tensions of Empire: Colonial Cultures in A Bourgeois World*, eds., Frederick Cooper and Ann Laura Stoler (Los Angeles: University of California Press, 1997), 87–151; Carolyn Steedman, *Childhood, Culture and Class in Britain: Margaret McMillan 1860–1931* (New Brunswick, New Jersey: Rutgers University Press, 1990); Cynthia Commachio, *"Nations Are Built of Babies": Saving Ontario's Mothers and Children, 1900–1940* (Montreal and Kingston: McGill-Queen's University Press, 1993).
70 Kanoerohnkwa/File, "Among the Six Nations," 9.
71 See, for example, Rayna Green, "The Tribe Called Wannabee: Playing Indian in America and Europe," *Folklore* 99 (1998): 30–55; Philip J. Deloria, *Playing Indian* (New Haven: Yale University Press, 1998).
72 Deloria, *Playing Indian*, 7.
73 Leslie Claus and Leo Hall to File, 22 June 1926, Celia File Papers, File 5.24, Correspondence 1923–34, Box 5, LAHS. Michelle Hamilton's point about First Nations' adoptions of non-Aboriginals – that they generally expressed respect for the individual person and not necessarily the project that brought them into contact with communities – may well have been the case here. See her *Collections and Objections: Aboriginal Material Culture in Southern Ontario* (Montreal and Kingston: McGill-Queen's University Press, 2010), 121–2.
74 Mrs. H. A. Brant to File, 8 September 1930, Celia File Papers, File 5.24, Correspondence 1923–34, Box 5, LAHS.
75 Clara Hill to File, 12 October 1930, Celia File Papers, File 5.24, Correspondence 1923–34, Box 5, LAHS.
76 Clara Hill to File, 20 October 1930, Celia File Papers, File 5.24, Correspondence 1923–34, Box 5, LAHS.

77 File's paper was published in 1961, possibly in a Department of Indian Affairs periodical. John Melling to File, 26 April 1961, Celia File Papers, File 5.26, Box 5, LAHS. Melling was the Executive Director of the Indian-Eskimo Association of Canada.
78 Kanoerohnkwa/ File, "Among the Six Nations," 7; Mrs. H. A. Brant to File, 8 September 1930 and Leslie Claus and Leo Hall to File, 22 June 1926, Celia File Papers, File 5.24, Correspondence 1923–34, Box 5, LAHS.
79 Mrs. G. D. Williams to File, 13 January 1966, Celia File Papers, File 5-26, Box 5, LAHS.
80 Mrs. G. D. Williams to File, 19 January 1966, Celia File Papers, File 5-26, Box 5, LAHS.
81 Donald M. Souter to File, 26 January 1966, Celia File Papers, File 5-26, Box 5, LAHS.
82 Wallace Havelock Robb to File, 1 February 1956, Celia B. File Fonds, Robb Correspondence, File 1, Box 1, QUA.
83 Robb to File, 10 February 1962 and 31 March 1972, Celia B. File Fonds, Robb Correspondence, File 1, Box 1, QUA.
84 For the concept of women's historians and the "better story," see Bonnie Smith, "The Birth of the Amateur," in her *The Gender of History: Men, Women, and Historical Practice* (Cambridge: Harvard University Press, 1998).
85 Antoinette Burton, *Dwelling in the Archive: Women Writing House, Home, and History in Late Colonial India* (Oxford: Oxford University Press, 2003), 7.

4 History, Tourism, and Landscape

1 John S. Clarke, *Illustrated Niagara-on-the-Lake Canada. Engravings of Some of Her Many Attractions* (Niagara-on-the-Lake: John S. Clarke, n.d.), 2–3.
2 Ibid., 30.
3 Ibid., 31.
4 Ibid., 2, 6.
5 Dona Brown, *Inventing New England: Regional Tourism in the 19th Century* (Washington and London: Smithsonian Institution, 1995), 204.
6 The literature in this area continues to expand. For Canada, see Patricia Jasen, *Wild Things: Nature, Culture, and Tourism in Ontario 1790-1914* (Toronto: University of Toronto Press, 1995); Ian McKay, *The Quest of the Folk: Antimodernism and Cultural Selection in Twentieth-Century Nova Scotia* (Montreal and Kingston: McGill-Queen's University Press, 1994); Ian McKay and Robin Bates, *In the Province of History: The Making of the Public Past in Twentieth-Century Nova Scotia* (Montreal and Kingston:

McGill-Queen's University Press, 2010); Karen Dubinsky, *The Second Greatest Disappointment: Honeymooning and Tourism in Niagara Falls* (Toronto: Between the Lines Press, 1999). Other influential work includes Mary Louise Pratt, *Imperial Eyes: Travel Writing and Transculturation* (London and New York: Routledge, 1992); Simon Schama, *Landscape and Memory* (New York: Alfred A. Knopf, 1995), and also W. J. T. Mitchell, ed., *Landscape and Power* (Chicago: University of Chicago Press, 1994).

7 While these approaches are not mutually exclusive, see Ian Ousby, *The Englishman's England: Taste, Travel, and the Rise of Tourism* (Cambridge: Cambridge University Press, 1990) for the first and Brown, *Inventing New England*, for the second.
8 See, for example, Dubinsky, *The Second Greatest Disappointment*.
9 Jasen, *Wild Things*, 38–43.
10 Janet Carnochan, *History of Niagara* (Toronto: William Briggs, 1914), 4.
11 "Old Niagara in 1836," *The Times*, 25 March 1898; "Recollections of Old Niagara," *The Times*, 8 April 1898; An Ex-Councilman, "What Niagara Needs," *The Times*, 3 February 1899.
12 Captain Beale, "To the People of Niagara," *The Times*, 25 November 25 1898.
13 J. W., "No Show for Manufactories," *The Times*, 9 December 1901.
14 F. Winthrop, "To the Ratepayers of the Town of Niagara," *The Times*, 28 December 1900. See also "Chautauqua and Lakeside Park Hotel," *The Times*, 28 May 1898 and "As Others See Us," *The Times*, 21 June 1901.
15 Rusticus, "Niagara 1886–1896," *The Times*, 2 July 1896.
16 "Something Must Be Done," *The Times*, 14 May 1896.
17 Citizens in favor of good roads, "A Cinder Path We Must Have," *The Times*, 18 March 1898.
18 An Ex-Councillor, "What Niagara Needs."
19 Percy Beale, "Trolley Line," *The Times*, 5 May 1899.
20 "Niagara and Port Dalhousie Rail Road," *The Times*, 22 March 22 1901.
21 "The Bicycle Path is Assured," *The Times*, 25 March 1898.
22 "Thoughts by the Wayside," *The Times*, 27 April 1898.
23 Unfortunately the Niagara Chamber of Commerce has not preserved its records. Neil Rumble (Chamber president), in discussion with the author, April 1996.
24 Many of these summer residences are still standing and occupied; a few homes take up entire blocks opposite the town's golf course. See *The Times*, 15 August 1895 and *The Times*, 24 May 1901 for a discussion of their ownership and real estate advertisements respectively. For Chautauqua, see "Chautauqua and Lakeside Park hotel," *The Times*, 28 May 1896; and

also Sheilagh S. Jameson, *Chautauqua in Canada* (Calgary: Glenbow-Alberta Institute, 1979), 93.
25 For example, "Chautauqua Guest List," *The Times*, 23 July 1898.
26 My research in the local papers, *The Times*, as well as its successor, *Niagara Advance*, shows ongoing coverage of the camp every summer from 1898 until the early 1970s. For example: "With the Boys in Camp," *The Times*, 10 June 1898; "Commons Alive with Militia," *The Times*, 13 June 1913; "Haldimand Rifles Stage Entertainment at Camp. Indians, in Ancient Costumes, Perform Ceremony of Giving Major Burns Tribal Name," *Niagara Advance*, 19 July 1934; "Military Camp Employs Chinese Cooks," *Niagara Advance*, 29 May 1941; "1700 Army Cadets Training at Niagara Military Camp," *Niagara Advance*, 20 June 1946. Other attractions included the World Boy Scout Jamboree of 1955.
27 "Niagara. Concluding Remarks About our Historical Town," *The Times*, 14 May 1896; Rusticus, "Niagara 1886 1896"; "News About Town and Vicinity," *The Times*, 1 July 1898. Of course, local boosterism probably shaped these writings – the town's paper constantly urged its residents to clean up their properties and welcome tourists.
28 "Chautauqua Breezes," *The Times*, 19 August 19 1898.
29 "Conference for the deepening of Spiritual Life," *The Times*, 6 July 1900.
30 "Lawn Tennis," *The Times*, 20 August 1896. A "calico cotillion" was one at which women wore dresses, and men vests, made out of the material.
31 Phillip Gordon Mackintosh, "A Bourgeois Geography of Domestic Bicycling: Using Public Space Responsibly in Toronto and Niagara-on-the-Lake, 1890–1900," *Journal of Historic Sociology* 20, no. 1/2 (March/June 2007): 126–57.
32 "Bicycle Tourney," *The Times*, 20 August 1896.
33 "Summer Sports at Niagara-on-the-Lake," *The Times*, 22 July 1900.
34 Henry Winnett to mayor of Niagara-on-the-Lake, c. 1914, Niagara Historical Museum, accessed 10 December 2014, http://niagarahistorical.pastperfect-online.com/33660cgi/mweb.exe?request=record;id=27AB77B9-86CA-4206-A5C7-581482123142;type=102.
35 For the New Woman and sports in Canada, see Michael J. Smith, "Graceful Athleticism or Robust Womanhood: The Sporting Culture of Women in Victorian Nova Scotia, 1870–1914," *Journal of Canadian Studies* 23, no. 1-2 (Spring/Summer 1988): 120–37; Helen Lenskyj, "Training for 'True Womanhood': Physical Education for Girls in Ontario Schools, 1890–1920," *Historical Studies in Education* 2, no. 2 (Fall 1990): 205–23.
36 Erika Rappaport, *Shopping for Pleasure: Women in the Making of London's West End* (Princeton: Princeton University Press, 2000); Susan Porter

Benson, *Counter Cultures: Saleswomen, Managers, and Customers in American Department Stores, 1890–1940* (Urbana and Chicago: University of Illinois Press, 1988); Cynthia Wright, "'The Most Prominent Rendezvous of Feminine Toronto': Eaton's College Street and the Organization of Shopping in Toronto, 1920–1950" (PhD diss., University of Toronto, 1992); Donica Belisle, *Retail Nation: Department Stores and the Making of Modern Canada* (Vancouver: University of British Columbia Press, 2011); Kathleen D. McCarthy, *Women's Culture: American Philanthropy and Art, 1830–1930* (Chicago: University of Chicago Press, 1991); Keith Walden, "Toronto Society's Response to Celebrity Performers, 1887–1914," *Canadian Historical Review* 89, no. 3 (September 2008): 374–97.

37 J. S. Clarke, "Niagara as a Summer Resort," *The Times*, 14 October 1900.
38 "Fort George. The Historic Old Place Will be Restored by the Golf Club – As Usual, Some Soreheads Are Kicking," *The Times*, 2 December 1900.
39 It is also difficult to find tourists' impressions, other than those that were sent to the local paper, that were in all likelihood mediated by its editor (for example, "As Others See Us," *The Times*, 21 June 1901, an account of a Washington women's delighted discovery of the town). The family papers of those who built large summer homes might shed light on their relation to the town, although that is beyond the scope of this chapter.
40 "Reminiscences, conducted 1981: Daisy Elliott, 6 July; Kitty Walsh, 24 June; Glen Bishop, 18 June." Transcribed by Joy Ormsby, Niagara Historical Museum. My thanks to Clark Bernat for bringing these interviews to my attention.
41 Ibid., Sigmond Smith, 7 July.
42 W. Goffat to Phillip Ellis, 31 July 1922 and Ellis to John Jackson, 2 August 1922, File 2, Box 30, NPC, General Manager's Office Correspondence, RG 38, Series 3-1, AO.
43 "Queen's Royal Property is Now in Town's Hands," *Niagara Advance*, 13 September 1934.
44 J. Musson, letter to the editor, *Niagara Advance*, 1 November 1934.
45 W. D. Caskey, letter to the editor, *Niagara Advance*, 27 December 1934.
46 D. A. R. Rodgers, letter to the editor, *Niagara Advance*, 22 November 1934.
47 William Kirby, letter to the editor, *Niagara Advance*, 9 July 1936. Kirby was likely the son of the writer, historian, and customs collector William Kirby, who died in 1906.
48 "A Serious Problem," *Niagara Advance*, 16 July 1936.
49 "Petition Against Sale of Queen's Property. Subject of Water Front Property Warmly Debated at Council Meeting," *Niagara Advance*, 9 July 1936.
50 "What Value Picnics?" *Niagara Advance*, 30 July 1936.

51 Progress, "Replies to "Producer," Niagara Advance, 6 August 1936.
52 Editorial, "Canada Steamship Line and Niagara-on-the-Lake," *Niagara Advance*, 25 June 1936.
53 Editorial, "Canada Steamship Line Passes Up Niagara," *Niagara Advance*, 19 May 1938.
54 John K. Walton, *The English Seaside Resort: A Social History 1750–1914* (Leicester: Leicester University Press, 1983); John F. Travis, *The Rise of the Devon Seaside Resorts 1750–1900* (Exeter: Exeter University Press, 1993).
55 "Request For Tourist Cabin Permit Was Strongly Protested," *Niagara Advance*, 17 August 1937.
56 The NPC files include a number of references to controlling the Queenston Heights environment. See John Languir, Chairman, to John Jackson, NPC Manager, 7 March 1911; Langmuir to F. H. Lowrey, 29 March 1911; Mr. Suess to Jackson, 11 April 191; Jackson to Mrs. Suess, 1 April 1912 and 30 April 1912. All letters in File 2, Box 17, NPC, Gen. Manager's Office Correspondence, RG 38, Series 3-1, AO. These letters concerned the lease of the concession stand at the park.
57 For the NPC's work at Victoria Park, see Dubinsky, "The Second Biggest Disappointment," 104.
58 See the correspondence April 1931–31 May 1934 in File 1-J, 1, Box 45, NPC, General. Manager's Office Correspondence, RG 38, Series 3-2, AO.
59 Musson to Phillip Ellis, NPC chair, 18 April 1922, File 1, Box 30, NPC, General Manager's Office Correspondence, RG 38, Series 3-1, AO.
60 Browne, 206–10; for the Canadian context, see Dubinsky, 186–90.
61 For example, James D. Chaplin to John Jackson, 23 June 1930, File I-I, Box 35, NPC, General Manager's Office Correspondence, RG 38, Series 3-2, AO; also J. E. Masters, Town Clerk, to Kaumeyer, 8 November 1939, File I-O, Box 46, NPC, General Manager's Office Correspondence, RG 38, Series 3-2, AO.
62 Jackson to Smith, 21 October 1929, File I-H, Box 44, NPC General Manager's Office Correspondence, RG 38, Series 3-2, AO; see also the correspondence between Niagara Township and the NPC, 10 January–17 April, which testifies to many fights between the two bodies over the costs of road repair and maintenance (File I-F, Box 44). The NPC and the village of Queenston had many run-ins in the 1900s over rights of way, road expropriations, and vendors; see, for example, Jackson to J. Clench, County Clerk, 22 July 1909; File 2, Box 29, NPC, General Manager's Office Correspondence, RG 38, Series 3-1, AO; F. H. Lowrey, Reeve, Niagara Township, 10 March 1911, NPC, General Manager's Office Correspondence, RG 38, Series 3-2, AO.

63 See correspondence of 1 January–31 August 1924, File I-A, Box 43, NPC, General Manager's Office Correspondence, RG 38, Series 3-2, AO; Kaumeyer to C. B. McNair, 8 January 1935, File I-K, Box 45, NPC, General Manager's Office Correspondence, RG 38, Series 3-2, AO; also the correspondence regarding Clark Shipston vs. the NPC (including a petition to the Ontario Supreme Court), 23 April-3 October 1938, File I-N, Box 46, NPC, General Manager's Office Correspondence, RG 38, Series 3-2, AO.

64 See correspondence of 14 July 1931–7 July 1932, File I-J, Box 45, NPC, General Manager's Office Correspondence, RG 38, Series 3-2, AO; also Anderson to Jackson, 21 April 1932; Bond to Smith, 3 May 1932.

65 See correspondence of 15 January 1934–30 May 1935, NPC, General Manager's Office Correspondence, RG 38, Series 3-2, AO.

66 Ronald Way, *Ontario's Niagara Parks: A History* (Niagara Falls: Niagara Parks Commission, 1946), 173.

67 For historic plaques, see Jackson to A. A. Pinard, Dominion Parks Branch, Department of the Interior, 29 October 1920, File 4, Box 17, NPC, General Manager's Office Correspondence, RG 38, Series 3 - 1, AO.

68 In 1898 the NHS petitioned the Dominion government that Forts Erie, George, and Mississauga be placed under Commissions' protection. See *Report of the Niagara Historical Society* (Niagara: Niagara Historical Society, February 1899).

69 See, for example, T. L. Church, MP to Charles Stewart, Minister of the Interior, 19 June 1922, File 1, Box 30, NPC, General Manager's Office Correspondence, RG 38, Series 3-1, AO; William Kirby and H. Smith, Niagara Historical Society, to Jackson, 9 December 1929, File I-H, Box 44, NPC, General Manager's Office Correspondence, RG 38, Series 3-2, AO; F. J. Keenan, Secretary, Niagara-on-the-Lake Golf Club, to Paul Pare, DND, n.d. (early 1950s?), File I-V, Box 96, NPC, General Manager's Office Correspondence, RG 38, Series 3-2, AO. The NPC refused to take over Fort Mississauga, which is still surrounded by the town's golf course. Navy Hall, used as a residence by the Simcoes in 1792, consists of a wooden structure enclosed in a twentieth-century stone building. Both it and Fort George were taken over by the National and Historic Parks Branch of the Department of Indian and Northern Affairs (now Parks Canada) in 1969.

70 See correspondence of 15 January 1934–30 May1935, File I-J, Box 45, NPC, General Manager's Office Correspondence, RG 38, Series 3-2, AO. For a discussion of the NPC's use of relief workers to build the Oakes theatre, see Dubinsky, "The Second Biggest Disappointment," 142.

71 K. Wisby, Ontario Employment Offices, Department of Labour to Kaumeyer, 1 December 1937, File I-L, Box 45, NPC, General Manager's

Office Correspondence, RG 38, Series 3-2, AO. Although no figures have been obtained for relief rolls in 1937, in March 1934 175 people received assistance in the township (Bond to Jackson, 15 March 1934, File I-J, Box 45, NPC, General Manager's Office Correspondence, RG 38, Series 3-2, AO).
72 Neale R. Ibbetson to Thomas B. McQueston, 19 November 1938, File I-N, Box 46, NPC, General Manager's Office Correspondence, RG 38, Series 3-2, AO.
73 See W. C. Brennan to Kaumeyer, 30 June 1938, File I-L, Box 45, NPC, General Manager's Office Correspondence, RG 38, Series 3-2, AO; also Brennan to Kaumeyer, 25 September 1939, File I-O, Box 45, NPC, General Manager's Office Correspondence, RG 38, Series 3-2, AO. Brennan Paving Company received $1.3 million in NPC contracts from 1937–1942, see John C. Best, *Thomas Baker McQuesten: Public Works, Politics, and Imagination* (Hamilton: Corinth Press, 1991), 177–9.
74 See correspondence between various teachers and the NPC, September 1945 to March 1948, File I-S, Box 95, NPC, General Manager's Office Correspondence, RG 38, Series 3-2, AO. These letters do not suggest that the teachers and principals were responding to any systematic advertising campaign mounted by the NPC.
75 Way, *Ontario's Niagara Parks*, 253.
76 Ibid., 338. The NPC often cited the Fort's location on the golf course as complicating matters. See Maxim Gray, Manager, to C. G. Childs, Superintendent of Historic Parks and Sites, 23 April 1952, File I-U, Box 95, NPC, General Manager's Office Correspondence, RG 38, Series 3-3, AO; also Gray to Kirby, 3 July 1953, Folder I-V, Box 96, NPC, General Manager's Office Correspondence, RG 38, Series 3-3, AO.
77 Mabel Burkholder, "Little Trips to Interesting Places in Niagara Peninsula," *Hamilton Spectator*, 26 January 1952; Bill Brown, "They still storm the ramparts at Old Fort George," *Weekend Magazine*, 21 May 1955; "History to discover: Fort George," *Discover Niagara-on-the-Lake* (Niagara-on-the-Lake: NOTL Chamber of Commerce, 1996), 18–19. See also "Old Forts Are Phonies, Archaeologist Believes," *The Globe*, 2 August 1957.
78 "Niagara. Concluding Remarks About our Historical Town," *The Times*, 14 May 1896. The Advance faithfully recorded annual May celebrations of Empire Day in Niagara until the early 1960s. In these events Canadians were reminded of their ties to Britain. For a discussion of Canadian cultural nationalism in the inter-war years, see John Herd Thompson and Allen Seager, "The Conundrum of Culture" chap. 8 in *Canada 1922–1939: Decades of Discord* (Toronto: McClelland and Stewart, 1985); see also Jonathan Vance, "The New Parliament of Art," and "Patron Saints of Culture,"

chaps. 11 and 12 in *A History of Canadian Culture* (Toronto: Oxford University Press, 2009).
79 See, for example, the NPC's 1920s brochure, Queenston Heights in File 4-I, 1 October 1928–31 January 1929, Box 60, NPC, General Manager's Office Correspondence, RG 38, Series 3-2, AO.
80 Ibid.
81 "House of 1800 Opened to Public This Sunday," *The Globe and Mail*, 29 May 1959; "Glimpse Into 'Good Old Days,'" *St. Catharines Standard*, 29 May 1959; "Historical 1800 Home To Be Opened Sunday," *Niagara Falls Review*, 28 May 1959 (see: NPC Scrapbook, Volume 6, 1958–9, RG 38 Acc 17741, AO). Other sites of "historical" interest in the area were recreated by the NPC, such as Fort Erie. The Commission also helped the Women's Wentworth Historical Society with funding for their maintenance of the Stoney Creek battlefield and house.
82 "P. M. To Dedicate Memorial Arch," *Niagara Advance*, 26 May 1938. Mackenzie King also opened Mackenzie House on this occasion; the paper pointed out there were plaques that showed William Lyon Mackenzie addressing the "Commons" one hundred years ago, as well as plaques to the executed Thomas Matthews and Samuel Lount.
83 In this commemoration of the military they were assisted by the town's apparently warm reception for the summer army camp, which helped to shape the idea of Niagara-on-the-Lake as a long-standing site for the military.
84 C. N. A. Ireson, "Brock's Indian Warriors Forgotten," *The Globe and Mail*, 30 July 1950 (see: NPC Scrapbook, Volume 1, 2 February 1949–8, December 1951, RG 38 Acc 17741, AO); "Haldimand Rifles Stage Entertainment at Camp. Indians, in Ancient Costumes, Perform Ceremony of Giving Major Burns Tribal Name," *Niagara Advance*, 19 July 1936.
85 For a brief discussion of Aboriginal Peoples' presence in the Niagara area, see Wesley B. Turner, "Early Settlement," in Niagara's Changing Landscapes, ed. Hugh J. Gayler, (Ottawa: Carleton University Press, 1994), 179–207. It would be difficult to know from NPC records and commemorations of this period that Colonel John Butler's Rangers included Senecas, although a number of re-enactments of the last five years have made that point. For a discussion of African-Canadians in Niagara, see Michael Power and Nancy Butler, *Slavery and Freedom in Niagara* (Niagara-on-the-Lake: Niagara Historical Society, 1993).
86 Janet Carnochan to John Jackson, NPC manager, 25 November 1925, File 1B C-3, Box 43, NPC, General Manager's Office Correspondence, RG 38, Series 3-2, AO; James D. Chaplin to Jackson, 15 January 1934, I-J, Box 45,

NPC, General Manager's Office Correspondence, RG 38, Series 3-2, AO; Arthur D. Armstrong to Ellison Kaumeyer, Manager, 26 September 1939, File I0, Box 46, NPC, General Manager's Office Correspondence, RG 38, Series 3-2, AO; V. J. Smith to NPC, 3 April 1951, File I-U, 95, NPC, General Manager's Office Correspondence, RG 38, Series 3-3, AO. And V. J. Smith, who in 1951 had recently finished building a home along the Niagara Parkway, hoped that the NPC would do something about a neighbour's tarpaper shack, which was in "deplorable condition" and sat on grounds that were littered with refuse; the NPC, however, could not (V. J. Smith to the NPC, 3 April 1951 and Gray to Smith, 5 April 1951; File I-U, Box 95, NPC, General Manager's Office Correspondence, RG 38, Series 3-3, AO.
87 R. B. Haley to Ellis, June 16 1926, File 30 I-C, Box 43, NPC, General Manager's Office Correspondence, RG 38, Series 3-2, AO.
88 Miss Onslow to NPC, 19 February 1947; Gray to Miss Onslow, 19 March 1947, File I-S, Box 95, NPC, General Manager's Office Correspondence, RG 38, Series 3-3, AO.
89 See, for example, Mrs. A. E. Cole to Hon. Wm. L. Houck, 10 July 1940, File 4-AC, Box 65, NPC, General Manager's Office Correspondence, RG 38, Series 3-2, AO. Mrs. Cole had busts of Brock and Tecumseh for sale.
90 Gray to Percy C. Band, 12 July 1945, File I-S, Box 95, NPC, General Manager's Office Correspondence, RG 38, Series 3-3, AO; Mary Weekes to NPC, 18 April 1946 and Gray to Weekes, 24 April 1946, File 4-AM, Box 99, NPC, General Manager's Office Correspondence, RG 38, Series 3-3, AO; Eva Tolen, Secretary, Lundy's Lane Historical Society to Carl Hanniwell, MP, 7 May 1948; Gray to Tolen, March 15, 1948 and A.W.S. Bennett, Manager, Greater Niagara Chamber of Commerce, 16 March 1948, File 4-AP, Box 101, NPC, General Manager's Office Correspondence, RG 38, Series 3-3, AO.
91 Dr. G. T. Field to Mackenzie King, 2 August 1941 and Kaumeyer to Field, 11 August 1942, File 4-AE, Box 66, NPC, General Manager's Office Correspondence, RG 38, Series 3-2; see also Field to Kaumeyer, 16 April 1942; Gray to Field, 11 May 1942; Field to Kaumeyer, 16 May 1942; Gray to Field, 20 June 1942; Field to McQueston, 22 June 1942; and Field to NPC, 26 June 1942, File 4-AF, Box 66, NPC, General Manager's Office Correspondence, RG 38, Series 3-2; see also Field to Gray, 19 February 1943; Gray to Field, 28 February 1943, File 4-A1, Box 67, Box 66, NPC, General Manager's Office Correspondence, RG 38, Series 3-2.
92 Palatine Hill was one of the oldest – possibly the oldest – surviving Loyalist homesteads; it also contained a number of late eighteenth and early nineteenth-century items. She also attempted to strengthen her

bargaining position by telling them that other organizations, including the Queenston Women's Institute, were interested. Mrs. M. E. O. J. Servos-Snider to NPC, 2 April 1931, File 4-M, Box 61, NPC, General Manager's Office Correspondence, RG 38, Series 3-2, AO; Servos-Snider to Jackson, 20 September 1932, 11 October 1932, File 4-O, Box 61, NPC, General Manager's Office Correspondence, RG 38, Series 3-2, AO; Servos-Snider to Jackson, 13 July 1933, 1 December 1933; Jackson to Servos-Snider, 5 December 1933, File 4-P, Box 62, NPC, General Manager's Office Correspondence, RG 38, Series 3-2, AO; Servos-Snider to Kaumeyer, 28 November 1935 and Kaumeyer to Servos-Snider, 30 November1935, File 4-R, Box 62, NPC, General Manager's Office Correspondence, RG 38, Series 3-2, AO; Lillian Walker, Provincial Secretary, United Empire Loyalist Association to the NPC, 13 December 1935; Servos-Snider to Kaumeyer, 18 March 1936; Kaumeyer to Servos-Snider, 5 May 1936, File 4-R, Box 62, NPC, General Manager's Office Correspondence, RG 38, Series 3-2, AO; L. C. Servos to Kaumeyer, 6 April 1940, File 4-AB, Box 65, NPC, General Manager's Office Correspondence, RG 38, Series 3-2, AO; Servos to Kaumeyer, 6 and 18 May, 3 June, 1940, File 4-AC, Box 65, NPC, General Manager's Office Correspondence, RG 38, Series 3-2, AO. See also A. D. Armstrong, Queenston Fruit Growers Association to Gray, 29 February 1944 and Gray to Armstrong, 15 March 1944, File 4-AI, Box 67, NPC, General Manager's Office Correspondence, RG 38, Series 3-2, AO.

93 C B Lindsey to Kaumeyer, 15 August 1938; Kaumeyer to Lindsey, 15 August 938; File 4-Y, Box 64, NPC, General Manager's Office Correspondence, RG 38, Series 3-2, AO.

94 Kaumeyer to Duff, 26 August 1938, File 4-Y, Box 64, NPC, General Manager's Office Correspondence, RG 38, Series 3 –2, AO.

95 Memorandum by A. F. to Gray, 25 August1942; Gray to Herbert Aiken, 31 August 1942; McQueston to Gray, 31 August 1942; Aiken to Gray, 31 August 1942, File 4-AG, Box 66, NPC, General Manager's Office Correspondence, RG 38 Series 3-3, AO. It's not clear whether these items were loaned or purchased, although the correspondence hints at the latter.

96 "Display Rare Museum Pieces," *Niagara Falls Review*, May 1950, NPC Scrapbook Vol. 1, RG 38 Acc 17741, AO.

97 Best, *Thomas Baker McQueston*, 96–8; see also the NPC scrapbooks for the 1970s for Donald MacDonald's accusations of NPC commissioners using Commission funds for private gain.

98 J. Lloyd Hughes and Gerald Noxon, *Niagara Preserved and Restored: A Brief for the Realization of the Historical, Architectural and Cultural Values of the Town of Niagara*, (Niagara-on-the-Lake: Historical Section of the Niagara

Post War Planning Commission, 1945), 4. The committee included a number of Niagara and some Toronto residents; Noxon's brother, Kenneth, a Toronto architect, had been hired by the town as a planning consultant. See Dana H. Porter, Ministry of Planning and Development to Gray, 27 October 1945, File I-S, Box 95, NPC, General Manager's Office Correspondence, RG 38 Series 3-3, AO.

99 Hughes and Noxon, *Niagara Preserved*, 4.
100 Ibid., 5. Williamsburg had been reconstructed in 1933. See Harry Scott, Commercial Counsellor, Canadian Embassy, Washington to Kenneth Chorley, Williamsburg, 12 November 1946, File I-S, Box 95, NPC, General Manager's Office Correspondence, RG 38 Series 3-3, AO. Scott wanted to build support for a similar restoration in Niagara that the NPC would supervise.
101 Noxon and Hughes, *Niagara Preserved*, 6.
102 Ibid., 7–8.
103 Ibid., 13–14.
104 Ibid., 17–18.
105 Ibid., 21.
106 For the federal government's participation in post–Second World War historic restoration and preservation, see C. J. Taylor, "The Board in Familiar Waters, 1934–54," and "The Politics of Historic Sites in the 1950s and 1960s," chaps. 6 and 7 in *Negotiating the Past: The Making of Canada's National Historic Parks and Sites* (Montreal and Kingston: McGill-Queen's University Press, 1990).
107 *Niagara Advance*, 1950.
108 Florence B. LeDoux, *Sketches of Niagara: "Where Yesterday Greets To-day."* (St. Catharines: Peninsula Press, 1955).
109 Carmen Pajak, "Lives Lived: Florence LeDoux," *The Globe and Mail*, 31 May 1996.
110 Some of the area's landmarks appeared on lists prepared by the department's D. F. McOuat (who was also the provincial archivist) for the Deputy Minister Guy Moore; these lists divided up the province's historic sites and buildings into either endangered or safe structures. It included the Secord homestead on the safe list, an assessment that would not have been greeted with unanimous approval in Niagara. See McOuat to Moore, 13 December 1963, Folder 16.6, MB 7, RG 5 Series A-1, AO.
111 T. C. Clarke to Auld, 28 January 1964, Folder 16.6, MB 7, RG 5 Series A-1, AO.
112 D. F. McOuat and Peter Klopchic, "Niagara – Historical Significance," 1966, Folder 3.11, MB 28, Ministry of Tourism, RG 5 Series A-3M, AO.

113 Niagara Foundation, "A Submission to the Commissioners Niagara Region Local Government Review," Folder 16.6, MB 7, Ministry of Tourism, RG 5 Series A-1, AO; "Historic Sites - Preservation - NOTL, 1963–71," MB 7, Ministry of Tourism, RG 5 Series A-1. Regional government came to Niagara in 1969. In 1959 former Toronto lawyer, Niagara resident, and NHS member Brian Doherty presented the town with the idea of a historical week for the benefit of town and Society. Doherty suggested a year later that the town should, among other things, beautify its main street with greenery and local merchants should use pioneer items from the museum for window displays. See Brian Doherty to Niagara-on-the-Lake Town Council, 28 September 1958 and 25 April 1960, Niagara Historical Society Minute Books 1895–1964, Vol. 4, 1952–1964, MS193, Appendix F Reel 7, AO.
114 Wool to Auld, 16 January 1967, Folder 25.2, NPC 1965–6, MB10, Ministry of Tourism, RG 5, Series A-1, AO.
115 Ibid. Several Foundation members had apparently given personal guarantees for the mortgage. See Robert Welch to Auld, 6 December 1966, Folder 25.2, NPC 1965–6, MB10, Ministry of Tourism, RG 5, Series A-1, AO.
116 "Apothecary Opening," *Niagara Advance*, 27 May 1971.
117 Paul Litt, "The Apotheosis of the Apothecary: Retailing and Consuming the Meaning of a Historic Site," *Journal of the Canadian Historical Association /Revue de la Société historique du Canada* New Series no. 10 (1999): 297–322.
118 Auld to James Allan, 8 February 1965, Folder 16.6, Historic Sites - Preservation - NOTL, 1963–71, MB7, Ministry of Tourism, RG 5, Series A-1, AO.
119 Mrs A. C. Temple to Bryan L. Cathcart, 5 August 1960, Folder 183, Preservation of Historic Sites and Buildings, 1960–1, MB 2, Ministry of Tourism, RG 5 Series A-1, AO; Kenneth Croft to Auld, 18 August 1965, Folder 16.6 Historic Sites - Preservation - NOTL, 1963–71, MB 7, Ministry of Tourism, RG 5 Series A-1, AO; "A Vacant Lot ... And History," *The Telegram*, 31 July 1965; Ralph Cunningham to John Robarts, 2 August 1965, Folder 16.6 Historic Sites – Preservation - NOTL, 1963–71, MB 7, Ministry of Tourism, RG 5 Series A-1, AO; John Bone to John Robarts, 8 February 1967, Folder 16.6 Historic Sites – Preservation - NOTL, 1963–71, MB 7, Ministry of Tourism, RG 5 Series A-1, AO.
120 See, for example, Welch to Auld, 6 April, May 4 1966, Folder 16.6, Historic Sites – Preservation - NOTL, 1963–71, MB 7, Ministry of Tourism, RG 5 Series A-1, AO; Welch to Allan, 29 January 1967, Folder 16.6, Historic Sites – Preservation - NOTL, 1963–71, MB 7, Ministry of Tourism, RG 5

Series A-1, AO; Welch to T. C. Clarke, Tourist Industry Development Branch, 28 October 1965, Folder 3.27, Proposals - NOTL, 1964–6, MB 38, Ministry of Tourism, RG 5, Series A-10, AO. Probably the impending Centennial celebrations helped prompt much of this interest; certainly residents and Welch were aware that there might be Centennial funds available for Niagara.

121 George Voth to Auld, 10 August 1970, Folder 15.8, Historic Sites-Preservation-Field Pharmacy - NOTL 1964–71, MB 6, Ministry of Tourism, RG 5 Series A-1, AO.

122 "Niagara Hotel Gets Government Expansion Loan," *Niagara Advance*, 17 June 1971.

123 L. W. Connolly and Jean German, eds., *Shaw Festival Production Record 1962–2007* (Oakville, ON: Mosaic Press, 2008), 14–15.

124 Nixon Brennan, "The Roaring (?) Twenties," in Bicentennial Stories of Niagara-on-the-Lake, ed. John L. Field (Lincoln, ON: Bicentennial Committee, 1981), 111.

125 "Niagara Playhouse Ends Season," *Niagara Advance*, 19 August 1948.

126 "Best Wishes for a Successful Season," *Niagara Advance*, 19 June 1969.

127 "Ottawa Becoming Disgusted. Threatens Spotlight Off Niagara," *Niagara Advance*, 23 July 1969; see also "The Town Has Been Deceived," *Niagara Advance*, 16 July 1969. These debates and controversies are also discussed in L. W. Connolly, *The Shaw Festival: The First Fifty Years* (Don Mills, ON: Oxford University Press, 2011), 48–52.

128 "Town Hall Foundation in Danger if Shaw Builds on Parking Lot," *Niagara Advance*, 1 July 1971.

129 Mrs. Grant Worthington, letter to the editor, *Niagara Advance*, 22 July 1971.

130 Jack Buchanan, "Make Queen Street a Mall," *Niagara Advance*, 5 August 1971.

131 Barbara Casselman, letter to the editor, *Niagara Advance*, 14 October 1971.

132 "Senior Citizens Voice Sentiment," *Niagara Advance*, 22 July 1971.

133 Shaw Festival Board of Directors, "Should Shaw Festival Pay Taxes?" *Niagara Advance*, 24 September 1970.

134 "Anonymous Report on Shaw Festival," File 25.4, Niagara Parks and Shaw Festival 1970–71, p. 1–3, RG5, Series A-1, MB10, AO.

135 "Mennonites Repudiate Hate Letter. Poison Pen 'Peter' Attacks Shaw Again," *Niagara Advance*, 21 January 1971.

136 Sardonicus, "Make Way for Ignoramus," and A Mennonite, "Will Not Bear False Witness," *Niagara Advance*, 28 January 1971; Betty Gullion, "Letter Lacked Backbone," and Crozier Iakyi, "Advance Has Retreated?" 4 February 1971. The anonymous distribution of the letter was the subject

of Don Dorling's letter to the editor, *Niagara Advance*, 15 October 1970; see also "Hate literature in town. Poison Attacks Against Shaw Council," and L. Wolofsky, "Unlawful Use of Mail Boxes," *Niagara Advance*, 15 October 1970.

137 Joan Phillips, "Shaw Festival Location, Tax-Exempt Status Protested," *The St. Catharines Standard*, 16 March 1971.

138 Leonard Connolly points to the controversy over the Festival's proposal to erect a tent theatre on the town Commons in 1980, when bicentennial celebrations of the town, which involved renovating the Court House, threatened Shaw's 1981 season (in the end, the renovations took place without relocating the theatre). Connolly, *The Shaw Festival*, 74–5.

139 The coverage of Project Niagara, as the proposed music festival was called, was extensive. See http://blog.projectniagara.org/archiveMartin Knelman, "Is Niagara-on-the-Lake Ready for a Major Music Festival," *Toronto Star*, 8 April 2010 and "TSO, NAC Pull the Plug on Project Niagara," *Toronto Star*, 13 July 2010; "What is Project Niagara?," Harmony Residents Groups blog, accessed 11 December 2014, http://harmonyresidentsgroup.blogspot.com/2008/03/who-we-are_15.html.

140 For example, Penny Coles, "NOTL tourism could be 'reinvented.' 1812 bicentennial celebrations could increase tourism for generations," Archives of *Niagara Advance*, accessed 11 December 2014, http://www.niagaraadvance.ca/articledisplay.aspx?archive=true&e=770640 http://www.niagaraadvance.ca/2011/02/02/notl-tourism-could-be-re-invented.

Conclusion

1 Geoff Eley, *A Crooked Line: From Cultural History to the History of Society* (Ann Arbor: University of Michigan Press, 2005), ix.

Index

archives, 7–8, 57–8, 103
Auld, James 151, 156–8

Bates, Robin, 38
Boyle, David, 21, 22, 24, 29, 31, 32, 62, 174
Brant family (Tyendinaga), 96, 107, 110
Brant Historical Society, 4, 5, 7, 62, 65, 73. *See also* Elliott Moses
Brant, Joseph, 26, 46, 49, 67, 80, 96
Brant, Mary (Molly), 45–6, 48, 93–6, 173,176
Brant-Monture, Ethel, 65, 83, 85
Brant-Sero John, 21, 62, 89
Brock, Isaac, 22, 26, 34, 45, 48, 55, 116, 122, 139, 142, 144, 146, 163
Burton, Antoinette, 111

Carnochan, Janet: African-Canadians in Niagara, 50–1; attitudes towards tourism, 101, 113, 150, 171; biography, 12–16; conceptions of the past, 9, 7–9, 11–12; relation to other commemorators, 14, 55, 174–6; *History of Niagara*, 33–52; Indigenous people, 45–50; memorialization of her, 52–3; Niagara Historical Museum, 16–33; womam's suffrage, 14; women in her writing of history, 39–48; War of 1812, 7, 12, 22, 23, 24, 26, 35, 52, 55
Chautauqua, 37, 38, 121, 122, 123, 124, 127, 136, 146, 171

Deloria, Phillip J., 88, 89, 107
Doherty, Brian, 160
Dubinsky, Karen, 139

Eley, Geoff, 172, 177

File, Celia B: biography, 91–3; conceptions of the past, 173, 177; family relationships, 98; friendship with Havelock Robb 110; McArthur, Duncan, 96; relationships with Six Nations (Grand River and Tyendinaga), 4, 5, 91, 97, 100–8; thesis on Mary (Molly Brant), 92–6; work as teacher, 98–100
Fort George, 14, 34, 37, 127, 129, 139, 141, 142–3, 144, 146, 147, 163, 172

Index

Fort Mississauga, 14, 34, 37, 44, 127, 128. 141, 161, 172
Fort Niagara, 34, 45, 50, 139

gender 9, 10, 12–14, 17–18, 20, 27, 29, 35, 39–48, 52, 55, 61, 63, 65, 92–6, 75–8, 85, 95, 98–108, 143, 144, 160, 161, 174–5
Glassberg, David, 6

Hill, Asa, 63–4
Hill family (Tyendinaga), 5, 97–8, 108

Indigenous/Native/Aboriginal/ First Nations, 4, 5, 6, 7, 9, 10, 21, 22, 39, 45–51, 55, 120, 123, 144, 146, 150, 151,173–7 *See also* File, Celia B.; Martin, Milton; Moses, Elliott

Jasen, Patricia, 115–16

LeDoux, Florence and Trellie, 150–1
local history, 5, 7,12, 22, 31, 32, 35, 36, 51, 64, 67 *See also* archives
Loft, Bernice, 4, 10, 67, 92, 93, 100
Loft, Frederick, 89

Mackintosh, Phillip Gordon 125
Maracle family (Tyendinaga), 5, 100–1, 104, 105
Martin, Milton: biography, 79, 88; conceptions of the past, 10, 67, 83, 175–6; enfranchisement, 82, 86, 87, 175; Indigenous peoples' status and history, 82, 84–8, 175; member of the Canadian military, 64, 79, 122; objections to textbooks, 5, 101, 102; representations in press, 80, 82; teacher and elementary school principal, 9

McKay Ian, 38
Moses, Elliott: biography, 67–9; Brant Historical Society, 65; conceptions of the past ,7, 8, 10, 67, 89–90, 173, 174; Delaware, 74–5, 177; enfranchisement, 90, 175; gender, 75–8; Indigenous peoples' status and history, 69–78; public educator, 9; relationship with other Indigenous people, 72–3, 78
Musson, J. 134, 139, 140, 145

national and imperial history, 5, 12, 14, 31, 35, 61, 64, 66, 67, 139, 141, 143
Navy Hall, 43, 130, 139, 141
Niagara Falls (New York), 49, 165
Niagara Falls (Ontario), 6, 12, 113, 115, 118, 119, 138, 139, 140, 156, 166, 175
Niagara Foundation, 156
Niagara Golf Course, 41, 125, 127, 128, 129, 130, 132, 141, 161
Niagara Historical Society and Museum, 13, 14, 16, 20–35, 39, 57–8, 122, 131, 138, 145, 171
Niagara Parks Commission, 113, 135, 176
Niagara-on-the-Lake: history and heritage, 5, 6, 11–12, 115, 139–58, 166–9, 173–4, 175; tourism, 5, 6, 113–14, 116–39,150–8, 173–4, 176. *See also* Janet Carnochan; Shaw Festival; Niagara Foundation; Niagara Parks Commission
Niagara-on-the-Lake Apothecary, 116–17, 156–7

Ontario Historical Society, 13, 21, 29, 49, 59, 60, 62, 176

progress, history of, 38, 60, 63, 67, 69, 75, 77 139

Queen's Royal Hotel/Queen's Royal Park, 38, 125, 127, 128, 132, 133–7

Rand, Calvin (and Rand family), 132–3, 160, 161, 164

Shaw Festival, 156, 158–66
Secord, Laura, 3, 4, 9, 17, 23, 37, 41, 55, 79, 139, 143, 145
settler society, 4, 5, 7, 10, 50, 82, 91, 93, 101, 108, 111, 149, 173, 175, 176, 177

Six Nations, 3, 4, 5, 7, 48, 49, 59–67. *See also* Brant Historical Society; Brant-Monture, Ethel; Brant-Sero, John; File, Celia B.; Loft, Bernice; Loft, Frederick; Martin, Milton; Moses, Elliott; Ontario Historical Society

teachers and history, 8–9. *See also* Carnochan, Janet; File, Celia B.
Tecumseh, 49, 101, 144, 146

www.ingramcontent.com/pod-product-compliance
Lightning Source LLC
Chambersburg PA
CBHW030317080526
44584CB00012B/594